C-7

3-

ONCE AROUND THE BLOCH

An Unauthorized Autobiography

TOR BOOKS BY ROBERT BLOCH

ROBERT BLOCH

A ONCE AROUND THE BLOCH

An Unauthorized Autobiography

A Tom Doherty Associates Book

New York

ONCE AROUND THE BLOCH

Copyright © 1993 by Robert Bloch

All rights reserved, including the right to reproduce this book, or portions thereof, in any form.

This book has been printed on acid-free paper.

A Tor Book
Published by Tom Doherty Associates, Inc.
175 Fifth Avenue
New York, N.Y. 10010

Tor® is a registered trademark of Tom Doherty Associates Inc.

Library of Congress Cataloging-in-Publication Data

Bloch, Robert.
    Once around the Bloch : an unauthorized autobiography /
Robert Bloch.
        p.   cm.
    "A Tom Doherty Associates book."
    ISBN 0-312-85373-4
    1. Bloch, Robert, 1917–   —Biography.   2. Authors,
American—20th century—Biography.   3. Science fiction—
Authorship.   I. Title.
PS3503.L718Z465   1993
813'.54—dc20
[B]   93-17047
                                                       CIP

First Tor edition: June 1993

Printed in the United States of America

0 9 8 7 6 5 4 3 2 1

This book is for the people in it
who have done so much to enrich
my life.

ONCE AROUND THE BLOCH

An Unauthorized Autobiography

ONE

1 was born with a silver spoon in my mouth.

The trouble is, it had somebody else's initials on it.

From what little I ever learned about family history, this was my grandfather's fault.

Simon Bloch and his brother Sol came to the United States as youngsters; the family emigrated from Darmstadt, in Hesse, around the time of the Civil War.

I was told that their father was a cigar maker, but they grew up to follow another trade. Somehow they settled in Chicago shortly before the Great Fire of 1871 and opened a wholesale grocery store. The two brothers met and married the two Mayer sisters—my grandfather got the pretty one—and their business prospered.

In 1884 my father was born. He was named Raphael, but inevitably called Ralph or Ray. His sister Lillian was several years younger. They lived in what was then a fashionable area of Chicago's South Side close to their cousins, Beatrice and Tess. Many more members of the Mayer clan settled in the city, but I know little of their background. As a child I gathered my grandmother's people considered themselves superior to a family descended from a lowly cigar maker. Who knows; maybe *their* family rolled joints.

But as Chicago entered the Gay Nineties—a term which in those days did not refer to sexual preference amongst nonagenarians—the family business boomed. My father's favorite memories centered around visits to the "Columbian Exposition" of 1893. At the age of nine, however, he was less interested in the hootchy-kootchy dancing of Little Egypt than in the equestrian feats of Buffalo Bill.

By this time my grandfather and my uncle were the owners of Bloch's Butter Store, at State and Madison streets, one of the choicest locations in Chicago's Loop. As well-to-do citizens, they sent their children to private schools. My father was enrolled in the Morgan Park Military Academy. He was there near the turn of the century when the proprietors sold Bloch's Butter Store for the staggering sum of $100,000 in cash.

He was still there when his father and uncle decided to invest their fortune in phony copper-mining stock. It was then that he lost his opportunity to graduate, and I lost the chance of being born with that properly initialed silver spoon in my mouth. Probably just as well; it would have complicated the delivery for my mother.

There wasn't much hope of getting silverware from the other side of my family.

I never knew my maternal grandparents, and learned little about them. Ferdinand Loeb was a shoemaker in the days when shoemakers actually made shoes instead of just slapping on a new pair of prefabricated soles and telling you that you could pick them up a week from Wednesday.

Grandpa Loeb was born in Alsace-Lorraine and probably came to America in the 1870s. I don't know if he'd married by then; I don't even know my maternal grandmother's first or maiden name. I do know that after marriage they settled in Attica, Indiana.

Their eldest son, Benjamin, went into the wrecking and salvage business and became the owner of a lumberyard. Eldest daughter Esther was a pioneer social worker in Chicago, an associate of Jane Addams at Hull House. She married Herman Falkenstein, who worked with Benjamin; he was killed by the collapse of a wall they were demolishing. Esther then opened her own home to poor immigrants, often literally starving herself to provide for them. When she died in 1914, the mayor and thirty thousand people joined the funeral procession. She is totally forgotten today.

What I know of her came from my mother, Stella, born in 1880. There were two other children. Her younger sister, Gertrude, was sickly, introverted, but devoted to a lifelong love of art and music. Her other brother, Lee, was also a music-lover. Unfortunately he was fonder of banjo-playing than of work. He left home in his teens and the family never heard from him again.*

In so doing he followed in his father's footsteps; Ferdinand Loeb disappeared when my mother was still a little girl, leaving Benjamin and Esther to support the household as best they could. With him went my last hope of ever seeing that silver spoon.

The Loeb family moved to Chicago, and it was there my mother grew up while working with her sister at the "settlement" houses. She had a fine singing voice and was an accomplished pianist; with these talents Stella supplemented the family income at weddings, funerals and church services of all denominations. Although of German-Jewish parentage like my father, her outlook was nonsectarian. My mother was diminutive and attractive, often described as a "beautiful" girl, probably because of an inner radiance as well as her physical attributes. Upon graduating from high school she was given an opportunity to enter a traveling light-opera company as a professional. The offer came from Florenz Ziegfeld's father, under whom she had studied at his Chicago College of

---

*Considering the banjo-playing, maybe it was just as well.

Music. Stella declined the offer, feeling obligated to support an ailing mother and sister Gertrude by finding steadier employment. She completed her education and became an elementary-school teacher.

Meanwhile my father had been yanked from the military academy before graduation and sent out to help support *his* family after dreams of silver spoons vanished amidst the whirlings of worthless copper-mine stocks. He found work as a bank messenger-boy. Over the next few years he advanced to a place behind the counter as a clerk.

Stella Loeb and Ray Bloch first met in 1904; by then my mother was teaching and my father was a handsome, self-educated young man, but still a lowly clerk. A year later my mother quit teaching to become a professional social worker. The position was an assistant directorship of the Jewish Settlement in Milwaukee.

What happened between 1905 and 1916 I don't know. What happened between Stella and Ray I also don't know. How much travel there was between Milwaukee and Chicago I don't know either.

I do know both had other romantic interests, though not the full extent of their involvements. One of the problems I face when writing about this period is that I can't throw in very much steamy sex. In those days their idea of steamy sex was kissing somebody in the back room of a dry-cleaning shop.

But whatever the case, they did see one another over the decade. In Milwaukee my mother's work expanded with a move to a new location at Ninth and Vine streets; she became full director of what was now called the Abraham Lincoln House. Here she lived-in and literally worked around the clock with immigrant families and their children. A large portion of the expense was defrayed by income from Mrs. Simon Kander's *Settlement Cookbook*, based on recipes originating in the Lincoln House kitchen. My mother became, in a sense, everyone's mother; she was teacher, mentor and protector; in later years many of her "boys" were business and community leaders in Milwaukee.

Meanwhile my father moved ahead in the financial world. Never a real threat to the Rockefellers, he advanced from bank clerk to teller, then became assistant cashier. I don't know his salary, but it was enough to provide modest support for a family.

And that's what Stella and Ray wanted. Both were already in their thirties and had worked for over half their lives. My mother resigned her position; she and my father were married in Chicago on June 6, 1916.

Their first residence was an apartment on Cullum Avenue. My mother's younger sister, Gertrude, lived with them, but only for a short time. They were in love, and wanted privacy. They wanted children.

Instead, they got me.

Two

On April 5, 1917, the *New York Tribune* published these front-page headlines:

SENATE 82 TO 6 FOR WAR: HOUSE TO ACT TO-DAY
LONDON SEIZED WITH HOPE FOR SUDDEN PEACE
GERMAN NEGRO PLOTS FEARED IN SIX STATES
GOVERNMENT ACTS TO ELIMINATE BIG PROFITS IN WAR
PACIFISTS START NATION-WIDE DRIVE TO HAMPER U.S. IN WAR

No word about my birth. That gives you some idea of where I stood.

Of course I was born in Chicago, not New York. And time has brought me consolations; the *New York Tribune* is dead, but I'm alive.

Alive in a world where we no longer hyphenate the word "to-day," London has given up hope for sudden peace, and there are no "Negroes" anymore, let alone "German" ones. The government has still not gotten around to eliminating big profits in war, and pacifists may continue to start nationwide drives, but aside from that, things have changed.

And so have I.

When I was six months old we moved to a larger apartment on Sunnyside Avenue in the Ravenswood area of Chicago's North Side. I suppose the furniture came in a van and we arrived by taxi. My family was the kind that always had a piano but never owned a car.

I retain no memory of moving. Nothing is left from that period except a few faded snapshots. One shows a baby in the arms of my great-grandmother. I don't remember her, but then I don't remember the baby, either. A portrait shot, taken a few months later, reveals it peering at the world with an expression of innocence which was all too soon to be erased. I see nothing of myself in these infant photographs. All they prove is that I was plumper in those days, and had more hair.

My sister Winifred was born bald on February 3, 1919. I was twenty-two months old and this is an event I do recall. While my mother was in the hospital my father and I stayed with Grandpa and Grandma in their Prairie Avenue apartment. Simon Bloch never bounced back after the loss of his fortune; he'd ended up a watchman in a furniture factory. I remember him as a bald-headed elderly man with a mustache. Kindly and dignified, he enjoyed having me sit on his lap and play with his heavy pocket-watch chain. Grandpa recited nursery rhymes to me in German, probably the way he himself had first heard them as a child. Grandma recited rhymes in English, holding me lovingly as she did so. Aunt Lil, my father's sister, worked as a dress clerk in a department store but still made her home with the family.

The same apartment building was also home to Grandpa's brother Sol and his wife, Grandma's sister Celia. Like Grandpa, Uncle Sol never recovered from the mining stock disaster. He worked downtown as a bookkeeper in some chain store. At least they told me that, but I didn't believe it, because he never brought home any chains. His wife, Aunt Cele, had a sour disposition; she could pickle a cucumber just by staring at it. Fortunately she was well disposed towards me, but to this day I retain an aversion to vinegar. Tessie, the older of their two children, had married; younger daughter Beatrice lived with them. Like Aunt Lil, she also worked as a sales clerk. Aunt Lil was heavyset and looked older than her years; Bea was slim, bobbed her hair and became a typical flapper during the twenties.

But I was about to describe memories of my sister's birth, and this is just a way of sneaking in some stuff about our relatives.

Let's get back to Winifred's arrival. Comprehending nothing about the facts of life at the time, I retain no realization of my mother's pregnancy. I do remember my father telling me why she had gone to the hospital and saying I would soon have a baby brother or sister. This news thrilled me not at all; the only thing I wanted was for Mama to come home again.

It came as a relief when my father arrived one evening by cab to announce the birth of a baby sister. I received this news standing at the head of the stairs in the hall outside the apartment, and immediately started to descend them.

"Bobby, come back here!" he shouted. "Where do you think you're going?"

"Home," I said.

Actually it was several days before we went back to Sunnyside Avenue, stopping en route at the hospital to pick up my mother and that strange, squalling, squirming little bundle which disappeared into my parents' bedroom as soon as we arrived.

I don't have any recollection of what is today called sibling rivalry. If Winnie and I competed for affection, it didn't traumatize either of us. And when she walked for the first time she came to me. That memory remains vivid; I can see the tiny child, blue-eyed, head finally crowned with long-awaited curls, taking her steps toward me with arms outthrust as she wavered for balance.

Soon came a trip to Milwaukee on an excursion boat called the *Christopher Columbus,* probably because it was old enough to have been used by him. If not, I could see replicas of his vessels in the Jackson Park lagoon. It was in nearby Washington Park, accompanying my Aunt Lil, that I went wading in the duck pond with my shoes on. And it was with my mother that I stood at the curb on sunnyside Avenue and urinated into the gutter. When she asked me the reason for this action I told her I was doing what I saw the horses doing every day. She then explained to me that little boys and horses were not the same. The chief difference seemed to be that little boys got spanked when they peed in the gutter. This is one of life's valuable lessons which I have never forgotten since.

Time passed. I grew out of rompers and into overalls. Mama had my picture taken riding a pony. We went to see Aunt Gertrude, who worked as a civil service clerk in City Hall. She took me to visit the studio of an artist named Sloan, who found out I scrawled crayon drawings; he gave me a small oil on wood, a painting of a sheep.

I was an ignorant child. My parents enticed me into card playing, thus teaching me numbers, and lured me into reading. But I knew little of what was happening in the outside world.

World War I had ended before my memory really began. My father was agitated upon reading about new developments in poison gas and germ warfare. I didn't see what all the fuss was about. If the germs wanted to kill each other that was okay by me.

It was a time of ignorance. One of the neighbor children with whom I played had a slight speech impediment which I failed to notice, accepting it as natural. As a result, it took me years to realize that the town of Athol, Massachusetts, was not named by someone with a lisp.

THREE

Most people never speak of the important moments of their childhood; perhaps they don't even remember such occasions. Adam and Eve had no childhood at all.

My own memories seem quite clear, though I was too young to attach dates to them at the time.

The discovery of separate identity came when I was two years old or thereabouts. One morning, while standing in the bathroom vacated by Dad after he'd finished shaving, a flash of comprehension suddenly occurred. I couldn't verbalize it, but the wordless certainty was overwhelming. For the very first time I realized that my consciousness was separate and distinct from Daddy's or from that of any other person to whom I'd previously communicated my reactions of pleasure or pain in sounds and gestures, taking it for granted they understood because they were in some way an extension of myself. I ran across to the bedroom where my father was putting on his shirt and pointed at him, trembling with excitement. "You!" I said. Then I jabbed a finger at my chest. "Me!"

He laughed and nodded. From that moment on I became an individual, self-aware and—though this was a more gradual process—aware of the selfhood of others.

I don't know what parlor psychoanalysts might make of my work and the experiences which shaped it. There are, however, a number of possible clues.

When still an infant I contracted what my parents described as "black measles"—whatever that is—and all I know is that it was regarded at the time as a serious ailment. Somehow I seem to have survived the flu epidemic of 1918, but my mother was stricken; fortunately, she recovered, though her illness undoubtedly disrupted my infant existence at the time.

As for death itself, my confrontations were gradual. My great-grandmother succumbed, but I was too young to understand what had happened. Shortly thereafter my grandmother had a sudden, fatal heart attack, but all that registered was the sorry fact that I wouldn't see her again. Then my grandfather was operated on for cancer of the prostate and confined to a nursing home; we visited him several times, and I was dismayed at his obvious illness and invalidism, as well as sickened by the overpowering smell of urine emanating from the pouchlike apparatus he wore. But when he died, it still wasn't enough to establish a definitive dread of the phenomenon itself.

At the age of six, in our new suburban home, I learned about death from a chicken.

One Sunday, when relatives gathered for dinner, someone—either an uncle or a cousin—brought a live rooster to the feast. He took it out into the backyard to prepare it for the stew pot and I, completely unaware of what to expect, followed to observe. The squawking creature's head was pressed down on a block of wood and the hatchet swung. A moment later—to my surprise and horror—the headless white chicken ran in a circle around the yard, gouts of blood spurting and spouting from the stump of its neck.

I wonder why so many of my stories involve decapitation . . .

It was only gradually, over the next few years, that I discovered the meaning of mortality and the facts of death: the probable prelude of pain and illness, the irreversible departure of consciousness in a slumber from which there would be no awakening save in this vague "heaven" which I couldn't locate or truly envision. God, I knew, was a disagreeable-looking old man with a long beard, very similar to those worn by the prophets in a picture which adorned our parlor wall, but what he had to do with death was unclear to me. Nor could I picture the mysterious realm in the sky where everyone who died sat around playing on harps rather than using their newly bestowed wings to fly free over the face of the earth.

I was not taken to funerals or funeral parlors, and it was only through hearsay that I learned of caskets and the business of burial. Although my parents were cautious and discreet in answering questions about mortality, I was beginning to obtain input from fairy tales, picture books, even films. It was all true, I decided; people *did* die and their bodies were buried in the ground in wooden boxes, alone in the dark. That was horrifying, and the explanation that they didn't mind because they were "asleep" offered no comfort to me, because this sleep was endless, without an awakening. Nor was I consoled by further talk of heaven. Nobody could answer my questions as to its exact location, nobody claimed to have been there and seen it, no one had even seen God. It occurred to me that maybe the stories about Heaven were just another fairy tale. But death was real, no doubt about it. People died in books, in newspaper accounts, and on the screen. And they died in daily life, strangers and relatives alike, filling up Rosehill and its counterparts all over the world.

The hardest thing to realize, let alone accept, was the fact that someday Mama and Daddy would die too, leaving me and my sister alone. What could we do without them? When directly confronted with the possibility, they admitted that this would happen someday, though by then I'd be a grown-up myself and able to cope. But I didn't *want* to cope, and I didn't even want to imagine a world without my parents. Death was something that happened to other people, not to my loved ones.

And of course it would never happen to me.

Somehow I survived my youth. And with luck, I may survive my old age.

FOUR

During my childhood the sound of the Roaring Twenties was only background music. The *plink* of ukuleles, the *awoogah* of auto horns on the Tin Lizzies, the scratchy syncopation of the Victrola record and the hammering foxtrot emanating from the player piano blended together in a medley almost unnoticed by my ears.

Although we lived in the Chicago of Al Capone, I never heard the bark of a pistol or the chatter of a machine gun until Warner Bros. incorporated these effects into the sound track of the motion picture screen—but back then the screen was still silent.

The world in which I dwelt was in a state of curious transition from uncomplicated past to complex present. Reminders and re-mainders of that past maintained a peaceful coexistence with more modern manifestations.

The horse—and his by-products—dotted the city streets. Bony nags pulled the wagons of junkmen and rag peddlers; a better breed furnished horsepower for the milkman's wagon, the ice-man's rig, the perambulating dispensaries of fresh fruit, produce and bakery goods. Galloping steeds dashed from doorways of firehouses, drawing hook-and-ladder equipment, and downtown traffic was patrolled by mounted police on handsome geldings. The tractor had not yet come into general use on the farm, and in hundreds of hamlets surrounding the city, the only service station was a blacksmith shop. Dollar bills were larger, both in size and purchasing power; they could be exchanged for gold coins at any bank. Silver coins were made of real silver; pennies were copper, and with ten of them you could buy enough cheap candy to make you sick for a week. Shoeshines cost a nickel. Domestic servants worked for as little as a dollar a day, if you could afford their services; our family couldn't. Everyone—men, women and children—wore hats. Men's hats were generally made of felt, though the workingman preferred a cloth cap. The once-popular derby disappeared after the defeat of 1928 presidential candidate Al Smith, and the top hat soon followed with the coming of the Great Depression. In summer the universal male headgear was the sailor straw; it vanished around the time of WWII.

Button shoes, thank God, were out of step in the march of progress, but youngsters trudged to school wearing rubbers when it rained and galoshes when it snowed. Most boys, myself included, attended classes garbed in sweaters and knickers which buckled below the knee, and our long stockings were secured by elastic garters or elaborate metal ones affixed to the legs of cotton or woolen underwear. It was a world of hairpins, celluloid, dollar watches, fur pieces, Kewpie dolls, incense, castor oil. Our school day started with the pledge of allegiance to the flag, followed by the singing of the national anthem—which was *America the Beautiful,* not *The Star-Spangled Banner.* Postcards cost a penny; regular mail (delivered twice a day in most communities) required a two-cent stamp. We kids went home for lunch—*walked* home, for virtually no one, including the teachers, used a car. Children who ate at school brought food in a brown paper bag; there were no school lunches. Newspapers cost two cents, three at most. Big weekly magazines sold for a nickel or a dime; "highbrow" literary monthlies and lowly pulps were priced from ten cents to a quarter. Books might cost seventy-five or ninety-five cents for reprints; new novels went for two dollars and nonfiction prices seldom ranged much higher. Both fiction and nonfiction presented a misleading picture of life in the Roaring Twenties; most of the content was written by college graduates who traveled abroad and reflected their own experience and background, but such experience was hardly typical. Actually less than five percent of the population had a college education, and only three percent ever set foot on foreign soil except in a WWI uniform. Only one family out of four owned an automobile, and we weren't among that number. And not one person out of a hundred thousand had ever left the ground in an "aeroplane."

In this quaint world of yesterday, all doctors made house calls, policemen and postmen performed their duties on foot, telegrams were delivered promptly by personal messenger on bicycle and most grocery stores had home delivery service too, at no extra charge. Women bought hats at "millinery" shops, purchased sewing material at "dry goods" stores. The five-and-ten-cent stores sold their wares for five or ten cents. Soda pop cost a nickel, sodas went for a dime. There were no laundromats, no supermarkets, motels, parking meters, stoplights; no dishwashers, refrigerators, tank vacuum cleaners, home air-conditioning units, electric stoves, stereos. Radio was primitive, TV didn't exist, nor antibiotics, radar or computers. The workweek generally ran until Saturday noon for privileged people like my bank-cashier father; many others toiled a full six days.

In the absence of video games, we kids spent time shooting marbles, jumping ropes, flying kites, playing hide-and-seek. Older boys rode bicycles; if lucky, they could earn money with them on a paper route. We youngsters awaited newspaper deliveries in order to read the comic strips. Comics were a lot funnier in those days, and also larger. The Sunday comic section boasted attractions equivalent to the rock stars of today. Everybody was familiar with

Mutt and Jeff, Barney Google, Andy Gump, the Katzenjammer Kids, Orphan Annie, "Bringing Up Father" and a dozen other favorites.

The dime stores sold sheet music of popular songs which millions like ourselves played and sang at home. On downtown streets uniformed monkeys held cups for pennies while their organ-grinder owners cranked out the strains of such immortal classics as "It Ain't Gonna Rain No More."

Children's books were not yet a major concern of the publishing industry; as a result of the cultural lag, libraries offered favorites of a previous generation. Tom Swift was still inventing, and G. A. Henty's heroes were busily saving a vanishing British Empire. My father would introduce me to the dime-novel demigods of his own boyhood, buying reprints which detailed the exploits of Buffalo Bill, Nick Carter and Frank Merriwell.

We children had little to fear in this bygone world. Gypsy caravans sometimes added a colorful touch in their journey through smaller communities, and we were yanked inside when they passed our door. According to ancient folklore these itinerants were dangerous—when not engaged in telling fortunes or stealing bedsheets off backyard clotheslines, they also kidnapped children. But tramps were welcomed without qualms; after Mother fed them in the kitchen they performed odd jobs and repairs as payment.

With the exception of a few urban youngsters who pilfered from fruit peddlers or the iceman's wagon, most children respected the law. And so did the majority of their elders. The cop on the beat was a familiar figure and the authority he represented was real. The phrases common to crime drama—"You're under arrest," "Take him away," "I sentence you to"—carried genuine clout. Plea bargaining, stays, appeals and commutation of sentences were rarities; jail meant disgrace. Litigation was so primitive that nobody ever brought suit for a hundred million dollars.

Of course the twenties weren't all that wonderful. In Washington the witch-hunters had a field day searching out modern bogeymen in the form of bearded, bomb-throwing "Bolsheviks" and did their best to bury the disgrace of the Teapot Dome oil scandals. Ordinary citizens were swindled in the stock market or the fake boom in Florida real estate. The Ku Klux Klan gave numskull nonentities in bedsheets an opportunity to conduct local witch-hunts on their own—not for godless "Reds" but for blacks, Jews and Catholics. Segregation and discrimination ranged from raw lynch-law tactics in the boondocks to polite urban ostracism; the "better-class" neighborhoods were policed by realtors who saw to it that homes were not rented or sold to niggers or kikes. In the South the "colored" were advised that it wasn't healthy to walk the streets after sundown; up north, the well-bred banned "sheenies" from country clubs and did their best to keep them from contaminating private schools.

My sister and I were blissfully unaware of such social inequities, but we heard rumors about things we didn't quite understand—the frequent bank crashes, the Prohibition bootleggers, rumrunners and gangsters, the woes of tenement dwellers and sweatshop workers, the relentless and murderous warfare which factory owners conducted against strikers and union organizers.

Because of the universal conspiracy of silence regarding sex, we didn't share grown-up concerns about prostitution, venereal disease or unwed mothers. That concern, such as it was, mostly revolved about methods of punishment. Prostitution was more or less tolerated as a necessary evil, and venereal ailments—easily acquired but hard to cure—served as a fitting fate for buyer and seller alike. A surprisingly large segment of the population knew absolutely nothing about homosexuality, except "pansies" portrayed as figures of fun on stage or screen. The worst treatment was accorded the unwed mother. "Fallen women" who avoided a prostitute's role usually ended up in the most menial occupations; illegitimate children were generally shut away in orphanages.

In addition to the "orphan asylum" there were "insane asylums" for the mentally ill, the "poorhouse" for the indigent, the "old people's home" for impoverished senior citizens. The physically disadvantaged were lumped together under the heading of "cripples" and many of them begged on the streets.

We youngsters had our minor illnesses treated by throat swabbings, oatmeal baths and purgatives; major childhood ailments might include measles, mumps, diphtheria, pneumonia and scarlet fever. Lacking today's medications, our family physicians could do little to decrease the high mortality rate other than monitoring the course of communicable disease and placing our homes under quarantine for several weeks at a time. The prevailing practice was to remove a youngster's tonsils and adenoids at the earliest opportunity (whatever became of adenoids, by the way?). Vaccination against smallpox was commonplace but my parents resisted it. Tuberculosis was a disaster, equivalent to a death sentence, and usually required permanent incarceration in a sanatorium.

Our elders were not always fortunate in their choice of medical practitioners and many fell prey to the hordes of quack doctors or even drugstore clerks who peddled sure cures for such mysterious conditions as strokes, heart attacks and cancer.

In retrospect, the general ignorance was appalling. My mother and father, despite their enlightened views on racial and religious tolerance and the high value they placed on education, still accepted certain popular beliefs about health care.

Thus we were solemnly warned that wearing rubbers or galoshes indoors was bad for the eyes. Just what connection existed between footwear and vision was never questioned or explained; the logical conclusion would be that anyone fortunate enough to go barefoot throughout a lifetime would never need glasses.

The folks also saw to it that our diet included plenty of fish, for everyone knew that fish was the world's best "brain food." No wonder performing seals were so smart; perhaps the country would have been better off if a walrus were elected president.

We were also cautioned never to leave home unless we wore

clean underwear. Apparently the theory was that if a kid became an accident victim while wearing dirty drawers, the ambulance attendants might spread gossip about parental neglect and very likely the doctors at the hospital would be so shocked that they'd refuse to render treatment.

My sister and I accepted these practices and beliefs without question, though we hated our sore throats being invaded by cotton swabs or having our chests coated with camphorated oil and covered with flannel. Our own sanitary precautions consisted largely of washing hands before each meal. It was okay to try avoiding an injunction to wash behind the ears—after all, what harm could germs do you way back there? In those days door and window screens were just coming into widespread use, so we spent a lot of time swatting mosquitoes and catching flies on sheets of evil-smelling, sticky flypaper.

Meanwhile my poor parents ran down into the basement at all hours of the day and night to shovel coal into the furnace and remove ashes. In summer they sweltered, in winter they shivered, and all year round they worked and worried about our welfare. My father rode clanging, crowded streetcars on long journeys to and from a job where he put in long hours and put up with short-tempered bosses and customers. My mother cooked and baked, ground her coffee beans by hand, washed our laundry in an iron tub and ran it through a wringer without the aid of a machine, did the ironing with an actual piece of iron heated on the stove, dumped a pan of water out from under the icebox every day, mopped the floors, cleaned the rugs with a manually operated carpet-sweeper, hung carpets on the clothesline to beat the dirt out of them, put up fruit and vegetables in jars as preserves, made the beds, changed the linen, dusted the furniture, did the dishes without a dishwasher, put up storm windows, ran to the market, and raised two hyperactive children.

Maybe the twenties did roar, for some people. But my parents never had time to listen.

FIVE

1n 1922 my family purchased a home at 305 South Ninth
Avenue in Maywood, Illinois. It was a green two-story "Queen
Anne" house: living room, dining room and kitchen downstairs,
three bedrooms and a single bathroom on the second floor, plus
the luxury of a laundry chute, a dumbwaiter and a cubbyhole
storage space which stored nothing but myself, playing hide-and-
seek with my sister. A basement housed the coal bin, furnace, iron
laundry tub and inevitable fruit cellar for storing preserves. Set on
a lot 120 feet deep, there was plenty of room for a garden and
outdoor recreation. Formerly the property of a circus performer,
the house's distinguishing feature was a poster of a lady bareback
rider displayed on the stairway landing which, despite my protests,
was painted over. To my sister and me our new residence was a
palace rivaling Versailles.

Although technically a suburb of Chicago, Maywood was
actually a typical small town of the twenties, and its 20,000 inhabi-
tants lived in an environment totally different from that of the
Windy City.

There was little traffic in the daytime hours, and youngsters found it safe to play on the streets or in vacant lots, which were abundant. Maywood had all the usual small-town delights, including a park complete with Civil War cannon memorial, a bandstand for Sunday concerts, and a pond to reflect the fireworks displays on the Fourth of July. Above all, it had a phenomenon new to me— friendly neighbors.

Everyone was warm and hospitable. My sister and I formed friendships with a dozen or more youngsters, and my parents joined in the social life. Its central ornament was a house party every two weeks, hosted by each family in turn. Games were played, the living-room rug was rolled back for dancing, and my mother took over the piano. In this innocent era, card-playing and community singing were the usual forms of entertainment—as was the big meal which followed. Every housewife cooked or baked something for the occasion, and there was often a birthday or anniversary to celebrate.

The rest of the social life centered largely around local churches. While religion was never discussed, and differences in faith played no part in daily relationships, the majority of the neighbors were Protestants. Soon after my family was welcomed into their activities it was suggested that we attend the Methodist church. The fact that we were Jewish made no difference to our newfound friends, and since we didn't observe the rituals of Judaism my parents had no objections. My sister and I enrolled in Methodist Sunday School, winning gold stars and bluebird seals for regular attendance and diligent application to our lessons.

Dad and Mom expanded their circle of acquaintances and before long my mother had taken over the church piano at various festivities. On New Year's Eve, a white-robed and bearded Father Time tottered onstage to welcome the infant New Year in the diminutive person of my sister Winifred, who scampered on clad in diapers and a pair of gold wings attached to her tiny shoulder blades. Church attendance had its blessings for us, too—the big stone two-story structure, with its refectory in the basement, proved an ideal place in which to play hide-and-seek with the minister's son on weekday afternoons when school was out. And we enjoyed the Sunday School picnics, riding to the park with our classmates crowded into the back of an open truck and joining in the chorus of "Onward, Christian Soldiers." Although religion never hooked me, I extended my devotions to form a friendship with Billy Wiechlin, son of the Baptist minister, and soon I was playing games in the spacious Baptist church as well.

But it was actually more fun to play in our own backyard. When we moved in, it was uncultivated, and the folks ordered several truckloads of earth, which, in those days, was still dirt-cheap. Before this could be leveled my playmates and I dug trenches and turned the yard into a no-man's-land for war games. My uncle then donated a great stack of double shutters salvaged from one of his wrecking jobs, and constructed a playhouse which served as a fort, a castle, or a clubhouse, depending on the mood of the moment. Sometimes, with the aid of clotheslines and old sheets, we erected a circus tent. The enclosed front porch of the house became the deck of a pirate ship, with the piano stool borrowed for the helm and an extra section of the dining-room table perched over the porch rail as a plank for prisoners to walk before they plunged into the ocean of the front lawn.

Emerson Grammar School was an ancient brick structure supplemented by a wooden barracks housing two additional class-rooms. The smell of chalk dust was everywhere, through the efforts of unruly pupils who stayed after school to write their sentences of penance fifty times on the blackboard and dispelled only by good students who were allowed to open the tall windows from the top with the aid of a long pole with a grooved end which fitted into the metal catch above. There was, of course, no air-conditioning; we baked in the summer heat and were saved from frostbite by woodstoves which burned in the barracks. Classroom desks were small, their tops fitted with recessed inkwells into which students dipped their pens; the fountain pen was reserved for businessmen and was just beginning to make its appearance at bar mitzvahs. Our teachers were angelic presences, and the principal was God.

In Chicago I'd attended kindergarten, where I earned considerable distinction as a musician—playing the triangle. But grade school was a whole new world. By the time I entered it I was already partially equipped for the experience. When I began to convert my early crayon scribbles into recognizable drawings, my mother artfully encouraged me to identify them with captions—and so I discovered the alphabet and word formation. The family library helped teach me to read, though I didn't always understand spellings and meanings. Running across a quotation that impressed me, I repeated it to my parents.

"Who wrote that?" Dad asked.

"Annie Mouse," I said.

It took a while for him to figure out that the writer I referred to was "Anonymous."

Armed with this educational advantage I came to first grade, but to amputate a long story, I was quickly shuttled on to second, third and then fourth grade, skipping ahead four semesters. In those medieval times there was little provision for the precocious: they were simply bulldozed forward and out of the way. The age difference between me and my classmates created an enormous gap; a seven-year-old is simply too small and physically undeveloped to compete with playmates who are bigger and older. That, plus growing myopia resulting from reading an average of a half-dozen books a week, excluded me from the no-win situation of competitive sports. Being a child in the 1920s was a full-time occupation and I don't recommend it—particularly to the young.

The game-playing routines I'd invented for neighborhood kids kept me from becoming a loner, but the lure of the public library was strong; at eight I was granted a special dispensation to borrow books from the adult section. What I found there—together with my parents' collections of Mark Twain, Poe, Hawthorne, O. Henry, Sir Walter Scott, Washington Irving, Francis

Parkman and a dozen other authors—augmented my classroom curriculum. In a remarkably short time I became a full-fledged, world-class smartass.

Of course not all my education came from books. As far back as I can remember, the folks made a regular practice of visiting the Lincoln Park Zoo or the Chicago Art Institute on alternate weekends. I loved animals, the wilder the better, and extended my affection by attempting to mount the stone lions guarding the portals of the Art Institute. Inside that wonderland I went bleary-eyed over sculpture and paintings. And it was there, one Sunday afternoon, that a distinguished-looking gentleman noted my rapt scrutiny of Seurat's *La Grande Jatte* and engaged me in conversation. We didn't worry about child molesters then, but only when he presented me with complimentary passes for his evening performance did I learn my fellow art-lover was the renowned magician Howard Thurston.

I knew the name well, for another aspect of my education was show biz. We children accompanied our parents to the theater; even after moving to Maywood the family generally spent Saturday afternoons or evenings at Chicago's vaudeville houses, the Majestic and the State-Lake.

The footlights were already sputtering and the stars themselves were dimming, but I arrived on the scene in time to see such living legends as Eva Tanguay, Sophie Tucker, Charlotte Greenwood, Harry Lauder, Gus Edwards's "School Days" act, Annette Kellerman's diving exhibitions, and Singer's Midgets (complete with a midget elephant).

I enjoyed Weber and Fields when they appeared at the opening of a new theater, the Palace Music Hall, performing their famous routines—the pool-table skit, the living-statuary act, and the cafe sketch. Along the way I caught a glimpse of a vanishing form of entertainment in an act featuring "Honey Boy" Evans, famous dancer Eddie Leonard, and a number of other greats. They opened in street clothes, seated at individual dressing tables and making up in blackface as they sang; then went into a full-stage miniature minstrel show.

It was heady stuff for a youngster, and so were our exposures to popular musicals like *Blossom Time,* such operas as *Samson and Delilah* or *Hansel and Gretel.*

I also saw the great Fred Stone, appearing with his wife and daughter Dorothy in the musical comedy *Stepping Stones.* From his entrance—descending from a high stepladder, headfirst and upside down—to his Raggedy Ann and Andy dance routine—I was completely captivated.

I heard John Philip Sousa conduct his band in Grant Park, and the music of Paul Whiteman, Ted Lewis and Fred Waring's Pennsylvanians at the Chicago Theatre.

One winter night Dad entrained with me to Chicago where the Sells-Floto Circus performed in the Coliseum. The route to the main arena led the crowd past the menagerie—but it didn't lead me. I halted at the elephant picket line, and there I stayed, refusing to budge. My poor father, who had braved the icy blasts to introduce me to the delights of the Big Top, was forced to spend the next two hours watching me feed and pet the pachyderms; we never did see the show.

But in the years that followed I saw them all—Ringling Brothers–Barnum and Bailey, with its chariot-race finale, Hagenback-Wallace, the great old-timers with the great stars.

Circuses visited Maywood, too, smaller outfits known as "mud shows" because they traveled by truck. One of them staged a parade which passed along the street just two doors away from our house. There was even a "Tom Show"—a dying breed of troupers presenting *Uncle Tom's Cabin,* complete with a pack of bored and indifferent bloodhounds. And I attended the once-mighty Chautauqua presentation in its last season. Legend has it that its principal attractions included the famed politician and orator William Jennings Bryan, plus a youthful Edgar Bergen, who was just teaching Charlie McCarthy how to talk. If I saw them, their impact was lost amongst the myriad marvels that followed. The youthful mind is like a cow patch, equally impressed by each footprint left on it. My personal involvement with the theatrical world began somewhere around this time, with an onstage appearance at the local public library. The play was *Mrs. Wiggs of the Cabbage Patch,* a drama which compared—though not too favorably—with the works of William Shakespeare. Memory does not dredge up the exact role I played, though I'm fairly certain it wasn't Mrs. Wiggs. Most likely I was one of the cabbages.

I do recall that I sang a "Chinese" song in appropriate costume, including a black tissue-paper pigtail, and that the production itself scored a resounding success. Unfortunately there were no Broadway impresarios in the audience to single me out for a starring contract, and I abandoned my theatrical career for several years to come.

Music was another source of learning. In addition to the piano which my mother played and which I plinked from time to time, we had a wind-up Victrola and a stock of records. The big twelve-inch ones offered the usual band-concert staples—the *1812 Overture,* Lizst's *Second Hungarian Rhapsody, Poet and Peasant Overture* and other noisemakers which usually required additional cranking midway to rewind the phonograph. There was opera, of course—Caruso, Galli-Curci and Alma Gluck. Orchestral medleys encapsulated *Babes in Toyland* and *Leave It to Jane.* Percy Grainger performed on the piano, Albert Spalding fiddled; there was even a recording titled *Bird Calls of Our Native Land.*

But bird imitations could scarcely compete with that marvel of sound effects, "The Whistler and His Dog," with its amazing climax in which the anonymous whistler is answered by an actual dog's bark. Science was indeed wonderful.

Along about this time my mother took us to visit her old friend Jane Addams, at Chicago's Hull House. Here an elderly lady offered to play and sing "When You Come to the End of a Perfect

Day." She was, of course, Carrie Jacobs Bond, the composer. Her fame didn't impress me but her performance did.

By 1926, however, we'd discovered radio—another source of music and the spoken word, to say nothing of static. Our Atwater-Kent "super-hetrodyne" was equipped with two sets of headphones and an astonishing array of knobs and dials. The combination brought in a lot of what was then known as "interference," but it also provided us with sound and fury from afar. Chicago's dance bands at the College Inn competed with the distant din of Coon-Sander's Nighthawks from Kansas City.

Radio offered history, too—the voice of President Calvin Coolidge, news accounts of the disarmament programs, the League of Nations and the World Court, which guaranteed peace in our time and forevermore. Politicians politicized, statesmen stated, and proponents of Prohibition prohibited over the airwaves at regular intervals, undeterred by the somewhat cynical observations of Will Rogers. Radio gave the younger generation a chance to eavesdrop on the world.

Holidays were also a part of the educational process. At Easter-time we colored eggs and hid them. The big event was the ingestion of indigestible jelly beans and the consumption of chocolate bunnies. If someone asked me to pinpoint the exact moment the world started to go to hell, I'd say it all began when greedy candy makers switched from solid chocolate rabbits to ones with hollow ears. Today the entire bunny body is hollow, and so is the laughter of youngsters who have never experienced the joy of breaking their baby teeth on a hard hare at Easter.

Memorial Day—then known as Decoration Day—was simply that, an occasion to bring flowers to graves of deceased relatives. Dead veterans were honored by live parades. The most impressive marches took place on Michigan Avenue in downtown Chicago, and the ranks of the first few I remember included survivors of the Civil War who still shuffled valiantly along on foot. Later, of course, they took to riding open cars, waving feebly at onlookers. As the then-popular song had it, old soldiers never die—they only fade away. And soon even the riders vanished from view, but they live in memory, for I literally saw the past parade before my eyes.

The Fourth of July was actually celebrated on the fourth of July. The afternoon was reserved for picnics in the park, where vast amounts of Orange Crush helped wash down the sandwiches and potato salad. In the evening, of course, we gathered on the banks of the park pond to *ooh* and *aah* at the fireworks display launched from the far side. Usually the spectacle culminated in a primitive pyrotechnical portraiture of George Washington and Abraham Lincoln, followed by the grand finale—Niagara Falls, glittering against a background of "bombs" bursting overhead. Wealthier communities might even invest in a three-color dazzlement vaguely resembling the American flag. It was, in retrospect, a somewhat touching spectacle—all those innocent young eyes gazing upward at Old Glory.

But those young eyes also focused on firecrackers sold at roadside stands or local shops. Weeks beforehand youthful patriots began saving their pennies to purchase an amazing assortment of noisemakers—thus enhancing the economy of China, where most of them were manufactured, and transforming America into one gigantic battlefield.

The twenty-four-hour explosion raised a dreadful din; our Aunt Gertrude fled her Chicago boardinghouse on the evening of July third to take refuge with us during the day that followed, but even in Maywood her sensitive ears were subjected to a continuous bombardment which was probably worse than any suffered during the Great War itself.

Sparklers were silent, and so were the sticks of punk which families usually kept in stock on the assumption that their fumes helped ward off mosquitoes. But the Fourth found a new use for punk—touching off the fuses of firecrackers.

By evening, of course, most of us had exhausted our stock,

along with the funds to purchase more. But if our parents were hosting a gathering of relatives and opted to skip the celebration in the park, it meant trouble for poor Aunt Gertrude. There was always some bachelor uncle or cousin who provided a private fireworks spectacle of his own. After dinner, with the coming of dusk, he would lug a cardboard carton into the backyard and proudly prove Thorstein Veblen's theory of conspicuous consumption by displaying as much as five or ten dollars' worth of loud and lethal weaponry.

We kids, limited to a budget, had to shop for quantity rather than quality—little strings of lady-crackers which were carefully separated from their tangle of fuses and ignited one at a time, or objects which gave off a crackling sound when ground underfoot. But the young adult relative—crazed by several glasses of "near-beer" or homemade fig wine—set off entire packages of lady-crackers at a time; instead of grinding snakes underfoot, he sent "nigger-chasers" darting along the sidewalk and with gay abandon tossed cherry bombs, two-inch salutes and even cannon-crackers into the air, followed by hissing rockets that exploded high above the clothesline. It was amazing just how much racket a few dollars' investment could produce—and even more amazing that the number of fingers, toes, eyes and ears lost during nationwide war games maimed only a fraction of the juvenile population. It was indeed a Glorious Fourth.

Veterans Day—then called Armistice Day—produced marches of a more militant nature. Middle-aged men who'd fought in the Spanish-American War competed for attention with still-youthful survivors of more recent carnage.

About Labor Day, the less said the better. While it may have represented a welcome day-off-with-pay for our elders, to youngsters it was a grim occasion, heralding the end of summer vacation and the beginning of our long incarceration in school.

Halloween was dress-up time, but the juveniles of the twenties weren't introduced to blackmailing tactics via the threats of trick-or-treat. We took our joy in improvising costumes and displaying them as we went from door to door, without any thought of extortion. The biggest thrill came simply from being allowed to stay up late on a weeknight.

Thanksgiving was even better than Halloween, because it was a real grown-up holiday. On Thursday we were free to feast and—since there was no school on Friday, either—spend the following day recovering from our gluttony. Of course there'd be a gathering of relatives, generally split by individual preferences for light or dark meat and decisions about dressing and side dishes. The leftovers usually lasted until Sunday, much to the delight of the family dog.

But Christmas was the best. At the time we moved to Maywood I was five and sister Winnie only three, so we greeted the occasion from different perspectives. On Christmas Eve, when Santa knocked on the door to greet us with a ho-ho-ho and helpings of candy canes, her little face lighted up immediately. I, in my worldly wisdom, cast a somewhat more jaundiced and jaded eye on his appearance—conducting an inspection of Santa's footwear, which was recognizable as the shoes of our neighbor across the street. But I held my peace, and only ventured mild comparisons between the resplendent Santas of Chicago's downtown department stores and the skinny, obviously false-bearded St. Nicholas portrayed by one Max Vodenoy at a local emporium.

Sunday School teachers said that it is better to give than to receive, but Christmas taught us that receiving is more fun. Although our parents and relatives were far from affluent, they went all-out for Winnie and me. There were paint sets, coloring books, windup cars and fire trucks, a box of magic tricks and a beginner's Erector Set which taught me nothing about sex.

Next, lead soldiers captured my fancy; during five years of birthdays and holidays I acquired an army of well over a hundred of the W. Britain hand-painted warriors—ninety-eight cents a box for eight infantrymen or five cavalrymen.

Now I began reconstructing famous battles, using our round

dining-room table which I covered with a dun-colored cloth beneath which was placed a variety of boxes to give the effect of a hilly terrain. I daubed the cloth with watercolors and red wax—after all, what's a battlefield without bloodstains? Sets of Lincoln logs served as fences and barricades, sandbags were fashioned from clay. I'd gotten into clay modeling, too, and often augmented my armies with the figures of denuded corpses.

As a stickler for reality I was forced to do research on the actual battles I strove to portray. Thus I painlessly acquired a smattering of historical information to supplement the skimpy coverage in our schoolbooks.

Before long I was as happy with the gift of a new book as I was with a squad of Gordon's Highlanders. From *Mother Goose* via the *Oz* books and Lamb's *Tales from Shakespeare* to Ridpath's *History of the World* seemed a surprisingly swift transition. My borrowings from the library now included nonfiction—though I was still getting a lot of inside information from the Tarzan books and the operations of that eminent physician Dr. Fu Manchu.

No chronicle of the twenties is complete without mention of the movies—for the movies *were* the twenties.

"Silent pictures" they were called, but although no sound emanated from the screen, there was always an accompaniment. Today that accompaniment is usually misrepresented as a piano offering schmaltzy "mood music." Actually, by the time the twenties rolled around, pianos had been relegated to only the cheapest theaters; most respectable neighborhood houses used organs. The big picture palaces boasted mighty Wurlitzers which rose on platforms, spotlighting well-known virtuosos like Jesse Crawford, a recording star in his own right. Some of the downtown cinemas had their own orchestras, and our suburban Lido Theatre boasted a five-piece combo on weekends, headed by local bandleader celebrity Johnny Parsons.

Organists and orchestras alike were generally provided with musical scores specially assembled or composed for the features to be shown—so despite the absence of dialogue, the films were far from silent. And on Saturday or Sunday afternoons we youngsters added sound effects—shrieks, whistles and laughter. Half the fun of attendance was audience participation.

Even local theaters had uniformed ushers who guided patrons to their places with flashlights at the ready, presided over by a real live manager whose eye was on the screening rather than the popcorn machine in the lobby. There was, in fact, no popcorn machine; no "refreshment" counter defaced the decor or permeated the picture-palace with rancid odors of overpriced junk food.

It was possible to smuggle small quantities of popcorn or sweets into theaters from the candy stores which frequently adjoined them, but the big deal was to visit them after the show for a ten-cent soda or sundae. We didn't go to the movies to eat—we went for mental nourishment.

My own patronage began early, in Chicago. I remember *The Kid*, with Chaplin and Jackie Coogan, and something called *The Bachelor Daddy*, starring now-forgotten Thomas Meighan. The latter offering gave me my first taste of terror when an on-screen locomotive rushed headlong toward the audience. Most of the audience, that is; by this time I was halfway under the seat.

But I stayed upright to enjoy episodes from the Saturday matinee serial *With Stanley in Africa*. As I recall it, Henry M. Stanley was a brawny young man who spent most of his time saving a curvaceous heroine from assorted lions, leopards, snakes, crocodiles, cannibals and Arab slave-traders. Though I don't recall him ever meeting Dr. Livingstone, I presume he did.

After we moved to Maywood, I began attending movies in earnest. The attractions I waited for with the greatest impatience were those of Douglas Fairbanks—*The Thief of Bagdad* was another special effects eye-popper. Fairbanks himself was a one-man special effect in *Don Q, Son of Zorro* and *The Black Pirate*, an early venture into Technicolor.

There were no "art houses" in those days, but many theaters played occasional revivals of earlier offerings. Thus I was able to catch up with Fairbanks as well as the work of his famous spouse, Mary Pickford, along with the past triumphs of Valentino.

All of this input had its effect; the pomp and pageantry, the revisionist historical dramas, the films set in exotic locales stimulated imagination and led me to seek out reading matter that enhanced awareness of the past and present. *The Lost World* seems crude indeed when compared to today's sfx state of the art, but it encouraged me to learn about dinosaurs and prehistoric life-forms. Even Bull Montana, playing an ape-man, inspired me to read up on the theory of evolution and then-current conjectures about "the missing link" in our ancestry.

But while I thirsted for education, my major appetite was for entertainment. Unlike most of my peer group, I never really got hooked on westerns. Instead I was turned on by comedy. Not the Keystone Kops, already scorned as old-fashioned, nor even Chaplin, whose two-reelers were in constant revival. My idols were Keaton and Harold Lloyd, together with a host of two-reel titans half forgotten today. Laurel and Hardy hadn't yet emerged, but I relished the talents of Harry Langdon, Charlie Chase, Lloyd Hamilton, Snub Pollard and Lupino Lane. Many comedians came from the theater for one or more films—Leon Errol, George Jessel, Eddie Cantor, Ed Wynn. W. C. Fields made silent features—some terrific, some atrocious. Bea Lillie's *Exit Smiling* is a neglected classic.

In a strange sort of way I learned something from the silent comedies. Despite overtones of slapstick there was a subliminal introduction to satire, irony, the part played in our lives by the vagaries of fate. The deflation of pomposity, the puncturing of inflated self-esteem, the caricature of conventional behavior patterns—all were food for thought as well as food for laughter.

Silent movies served as a postgraduate course in human

behavior. My teachers formed a faculty ranging from Marion Davies to Lillian Gish, from John Gilbert to Noah Beery.

Parenthetically, I must add that today's retrospective screenings cast only a pale shadow of what we saw. The original nitrate prints often offered superb cinematography, unmarred by scratches and light streaks. Night scenes were usually on blue stock; fires and disasters were in red; romantic interludes were bathed with the golden glow of amber. In the general absence of Technicolor, some spectacular sequences might be hand-tinted. Few such prints survive, and most present-day audiences are unaware of their original visual impact. In addition, the films were run at their proper speed. Today's projectors, designed for sound, unreel them at a rate which destroys the pace of pantomime, distorts drama and turns comedy into frantic frenzy.

But when we entered the darkness of a picture palace in the twenties and listened to appropriate organ accompaniment, what we saw on screen seemed quite real.

This I discovered for myself when I attended my first movie alone at night. At the age of nine I was not yet a film buff and I was more excited by the prospect of joining an adult audience at an evening performance than by what I was about to see. In fact I knew nothing of the picture or its star, but the learning process began quickly.

It started when I discovered that the ushers at the Lido Theater that night were wearing masks. As I settled somewhat uneasily into my seat, my apprehension was allayed by the usual prologue of short subjects. There was a newsreel, a crude animated cartoon featuring the even cruder antics of Felix the Cat, and an educational comedy—so-called because its producer had originally formed the company to make films for schools, then abandoned his purpose in favor of two-reelers starring Bobby Vernon, Jack Duffy, Billy Dooley and other now-forgotten fun makers. I don't recall who manufactured the mirth in this particular picture, but I know I laughed.

My laughter halted abruptly when the comedy flickered to a finish and the jazzy strains of its organ accompaniment gave way to a rumbling roar. A green spotlight from the projection booth swept over the screen as the title of the feature appeared: *The Phantom of the Opera*. The name of its star, Lon Chaney, was new to me.

And so was the world in which I found myself as I watched the opening sequences. Here was the Paris Opera House of a bygone day, or more properly, bygone nights, when it was apparently haunted by a ghost. This invisible presence, feared by performers and stagehands alike, left messages for the new management, warning them to dismiss their star soprano and substitute the young heroine in her role. This girl had apparently been trained by the ghost himself, acting as an invisible vocal coach, a self-proclaimed Angel of Music whose voice sounded through the walls of her dressing room.

But somehow the single glimpse of him, a cloaked figure seated back-to-camera in a theater box, didn't seem all that angelic. And when the managers who sought him there took a second look, he'd disappeared. When the prima donna sang, the cloaked figure brought the chandelier down to crush the audience—a distinctly unfriendly gesture. He also hung a backstage property-man who claimed to have once seen him lurking there.

Eventually, after the heroine's debut performance, the strange being—ghost or angel—manifested himself to her when she walked through a trick mirror from her dressing room to the labyrinth beyond, much to the puzzlement of the hero, a young military officer. Clad in the cloak, wearing a black slouch hat, the mysterious figure's face was hidden by a grotesquely mustached mask, immobile save for movement of the lips hidden beneath.

It was in the company of this creature that the heroine and I were led through the twisted tunnels and cavernous catacombs to the cellar concealed five levels below the Opera House. Here, after gliding by boat across a subterranean lake, the masked entity ushered us into his lair—a gloomy, dungeonlike stone chamber dominated by a massive organ on which he played the proclamation of his love.

The distraught heroine took refuge in an adjoining chamber, only to discover that it contained an open coffin. Fleeing from the sight, she confronted the ghost—by this time I knew for damn sure he wasn't an angel—and he calmly informed her that in the coffin he enjoyed his nightly rest. Neither the heroine nor I appreciated his choice of sleeping arrangements; in fact her disapproval was so great that she subsequently fainted.

Conducted to another bedchamber, she awoke the following day to find herself in a lavish boudoir equipped with a closetful of clothing and accessories bearing her initials. In the main chamber her host was playing the organ. While thus distracted she approached him from behind and—unable to resist the temptation—removed his mask.

It was then, in a gigantic series of close-ups, that I got my first look at the hideous living skull-face of the Phantom of the Opera.

On some occasions, when describing the effect on me, I have stated that I paid Chaney the greatest tribute a small boy could possibly bestow—I wet my pants. Now I must confess this wasn't exactly true; merely poetic license, you might say. But I did close my eyes, opening them from time to time only to observe more horrors. Their visual impact was effective, but when I ran all the way home through the dark after the film ended, the image that floated behind me was the Phantom's face. He kept me company in bed and haunted my dreams.

He also made me a Chaney fan, and a fan of the other horror pictures which played during that era, epics like *The Bat, The Gorilla, The Cat and the Canary*. Actually they were quite mild in terms of today's taste, or lack of it; apparently all you needed to make a horror film back then was a maniac who ran around in an old dark house disguised as an animal. None of these efforts, or

Chaney's, had a supernatural premise, and there was little on-screen violence. The emphasis was on atmosphere conveyed by setting and cinematography. Chaney achieved his effects through makeup and contortions emphasizing physical defects or deformity, supplemented with superb pantomime which conveyed the humanity of characters crazed by wrongs inflicted on them by others.

He did all his own makeup, and soon I was doing mine—strapping my arms to my sides, doubling my legs at the knees, donning a hump as a hunchback, slithering across the floor as a paralytic, disfiguring my face as a one-eyed criminal or an evil Chinese mandarin.

My parents, bless them, indulged me in this catharsis. And while familiarity with role-playing didn't bring contempt, it helped to exorcise my fears.

My inability to identify with heroes had an obvious source—the mirror which revealed quite clearly that I was not destined to enjoy the physical requirements of a leader of men or a follower of women. With this in mind, you don't have to be a psychology major to figure out why I came increasingly to empathize with comics or villains on the screen, or why comedy and villainy eventually became dominant *motifs* in my work. But that development was yet to come.

Sometime late in the summer of 1927 the family, accompanied by my father's sister, entered Chicago's Northwestern Railroad Station to entrain for a suburban destination. Where we were going eludes memory, and it's not important. What matters is that we passed the huge magazine stand in the terminal.

Here literally hundreds of periodicals—including the then-popular weekly and monthly "pulp" magazines—were ranked in gaudy array. Row after row of garish covers caught the eye; comparatively respectable offerings like *Argosy, Blue Book, All-Story* and *Adventure* competed for attention with scores of titles featuring romance, mystery, detective stories, westerns, and every variety of sports. There were even pulps devoted exclusively to railroad yarns, pirates, WWI air combat. I stared at them, fascinated by this abundance of riches.

It was then that Aunt Lil, with her usual generosity, offered to buy me a magazine to read during the train journey. Scanning titles and covers, I stood poised in delicious indecision. Here was a mustached member of the French Foreign Legion battling a bearded Arab armed with a wicked-looking scimitar . . . beside it, an Indian chief preparing to discharge a flaming arrow at an ambushed wagon train . . . directly overhead, a helpless maiden struggling in the clutches of a gigantic gorilla whose glaring red eyes indicated his zooreastic intentions. Salivating, I surveyed this feast of literature. For a dime I could devour the exploits of a master detective; fifteen cents would satisfy my appetite for mutiny on the high seas; twenty cents might gorge me with a huge helping of Secret Service operatives foiling the hellish Huns who presumably had substituted a bomb for the torch held by the Statue of Liberty.

But in the face of these attractions, what more might be offered for an entire quarter?

That price was imprinted on the cover of a magazine featuring a cloaked, bearded, evil-looking man confronting a recumbent, half-naked girl clad in Oriental garb against a background of Egyptian hieroglyphs. The featured story was "The Bride of Osiris," by one Otis Adelbert Kline.

Snatching the magazine from the rack, I paged through it quickly, noting such promising titles as "Satan's Fiddle," "Creeping Shadows," "The Phantom Photoplay" and "The Man with a Thousand Legs."

That did it. "This is the one I want," I said.

And it was thus that I was introduced to a magazine which changed my life, my very first copy of *Weird Tales*.

Six

At the time I acquired my first copy, *Weird Tales* was scarcely a household name, and during the thirty-odd years of the magazine's existence it never became one. And despite posthumous fame many of those who wrote about it later referred to the publication as *Wierd Tales*. In todays' drug culture it's *Wired Tales*.

Come to think of it, to many people this last title might have seemed accurate enough, even in 1927 when my own readership began. The cover which attracted my attention at that time illustrated a serial which dealt with an ancient Egyptian city still flourishing today directly below Chicago, unbeknownst even to Al Capone.

In issues to come I read the adventures of a French physician and amateur detective whose monthly confrontations with the supernatural occurred aboveground. Every thirty days he staked out a vampire, neutered a werewolf, exorcised a demon or laid a ghost—the latter procedure, in those days, was nonsexual. All these activities took place on the streets and in the dwellings of Harrisonville, New Jersey, a community which seemed to be inhabited by almost as many monsters as Beverly Hills. It took me several years to learn that the city of Harrisonville was a fictitious creation, and several more to discover that the same thing was true of Beverly Hills.

But by far the most horrifying concept, and to me the most convincing, was an account of ghouls feasting in their burrows below the cemeteries and subways of modern Boston. The story, "Pickman's Model," was credited to one H. P. Lovecraft, and I made a mental note to remember both the title and the name of the author.

This is neither the time nor the place to go into the publishing history of what its masthead first described as "The Unique Magazine" and then as "A Magazine of the Bizarre and Unusual." It was all these things and more; to me personally *Weird Tales* became a sort of nontheological *Book of Revelation*. What it revealed was that fantastic fiction was not necessarily the work of long-deceased authors like Poe, Hawthorne or de Maupassant; its prose and poetry were not entombed in pages from the past. Death was alive and well and living in Chicago.

To be exact, its present address was 840 North Michigan Avenue. Here *Weird Tales* maintained editorial offices, but not quite as well as I then imagined. Although the magazine never expired, a lot of its subscriptions did. Battling circulation problems, the publication seemed chronically moribund and constantly hooked up to a life-support system on which creditors kept threatening to pull the plug.

All this, of course, I learned much later. Living in the suburbs made it difficult to venture into the downtown Loop on my own, and it never entered my mind to seek out the lair where monsters lurked, whether as gangsters aboveground or as Egyptians below.

What my parents thought of my taste remains unclear to me. Although they seemed uninterested in reading my favorite magazine they offered no objections to cover illustrations of damsels in various stages of distress and undress, and continued to supply me with quarters for the monthly issues. Their own preferences were the *Saturday Evening Post, Liberty Magazine,* the *Literary Digest* and the *Ladies' Home Journal,* none of which specialized in the supernatural. Once in a while my mother purchased a copy of a magazine called *Harper's Bazaar,* but if there was a periodical called *Harper's Bizarre* I never got to see it.

Nor did I see the byline of H. P. Lovecraft anywhere except in the pages of *Weird Tales.* Bookstore clerks couldn't place his name, public libraries had never heard of him, schoolteachers—when I tried explaining the sort of thing he wrote—didn't want to.

It took years before I learned the background of my favorite writer of horror fiction. Again, this is not the time or place to delve into details, nor is it necessary. Today biographical material on Lovecraft and critical evaluations of his efforts abound, and most of his work remains in print.

Suffice it to say that Howard Phillips Lovecraft was born in Providence, Rhode Island, in 1890 and, with the exception of a brief residence in New York during his marriage in the mid-twenties, lived there throughout his life. Of longtime New England stock, his parents were short-lived, and both suffered from mental illness in their latter years. Judged a sickly child by his mother, Lovecraft was removed from school, but his phenomenal precocity aided him in an impressive self-education. As a young man he dabbled in writing—his articles, essays, poetry and short fantasies in prose contributed to the field of amateur journalism. A dwindling income from a small family inheritance and the necessity of helping support two spinster aunts forced him to turn his talents toward professional markets which published fantasy and supernatural horror fiction.

Such markets proved few and far between. In fact the only consistent outlet for the outré was *Weird Tales.* Lovecraft wrote and sold what he could of his own work and did revisions and ghostwriting for others, but he never rose above the poverty level nor surfaced to general recognition or critical acclaim. Only a very few of his stories found publication outside the pages of *Weird Tales,* and even there a number were rejected.

In a professional career spanning a mere fifteen years he gradually graduated from the early, abbreviated poetic prose to longer—though sometimes equally lurid—tales of horror. Then, about the time I discovered him, he began a cycle of stories loosely linked to a common background, a cosmos of his own creation based on what has become known as the "Cthulhu Mythos."

His vision of a universe ruled by monstrous entities which once claimed earth as their own had a persuasive paranoid logic. Lovecraft, himself a strict materialist, bridged the gap between fantasy and reality by the introduction of modern science into many of these tales. Hidden horrors were hinted at by scholars, researchers, astronomers and astrophysicists, hunted down by teams of explorers using the resources of contemporary technology.

It was with these tales that Lovecraft came into his own. *The Call of Cthulhu, The Dunwich Horror, The Whisperer in Darkness, At the Mountains of Madness, The Shadow Out of Time*—these, plus a half dozen others, form the basis of an enduring concept. Enduring, and endearing to literally dozens of other writers who have since borrowed Lovecraft's Mythos, monsters, and in many cases, mannerisms of style and presentation. Some of them made use of his imaginary New England locales, including Dunwich, Innsmouth, Kingsport and the city of Arkham. The latter is the home of Miskatonic University, which owns a translation of *The Necronomicon.* This is the sourcebook for Mythos lore and the spells and incantations that can presumably conjure up or cast down its immortal monstrosities.

Lovecraft had a lot of fun inventing the Mythos, but some of the succeeding generations of readers tended to take it more seriously. References to Cthulhu have been incorporated into the rituals of several cults, and years ago a few unscrupulous dealers in rare books claimed to actually possess copies of the *Necronomicon.*

I imagine all this might have amused Lovecraft, as well as

helping to confirm his views regarding the intellectual and cultural decadence of modern society. As a result of both physical and financial limitations his travels and social context were curtailed. He communicated with the outside world largely through correspondence so widespread and voluminous as to be almost legendary. And it was in letters that he created a legendary persona, that of a New England gentleman displaced in time. Pen in hand and tongue in cheek, he proclaimed himself a Tory, a loyal subject of His Majesty, King George III. He frequently affected the grammar and spelling of colonial days and began referring to himself as an elderly person while still in his thirties.

He was, in reality, a kind, considerate, courteous man, generous to a fault with his time and talent. Since his death more than a half century ago Lovecraft and his work have been both revered and reviled. But two facts remain indisputable. Professionally, his influence on the field of supernatural horror fiction was equal to that of Edgar Allan Poe; personally, he was one of the last true gentlemen.

Mind you, back in 1927 I didn't know all that much about either Lovecraft or *Weird Tales,* and probably wouldn't have cared if I did. What mattered to me was that this guy wrote good stuff in a swell magazine.

In school I was forced to squirm my way through the works of Oliver Wendell Holmes, James Lowell and Henry Wadsworth Longfellow.

In "Pickman's Model," the ghouls ate all three.

Now that, I decided, was poetic justice. And I still think so today.

SEVEN

Over the months that followed I read *Weird Tales* regularly, then sporadically, then not at all.

Because very shortly, my family ran out of quarters. As a matter of fact, once the cash flow dried up, we ran out of Maywood.

My mother had formerly been head of the Abraham Lincoln House, as previously mentioned. Since 1916 she'd been a housewife, and my father had advanced from bank teller to cashier at the Home Savings Bank in Chicago. When it went under—thanks to the machinations of the owners—he'd found a position at the Madison Square State Bank. Here, as head cashier, he'd been able to afford the down payment on our new home in Maywood.

But history repeats itself, and in the words of that great philosopher, the Shadow, the weeds of crime bear bitter fruit. The Madison Square State Bank was also trashed by its proprietors, and when it failed my father was suddenly out of a job.

As luck would have it, the Abraham Lincoln House contacted my mother. Would she consider returning to Milwaukee and become assistant to the director of the settlement again? Since my father was having trouble finding a job in another bank and mortgage payments loomed threateningly on the horizon, this offer seemed like a godsend. It would, of course, be only a short-term stopgap. Even though we'd move to Milwaukee, my father would continue to look for a banking position in Chicago. And instead of selling our house, we'd lease it for a year to a responsible citizen, Maywood's new superintendent of schools.

So it was that after fond farewells we entrained for Milwaukee and took up temporary residence on Thirteenth Street, behind Schuster's Department Store. The crowded three-room flat on the second floor of an old house in a dingy neighborhood was a far cry from our suburban home, but more importantly it was within walking distance of Lincoln House, a half-mile away. The neighborhood was even dingier there, and my mother worked evenings, but in those unenlightened times it was perfectly safe for a woman to venture forth alone at night, even in the so-called slum areas of a big city.

She went to work with her customary skill and enthusiasm, and the faltering social center—catering to the needs of Eastern European immigrants and their youngsters—soon flourished. Meanwhile my father roomed in Chicago while job-hunting and visited us on weekends. It wasn't an ideal arrangement, but my parents made the best of it.

For my sister and me, the best was none too good. Gone was our familiar home, our backyard playground, our friends and neighbors and relatives. Our household furniture, even most of our toys, had vanished in the move. In the absence of lead soldiers, I made armies out of painted figures which I cut from cardboard. We had no backyard now in which to romp outdoors, though sometimes we went across the street to Schuster's Department Store and played hide-and-seek throughout its three floors and basement. Winifred was eight and I was ten; although the landlady's teenage daughter kept an eye on us at night, I suddenly found myself responsible for the welfare of a younger sister. We began to learn the art of housekeeping—washing dishes, making beds, grocery shopping.

I got along well enough: I was president of my sixth-grade class when graduating from Fourteenth Street School prior to entering junior high. Still, we endured our dreary first year in Milwaukee only because we knew our stay was temporary. Just as soon as my father found a job we'd be returning to our house in Maywood.

But my father didn't land a banking position. He was over forty, and despite his acknowledged innocence of wrongdoing, the fact that he had been employed by two failed banks undoubtedly clouded his résumé. Despite the efforts of fellow Masons—he was a member of the Ancient Crafts Lodge—nothing was offered to him, and gradually he began to accept the fact that as far as banks were concerned, he simply wasn't bankable.

And even if he'd found employment, we wouldn't be returning to our home in Maywood, because it wasn't ours anymore. The superintendent of schools who leased it was six months behind in his rent. When pressed for payment, this respectable tenant promptly disappeared, leaving behind him a trail of bad debts and—some said—his wife and children as well. Unable to keep up mortgage payments, we lost the house.

So we were stuck in Milwaukee. Dad joined us there, to continue a fruitless round of job hunting, while my mother stayed on the job. The only mitigating factor was that the head of the Abraham Lincoln House was discharged and my mother became the director at a slight increase in salary. It was enough to enable us to move, first to an upstairs flat on Thirty-ninth Street, then to a similar residence on Fortieth. It meant my mother had to travel to and from work on the streetcar, but she did so willingly, with the assurance that we kids were living in a better neighborhood.

Here in our new home, Winnie and I attended the Thirty-seventh Street School and gradually settled into a much more pleasant life-style. We had a backyard to play in and neighborhood kids to play with. A few short blocks away was the vast wooded expanse of Washington Park, with its harness-racing track, its lagoon for boating, its playground facilities, and the Washington Park Zoo.

At school I squinted at the blackboard with increasing myopia. It reached a crucial point after a severe bout with scarlet fever, during which my father—bless him!—spent two weeks of quarantine with me in the bedroom. I emerged cured but obviously in need of glasses. Glasses were traumatizing; in those days only "sissies" wore spectacles, and were generally designated as "four-eyes." But the knowledge that I could see again overrode all ridicule—and the first day I wore my badge of shame we went to the state fairground to attend the Al G. Barnes Circus. Never have the tigers' stripes been so vivid nor the clowns' makeup so fantastic.

The years seemed to speed by. My sister was a homebody, but I roller-skated five miles downtown and back after school to visit the library, became interested in my father's stamp collection, played with Ralph Kufahl and other schoolmates. In winter Winnie and I listened to the radio—now a much more sophisticated medium of entertainment—and went to the new talking pictures regularly. After graduation I attended Steuben Junior High School, walking a mile both ways in snow, sleet, hail and galoshes, then entered my sophomore year at Washington High. By this time I'd discovered science fiction through the magazine *Amazing Stories* and renewed my interest in *Weird Tales*.

It was a comparatively happy interlude, and a heartless one. I'm afraid neither Winnie nor I, protected as we were by our fond parents, ever realized what they were going through. My father found temporary work, filling in for bank employees on vacation, but nothing more. Around 1931 he suffered a severe inflammation in the arm and was cured by—you guessed it—the removal of his tonsils. But from then on he began to develop symptoms of a mysterious malady which gradually affected his right leg with partial paralysis. Meanwhile my mother worked—nights, weekends, sometimes holidays.

And over all hung the pall of the Great Depression as the stock market crash of '29 heralded the horrors of the decade to come. Again, my parents made the best of it; my only firsthand evidence of economic tragedy came when *Weird Tales* cut back to bimonthly publication—and I couldn't stretch my diminished allowance enough to purchase it any longer.

Then the Lincoln House moved to Milwaukee's East Side and became the Milwaukee Jewish Center, in a much more modern building. I suppose it was then that I began to realize the facts of life, when we moved from our large upstairs flat to smaller third-floor quarters in an apartment at 620 East Knapp Street. It was within walking distance of the center, and only two blocks from Lincoln High School.

Again there was a disruption in our life-style. My father finally found a position as a cashier—not in a bank, but in the downtown Thompson's Cafeteria, where he worked all night. His salary was a princely fifteen dollars a week.

Winnie and I were more alone than ever, but now the Depression was a familiar and constant companion. Its impact was forcefully brought home to me when Dad told about the restaurant's employment policies. Whenever the cafeteria had an opening for a dishwasher, the boss always gave first choice to a university graduate, on the theory that anyone who'd spent four extra years to get a college degree was more deserving of an opportunity to earn thirty cents an hour.

Incidentally, one of the dishwashers was yanked off the job by police and charged with statutory rape. Why anybody would want to rape a statue I'll never know.

EIGHT

*T*he Crash of 1929 was still echoing as the nation was dragged, kicking and screaming, into the next decade. The Age of Innocence ended abruptly for the country and gradually for my sister and me.

The view from the third floor of 620 East Knapp Street was for the most part rather bleak. The neighborhood was aging less gracefully than the residential area Winnie and I had learned to accept as home. But there were certain advantages in the new location. My father made a gradual transition from limp to cane to single crutch over the years ahead, but at least the streetcar line which he traveled to and from work was only a half-block away. My mother walked the five blocks to the center. Winnie and I were close to Lincoln High School. A stroll could bring me to the lakefront, half a mile to our east; going downtown merely involved walking a mile in another direction.

Life had become more pedestrian. And for my parents, there were additional bills to foot. What they went through while Winnie and I frittered our lives away in high school is painful to contemplate even today. Somehow, despite physical and financial reverses, they found time to preserve our sense of family.

Often the time came at an odd hour. My father worked nights and went to bed when we went to school; we were together with him in the late afternoon and the evening meal before his return to work. My mother had a staggered schedule, but many times it involved night shifts from seven to ten P.M. I often walked over to escort her home, and sometime during the later years we might stop at the local tavern for a sandwich and a glass of beer. And there were nights when I'd head downtown just to pay a short visit to my father.

School, of course, was the big diversion for me. I was able to sail through most of my classes, foundering only upon the rocks of mathematics. During my last year of high school I attended a typing class which did nothing for me but did drive my instructor into a lifetime of analysis.

Early on I discovered that if my grades met certain requirements I could avoid the dreaded "three-mark" periodic examinations. I could also avoid the otherwise obligatory attendance at daily study-hall sessions by becoming involved in extracurricular dramatic activities; that time could be spent in comparative freedom, writing and rehearsing skits for what were termed pep rallies, which supposedly activated the gonads of the jocks involved in football or basketball games the following day. This led to participation in the annual minstrel shows and several senior plays. These activities, together with a stint as so-called humor editor for the monthly magazine and four semesters as president of the Student Council, kept me into mischief.

Since arriving at Lincoln High I'd become a member of the Harlequin Club, a drama society presided over by one Laura C. Boyle, a good drama coach and a skilled director with only one noticeable deficiency. She had no sense of humor. This turned out to be my own personal salvation; since her comedic judgment was flawed, I was allowed to do more or less what I pleased as long as the audience laughed. The outdated joke-book wheezes she supplied to the minstrel end-men didn't get the response of my monologues, which were filled with original material, mostly stolen from radio programs.

Let me hasten to add that I was by no means the brightest star in Miss Boyle's constellation; she attracted the most talented performers and extracted from them their best performances. The result being that now, even in the depth of the Depression and at a high school attended largely by kids from low-income or no-income families, Miss Boyle's productions always made a profit and often were held over for an extra showing. During the previous two years the box office returns had enabled the school to equip itself for talking pictures and a modern stage-lighting system, with enough left over to supply rather lavish costumery and elaborate props for the assembly sessions and rallies which I frequently was responsible for writing. I mean, after all, with the economy in such bad shape, what other high school could afford to supply me with a Napoleon outfit or two live chickens to carry onstage?

During those years it was evident to me that what I'd achieved was notoriety, not popularity. While I had an ample supply of friends within the student body and among the graduates therefrom, my onstage self-confidence and my offstage shyness made for some puzzled judgment calls. I was a tall, skinny kid who wore glasses; not being interested in sports was one handicap, and being interested in the curriculum was another. I knew too many answers in some classes and none at all in others. I had girlfriends, but no steady girl. I was supposedly Jewish but not a Jew. I smoked, I drank, but I didn't steal hubcaps. As a result, opinions about me were widely divided, with but a single general consensus—I was some kind of nut. In reality I was a centaur—half man and half a horse's ass.

Miss Boyle asked I stay on an extra semester. During the mornings I spent more time in rehearsal than in classes. In the afternoons I played bridge with ex-classmates Tony Balestrieri and Shanah Levant, and a young lady named Althea. The minstrel show and the senior play I stayed on to appear in both made a bundle; somewhere along the line I suddenly turned seventeen. And then, in June, everything was over. Or just beginning.

Because all this time I'd been leading a secret life.

NINE

The apartment building in which we dwelt was bordered by an alley just one block long, ending at the street to our north. This poorly paved stretch was flanked on the east by the backyards of other apartment buildings and the trash bins of their occupants. Standing beside the bins were long lines of garbage cans that served as condominiums for flies.

The west side of the alley offered a rear view of the local movie theater, which didn't look all that good from the front, either. Adjoining it was a massive soot-blackened structure which had once been a brewery; now, during the years of Prohibition, it had become a dairy. How they trained the cows to stop giving beer and produce milk instead is something I never knew.

During winter the alley was a wind tunnel; in summer it became a heat-retaining inferno. But for one day on or about the first of each month, the alleyway was transformed for me into a path to paradise.

At the far end of the alley was Ogden Avenue, and there, directly across the street, was the Ogden Smoke Shop. Despite its name, the shop didn't sell any smoke, although it was possible to purchase cigars, cigarettes, pipe tobacco and assorted merchandise from two elderly spinster ladies. I never learned to identify them; for all I know, their names could have been Nieman and Marcus. But that didn't matter to me. What was important was that they also stocked magazines. And one of the magazines they sold was *Weird Tales.*

It was after our move to 620 East Knapp Street that I resumed my perusal of this periodical on a regular basis. Despite the economic effects of the Depression, *Weird Tales* still cost twenty-five cents, but that was one of the facts (or figures) of life I had to live with. Most drugstores and newsstands didn't bother to handle this exorbitantly priced pulp magazine; the Ogden Smoke Shop was just about the only place where I could purchase the current issue. And purchase I must, because it was impossible to just stand there and consume the entire contents of the magazine with one or both of the shop's proprietors plunging their ocular daggers into my back. The message was clear; I had better buy because they would spare me no quarter.

In keeping with my exalted position as a high school student, my parents maintained me on an allowance of, roughly, a dollar a month. This sum I was permitted to squander as I saw fit, on sodas, candy, carfare, movie tickets and designer drugs of my choice. By cutting down on my consumption of carbohydrates, borrowing streetcar passes and confining motion picture attendance to nights when tickets were ten or fifteen cents, I managed to keep the necessary quarter in reserve for the next issue of *Weird Tales.*

But that didn't completely solve my problem. The anonymous ladies who ran the shop (could they have been Emma and Lizzie Borden, I wonder?) ordered only two copies of the magazine each month. This meant I had to get mine before the supply was exhausted, even if I exhausted myself in the process, which was usually the case.

On the morning which marked the first of each month—or

the second, if the first happened to fall on a Sunday—I would roll out of bed promptly at six-thirty. I dressed quickly and sneaked out quietly. Whatever the weather, I took the shortcut up the alley and usually reached the door of the shop just as it was being unlocked. Sometimes I even lugged in the bundles of magazines which had been dumped there, the sooner to stake my claim.

Many times I mused upon the possibility of sparing myself all this time, effort and stress by subscribing to the magazine instead of making individual monthly purchases. For $2.50 a year *Weird Tales* would be delivered directly to my door, and I'd be saving a whole half-dollar per annum, if you'll pardon the expression. But what if an issue got lost in the mail? What if some other resident of our building stole a copy from the downstairs mailbox? And, not to put too fine a point upon it, just where the hell would I get $2.50 together at one time in order to take out a subscription?

Matters of high finance were always a problem. As I previously mentioned, there was an interlude during which my monthly purchases of the magazine ceased. But though I told myself I'd sworn off (as I later did in regards to LSD, PCP, AT&T and other recreational drugs) I was still hooked.

In particular, my addiction to the work of H. P. Lovecraft increased. By the time I resumed reading *Weird Tales* his output had slowed, frequently leaving me frantic for a fix.

In the letter column of the magazine longtime readers frequently referred to Lovecraft's stories which had seen publication long ago and had not been reprinted. As far as I knew, none of his work appeared in book form although two of his efforts had received honorable mentions in annual anthologies purporting to represent the best short stories of the year. A fair number of back issues were still available from the publisher at cover price, but few contained the titles I was searching for. A Lovecraft junkie, I was hungry for more highs. What could I do?

As it has so frequently during a long lifetime, sheer stupidity came to my rescue. I sat down and—using the Palmer Method of

Penmanship, which I haven't mastered to this day—scrawled out a letter to Mr. Lovecraft care of the magazine. Identifying myself as an ardent fan (and a brash, presumptuous teenage idiot), I inquired if he might inform me as to where I could locate some of his stories presently out of print.

There came a time, some years later, when I myself received similar letters from readers or would-be readers. Invariably I replied, advising them to drop dead, get stuffed, or save on funeral expenses by willing their bodies to a cannibal.

Fortunately for me, Mr. Lovecraft proved to be far more charitable. There was nothing in his nature to sour the milk of human kindness. Within a remarkably short time I received a reply from 10 Barnes Street in Providence, Rhode Island, dated April 23, 1933.

In his minute, distinctive calligraphy (penned by a method unbeknownst to Palmer) the writer informed me that he and his two maiden aunts were in the process of packing and moving to a new address, 66 College Street. He had just finished taking inventory of his magazine stories and book collection, and was enclosing copies of both. If there were any stories on the list which I wanted to read he would be happy to lend me tear sheets. If there were any books in his library which might interest me he would be glad to lend me his copies.

To state that this response had a traumatic effect on me is to put it mildly, not to say tritely. The notion that a full-fledged adult literary celebrity would make such an offer to a half-fledged teenage nonentity was as astonishing to me as it was commonplace to Lovecraft.

Needless to say I jumped at the offer after first hurdling the problems of postage and parental approval. I never borrowed any books but I did solicit a loan of such stories as "The Rats in the Walls," "The Outsider" and "The Picture in the House." Formerly a Lovecraft fan, I was now a Lovecraft devotee.

More significantly, I had become a regular correspondent

with the man who variously referred to himself as "Grandpa Theobald" or "The Old Gentleman," he having reached the venerable age of forty-two. I had also thus unwittingly become a member of what was later styled the Lovecraft Circle—a group of friends and fans, many of whom were themselves writers or aspired to be.

Soon Lovecraft introduced me to some of them by mail, including such well-known *Weird Tales* writers as Clark Ashton Smith, Henry S. Whitehead, E. Hoffmann Price and August W. Derleth. Smith, a poet, artist and sculptor, wrote stories which many readers compared favorably to Lovecraft's; he lived in faraway California and we never met. Whitehead had been an Episcopal minister in the West Indies whose fantasy fiction frequently dealt with voodoo and similar beliefs; he died soon after we conducted our brief correspondence. E. Hoffmann Price saw military service in the Philippines, France and Mexico; an expert swordsman, Orientalist and astrologer, he lived eighty-nine full years. August W. Derleth, who later discarded his middle initial, was a poet, critic, essayist, budding novelist and near-neighbor; his home was Sauk City, Wisconsin, 120 miles west of me as the crow flies. But owing to governmental deregulation of birds the crows weren't flying all that often in 1933. It would be several years before we met face to face, and even then I traveled by Greyhound instead of crow.

It was much easier for me to journey via streetcar to see another Lovecraft friend, a gentleman named Maurice W. Moe who taught English at West Division High School. The idea of a student visiting a teacher in his family home was in itself rather heady stuff at the time, as was corresponding with grown-up fans like Bernard Austin Dwyer and J. Vernon Shea, Jr.

There were perhaps a dozen other members of the Circle; with a few I had peripheral contact, others I met years later or not at all. But I learned quite a bit about most of them and a great deal more about Lovecraft himself, whom they commonly referred to as "HPL."

Lack of funds generally prevented him from traveling, so

many of his friendships were made and maintained by mail. Diurnal duties included his own ventures into prose or poetry and all-too-underpaid ghostwriting or rewriting the work of others. Nocturnally, chronic insomnia aided and abetted his devotion to correspondence. The length and literacy of his letters are legendary; five thick volumes of them have been selected and published, representing only a tiny fraction of his output. If he'd diverted that time and effort to tales instead of the mails, fantasy literature would be the richer.

But people like myself would be the poorer. One of HPL's stories was titled "The Silver Key," and a sequel—written in collaboration with E. Hoffmann Price—was "Through the Gates with the Silver Key." In these stories Lovecraft himself appears as a character named Randolph Carter, whose silver key unlocks the gates of dreams.

To me those two tales and their titles came to assume a personal and particular significance, for it was Lovecraft who gave me a key and opened the doorway to my dreams. Quite early in our correspondence HPL suggested I might be interested in trying my own hand at writing with an eye to publication. A quick inventory of physical assets confirmed that I did indeed possess a hand and an eye, plus backups. And since Lovecraft's suggestion generously included his willingness to inspect my efforts, what more did I need?

Talent, ideas and experience, for starters. In the absence of all three, I unwittingly elected to follow in Lovecraft's footsteps—a route since chosen by dozens of future fantasists. Lacking a style of my own, I imitated HPL's; devoid of original concepts, my sketchy plots were, to put it charitably, derivative; as for experience, hadn't I written a school project, a short piece about life in the future, when I was only eleven years old? Surely now, having survived to become sixteen, I ought to have the ability to toss off five hundred or even a thousand words of masterpieces like "The Madness of Lucian Gray."

Effusions of this sort, which should have been tossed directly into the wastebasket, I sent off to my literary mentor. If he discovered grammatical or factual errors he offered gentle correction. I must have perpetrated four or five such pieces over as many months, in return for which he offered encouragement instead of criticism. And encouragement was precisely what I needed. Early on, at HPL's instigation, I sent one of my efforts to August Derleth, whose reaction was not quite as favorable. To put it bluntly—and he did—Derleth told me flat out that I would never become a professional writer.

As a matter of fact, it was to take eleven more years before my first hardcover book collection of short stories was published—by August Derleth.

But I anticipate, which is something I could scarcely do back then in the early months of 1934. By this time, again at HPL's suggestion, I'd sent several stories to William L. Crawford, a printer who aspired to become a publisher. In the faraway metropolis of Everett, Pennsylvania, he produced digest-sized magazines which featured a number of professional writers but paid zilch for contributions. Crawford, having nothing to lose, put my first story into print in 1934; its title was "Lilies" and the periodical was called *Marvel Tales*. Another of his short-lived publications, *Unusual Stories,* brought out something which I christened "The Black Lotus."

While Crawford had nothing to lose, it turned out I had little to gain. The so-called magazines bore little or no resemblance to anything found on the newsstands or even produced from under the overcoats of pornography peddlers, where their wares were concealed in that puritanical period. Showing copies of these crudely printed periodicals around would scarcely serve to establish my credentials as a "published" writer. Meanwhile, back at the school, I was still struggling to learn how to type properly. And time was running out; my extra semester had almost ended.

Then, all too suddenly it did end, with both a bang and a

whimper. The bang came from an all-night graduation party, and the whimper came from me.

Okay, I was seventeen years old, a high school graduate, and that just about summed it up. I owned one suit, an extra jacket, a hat, two pairs of worn-down shoes and a run-down watch. I had no job, no prospect of getting one, and no aptitude or special skills to offer.

To tell the truth, I was beginning to feel somewhat guilty about refusing a university scholarship. After all, my mother had been a grammar school teacher before she entered social work, and my father spoke highly of higher education. Undoubtedly both of them would have been pleased if I had chosen to obtain a degree and go into a teaching career; pleased, and in those deepest and darkest days of the Depression, probably relieved concerning my future.

But right now I didn't have any future. All I had was a somewhat willful and stubborn conviction which, after taking a deep breath, I conveyed to them directly.

"If you want to be a writer, give it a try," my father said.

"It's your life. You must do what you think best," my mother told me.

I was greatly relieved, but I should have expected those answers. When the Prohibition law was repealed, I joined various of my older friends in sampling alcoholic pleasures. These experiments culminated in an epic binge with a classmate which resulted in a lifelong distaste for gin. More immediately, it resulted in a burst of parental disapproval. My mother made it plain to me that she didn't want her son to win a gold medal at the Olympics for diving into a drunk tank. And yet on my following birthday, one of my gifts was a pint of whiskey—from my mother. It was her way of letting me know that I was responsible for my own actions and that she had faith in me.

This attitude on the part of my parents never faltered, and as a result I seldom faltered either. Once I completed the summit meeting concerning my plans for the future, the next step was comparatively easy. I'd accumulated a few dollars as graduation gifts from Chicago relatives; with them I purchased a secondhand typewriter and a secondhand card table and set up shop in a corner of my bedroom. Unable to find a source of used carbons and secondhand typing paper, I boldly rushed down to the nearest Woolworth's and purchased close to a dollar's worth of this material, together with several manila envelopes. For approximately twenty-two dollars I had assembled a complete armamentarium with which to wage a war against poverty, and now, all I had to do was write.

I trained my sights on the most obvious and visible target, *Weird Tales*. Instead of bombarding them with contributions, I took careful aim before shooting off a story in their direction. This cautious approach didn't reflect any particular intelligence on my part. What it demonstrated was that in addition to teaching myself how to write I had to teach myself how to type properly at the same time.

The secondhand card table was rickety and at times its legs seemed ready to give way as I pounded the machine it supported. The secondhand machine wasn't all that spry either—as a matter of fact, I believe it was one of the first typewriters William Shakespeare ever used—and frequently its keys jammed and the carriage lever had a miscarriage.

Words are weapons, too. Assembling several thousand of them, I constructed a story called "The Secret in the Tomb," which was a real bomb.

From what I later learned, many hundreds of such bombs were dropped every month upon the desk of the magazine's sole editor and reader. Since the magazine published a mere dozen or so stories in each issue, most of the bombs were effective only in exploding the hopes of their writers.

Why a battle-scarred veteran of longtime literary warfare would notice the feeble dud I delivered remains a mystery to this day. But in July, 1934, less than a month after graduating from high school, I received a letter of acceptance for my story. I would be recompensed at the standard rate, a penny a word, which added up to the substantial sum of twenty dollars.

Even though payment would not be made until publication, in four short weeks I had already earned back all but two dollars of my reckless initial investment towards a career.

More important to me was the fact that I had suddenly and almost miraculously become a professional writer, a contributor for the very magazine which published the work of my favorite author and present pen pal. On the day the letter of acceptance arrived I informed my parents, and sent off word to Lovecraft. Then, as visions of megabucks danced in my head, I sat down and started to write another story.

In the period that followed I sold four stories for a grand total of one hundred dollars. If I could keep up the pace during the twelve months thereafter and write longer pieces, I might escalate my income to as much as three hundred dollars a year. Of course this wouldn't be a sufficient amount to make me totally self-supporting, but then I was never any good at mathematics. All I knew was if I could step up my output, perhaps in five or six years I'd make enough money to starve to death.

Quickly writing (and selling) that second story turned out to be a good idea. "The Feast in the Abbey" was five hundred words longer and a smidge better than its predecessor. The editor decided to use it as my first appearance in the magazine, and this proved providential. It attracted enough favorable comment in the letter column to take the curse off my own letter which appeared several months before I became a published writer. In it, as a fan and reader, I had taken somewhat humorous but unmistakable exception to a character called Conan the Barbarian, hero of a series of stories written by Robert E. Howard. Mr. Howard was also a correspondent of Lovecraft's and had written many other tales which I admired, but I found Conan much too barbaric for my tastes.

Mr. Howard and his barbarous creation had many partisans, all of whom waited in ambush for my own debut. Like Conan himself they were equally adept with broadswords and bludgeons, led by a gentleman whose surname, appropriately enough, was Anger.

Using missives as missiles they skewered me for my opinion and the even more heinous crime of criticizing a fellow author. The fact that my letter had appeared in an earlier issue, when I was still a fan, didn't save my neck. I believe execution was avoided only because that second story of mine was printed first. Had the other preceded it, the Conanites might well have argued that anyone who wrote that badly himself had no right to censure the work of his peers. But somehow my story saved me from such a verdict and the literary lynching which might have followed.

It also taught me a valuable lesson. From that point on and to this very day I have avoided public criticism of my fellow writers, no matter how lousy and rotten their crummy efforts may be.

My status achieved public attention on my eighteenth birthday, April 5, 1935. That day a photograph and feature article appeared in the *Milwaukee Journal*'s popular Green Sheet. An interview by a lady journalist disclosed the sort of data no one would come up with until almost half a century later when somebody invented Trivial Pursuit. One of the nuggets in this gold mine of information was the disclosure that I had once spent the night seeking inspiration in a cemetery.

This was not entirely accurate. I had indeed climbed over the wall of Concordia Cemetery one evening during the past summer, but I didn't spend the night there. Nor did I intend to; if so I would have brought a midnight snack. As far as I was concerned the cemetery was a nice place to visit but I didn't want to die there.

The newspaper article escalated my ego but not my sales. That year saw the publication of three more tales, but it wasn't until the end of 1935 that I began (and continued) selling on a frequent and regular basis. The real benefits of publicity came about a week after the article appeared, in the form of an invitation to attend a meeting of the Milwaukee Fictioneers.

TEN

As far as I knew, all the members of the Milwaukee Fictioneers were vampires. They only came out at night.

Actually, most of them were moonlighters. Although the term had not yet been invented, the practice was widespread. You had to spread things pretty wide back then if you wanted to make a living as a writer. This was particularly true for those whose writing income, if any, was derived from the pulp magazines.

In faraway New York there were full-time professional writers who sat down to double-martini luncheons with double-dealing editors who reciprocated by giving them story assignments for their magazines. Several scores of these writers ground out wordage at roughly the same rate McDonald's grinds out hamburger meat today. Roughly, but not precisely; the rate for pulp fiction varied from one-tenth of a cent to as much as three cents a word, though a penny a word was generally regarded as the acceptable standard.

But the standard problem was how to make one's work acceptable.

Milwaukee was a far and despairing cry from New York. The number of pulp magazines published there could be counted on the fingers of one sardine. Milwaukee writers had no editors to buy martinis for, or the money to buy them with—a statement which, however ungrammatical, happens to be true.

As a result the city could boast of few published writers. It could, but it didn't. Milwaukee rewarded local authors with a long face and granted them short shrift. Even the latter was hard to come by; during all the years I lived there, the city never gave me any shrift at all. I had to buy my own, which wasn't all that easy, because I couldn't find out what stores to go to, and I didn't know what the hell a shrift was in the first place.

I didn't know what the Fictioneers were, either, when I received a mysterious phone call inviting me to attend their next meeting. Some kind of literary society, I guessed; maybe there'd be some girls. In any case I had little to lose aside from the carfare which transported me to a duly designated stop on the near South Side of the city.

Here, stepping out of the shadows to escort me to the meeting site, was a dwarf.

At least that was my first impression of Raymond A. Palmer, an impression quickly dispelled and displaced by the warmth and wit of his personality. Actually he was diminutive rather than dwarfed, a moonlighting science fiction writer who daylighted as a roofer and tinsmith. The evening meeting took place at his family's home.

It was there that I met Ray's fellow Fictioneers. The all-male unorganized organization had been founded three years previously by its perennial president, Lawrence A. Keating, who specialized in western stories, presumably based upon his own career as a cowboy in La Grange, Illinois. Morry Zenoff and Al Nelson were journalists, which gave them license to write about anything. Larry Sternig was honestly employed, but later turned against humanity by becoming a literary agent. Three members—Leo Schmidt, Bernard Wirth and Dudley Brooks—were university professors, but otherwise decent, law-abiding citizens. Gus Marx and Arthur Tofte churned out fiction on a daily basis as advertising copywriters.

Roger Sherman Hoar was a descendant of Roger Sherman, one of the signers of the Declaration of Independence. As corporation attorney for Bucyrus-Erie, he enjoyed train trips across the country accompanied by a secretary to whom he dictated stories under the pen name of Ralph Milne Farley. A pioneer in science fiction magazines of the twenties, he was now facing writers who brought new concepts to the field.

One of those younger writers was Stanley G. Weinbaum, who had become a Fictioneer only a year or so earlier. In that short span he had changed the face of science fiction without resorting to plastic surgery. Adding badly needed cosmetic touches of humor, his major operation transformed conventional "bug-eyed monsters" into characters. Where they were usually portrayed as threats, he gave them traits; instead of confining extraterrestrials to actions, he allowed them reactions. All this, mind you, before George Lucas was born.

Taken as a whole, the Milwaukee Fictioneers made quite an impression on me. I learned that they met on Thursday evenings, twice a month, each member playing host in rotation. Coffee and dessert were served, but no alcoholic refreshments. The meetings themselves were informal; reading one's efforts aloud was not allowed. These gatherings were to discuss problems encountered by those who had work in progress, and to help suggest story ideas for those who did not. It was in many ways the forerunner of today's writers' workshops. Most certainly it was a mutual-aid society; there was never any feeling of competition in the open-floor comments and criticism offered. Despite the disparity in backgrounds, education and income levels there seemed to be a genuine fraternity among these men, whose ages ranged from the mature mid-twenties to the elderly mid-forties.

I was later to learn that my role at this meeting was that of a prisoner summoned to a hearing before a probation board. Only after passing inspection was a writer free to become a member of the Fictioneers. What sort of discussion took place following my first appearance can only be imagined, but apparently there was no objection to a teenage weirdo who wrote weirdo stories.

Thus I became a full-fledged member of the Milwaukee Fictioneers at the age of eighteen and so remained for another eighteen years. During that time old members passed on and newcomers, some female, joined the group.

The Fictioneers did a great deal to sustain my feelings of identity at a time and place where writers were regarded—or, more accurately, disregarded—as nonpersons. Although only Farley had ever sold a story to *Weird Tales*, I discovered that Weinbaum wanted very much to appear in its pages. We frequently discussed the matter at impromptu interim meetings, during which times he came up with a variety of fascinating story premises he was never to work on. He died, tragically, a victim of cancer before the year's end, at the age of thirty-three.

Later I rewrote and sold stories which appeared under the bylines of Ralph Milne Farley and another member, Jim Kjelgaard. But at regular meetings I seldom discussed my own work problems and was never offered a story premise, matters which didn't disturb me in the least. What the Fictioneers gave me was the opportunity to learn about writing in other fields and find solutions to the problems involved in plotting and characterization.

In due time I collaborated on a play with Lawrence Keating, which we never sold, but it was heartening to be treated as an equal by an older and more experienced writer. Before his death Farley honored me in the introduction to a collection of his stories, referring to my scientific definitions—"Time is longer than anything" and "Space is just a lot of nothing between stuff." These postulates have yet to be refuted; neither has my gratitude for the help the Fictioneers gave me.

After joining them I began to take a more professional approach to my own efforts. The first thing I did was invest several dollars in round-trip trainfare to Chicago, then famed as hog butcher to the world, second largest city in the United States and home of *Weird Tales*. The magazine resided in a fifth-floor, three-room office a few blocks north of the old Chicago Water Tower. One of the inner offices was occupied by editor Farnsworth Wright, the other by managing editor William R. Sprenger. The outer office held a secretary and me, until I was duly summoned to step inside.

Farnsworth Wright was a tall, thin man with a small, thin voice. The latter, together with a persistent palsy, was probably due to the effects of Parkinson's disease, an affliction which had plagued him since wartime military service. An authority on Shakespeare and formerly a music critic, this soft-spoken, balding, prematurely aged man seemed miscast as editor of a publication featuring bimbos uncovered on its covers and horrors concealed within its pages. Bill Sprenger was more boyish and buoyant, but hardly the business-manager type. And yet between the two they created a magazine which fulfilled the promise of its masthead—a magazine so truly unique, bizarre and unusual that its name and reputation survive today.

Thanks to their warm welcome, I survived my first meeting and, during the years that followed, came back for more. Both men had a rare sense of humor, which is probably why they tolerated a teenage interloper like myself.

It was prior to this meeting that I'd sold them "The Shambler from the Stars," a story in which Lovecraft himself appeared under a pseudonym and a heavy cloud of purple prose. Naturally I had written to Mr. Lovecraft, asking if I could use him as a character and, incidentally, kill him off. He not only agreed but also sent me an official note of permission signed by a number of *his* Cthulhu Mythos characters.

Shortly after my story appeared, one of the readers wrote to the letter column of the magazine and suggested that Lovecraft might retaliate with a sequel. The notion appealed to him and he promptly set to work on a tale about one Robert Blake, of 620 East Knapp Street, Milwaukee, Wisconsin, who came to Providence and occupied a house which bore more than a passing resemblance to Lovecraft's own. In the end, needless to say, it would have been a lot better for young Mr. Blake if he'd chosen to stay at a Holiday Inn. Luckily for Lovecraft fans, Holiday Inns had not yet been created, or I might not have been destroyed. As it was, "The Haunter of the Dark" saw print in *Weird Tales*. Lovecraft dedicated it to me—the only story of his ever bearing a dedication—and for this I am forever grateful.

Following my Lovecraft pastiche it was time to move on. Not yet confident enough to shake off the influence of his style, I could at least explore fresh subject matter. After a slow start I wrote a yarn dealing with druids, although at that time I had never met one. Then I wrote a story about ghouls, though I had never met one of those either, and didn't until much later, when I went to work in a Hollywood studio. After that I tried a tale with an Egyptian background and subsequently pyramided it into a sequence of stories connected only by common (and all too often incorrect) mythology. Occasionally there were relapses into Lovecraftean settings but I was gradually undergoing a write of passage.

By now I was becoming somewhat established as a *Weird Tales* contributor and even had a few fans. One of them was a young California resident named Henry Kuttner who worked for his uncle's literary agency but had yet to sell a story of his own. When he did, shortly thereafter, he at once achieved a reputation for himself at *Weird Tales*, a correspondence with Lovecraft, and the basis for a lifetime career. He sent me one of his rejected stories and asked if I'd rewrite it as a collaboration; I did, and "The Black Kiss" was accepted. Years later he suggested his byline be dropped from reprintings because of the degree to which I'd altered the original draft.

Oddly enough, one of my most constant pen pals was none other than August Derleth, who had only a few years previously offered his critical opinion that I would spend the rest of my life as an unpublished person.

Augie, as he was generally known to his fellow residents in Sauk City, Wisconsin, was eight years my senior and he too had made his first appearance in *Weird Tales* at the age of seventeen. After university graduation he worked briefly as an editor and critic, then became a full-time free-lance short story writer, poet, essayist, dramatist and lecturer, and began a series of historical novels in a regional Wisconsin setting. The first of these had been praised by the eminent Sinclair Lewis, and thus Augie achieved a stature beyond that of his fellow writers in *Weird Tales*. He was prodigiously prolific and turned out a book faster than you can say "Stephen King."

On the day I rode the bus to Sauk City for our first meeting, Augie took the day off. He received me at the family home clad in a smoking jacket. This seemed a bit unusual to me, inasmuch as Augie didn't smoke. It did, however, contribute to his image as an Established Author, although in later years he abandoned neckties, long-sleeved shirts and ordinary footwear, even when fulfilling speaking engagements. Burly and barrel-chested, with a booming voice, Derleth was the antithesis of the "artistic type" then envisioned by the general public. He was a man of hearty appetites which he promptly satisfied, as demonstrated when he led me to the local restaurant for lunch and sent the waitress to the corner grocery to buy strawberries for his dessert.

During our meal he expressed hopes of subsidizing a Wisconsin visit for Lovecraft the following summer. Contrary to legend, HPL was not a recluse by choice. In past years I'd received postcards from Quebec, Florida and New Orleans, but his excursions were limited by economics. Derleth proposed bringing him out to the Midwest where, along with us, he could meet Maurice Moe in Milwaukee and Minnesota resident Donald Wandrei. Naturally he'd also stop by the *Weird Tales* office in Chicago.

I departed from Sauk City in good spirits and a Greyhound

bus. Back home, life followed its usual ups and downs. My father and mother continued working, but there were a few compensations. Sister Winifred was attending State Teachers' College, thanks to the generosity of the family friend who had offered a scholastic subsidy to me, which I'd refused.

My own earnings from writing were still limited, but sufficient to pay for the basics and such luxuries as a secondhand (or perhaps eighthhand) phonograph. Together with our radio and the upright piano which was always a parlor fixture, this massive mechanism provided hand-cranked entertainment. The seventy-eight-RPM records had a playing time of five minutes or less—*much* less if the instrument wasn't constantly rewound. I now had an opportunity to seek out and purchase a few of the compositions heard in radio concerts. My first selection was the Whiteman recording of *Rhapsody in Blue,* my second the first scene from *Swan Lake.* After that my choices were eclectic and eventually my phonograph became electric.

Meanwhile, music was a comfort, particularly during the sieges of respiratory infections which had plagued me since childhood. Colds were a constant problem when winter arrived. As a veteran Milwaukee pedestrian I had long since learned that when venturing outside at any time between November and March it was advisable to walk backwards. This effectively kept the wind from blowing your nose off. In those days, before the dawn of history, the windchill factor had yet to be invented. All we knew was that it was time for hats, earmuffs, gloves, scarves, overcoats and long underwear. Rubbers or galoshes were also de rigueur if one wanted to avoid rigor mortis.

But walking backwards was the real secret, though special skills were needed to avoid slipping on the ice which frequently covered sidewalks and crosswalks. It also helped to plan one's journey in advance, mapping out a route which included opportunities to duck into doorways and take momentary shelter.

When not under the weather I was out in the weather, making regular trips to the Brady Street residence of Harold Gauer.

ELEVEN

first met Harold Gauer in 1932, at Lincoln High School. He was a senior, contributing humorous pieces to the monthly *Quill* magazine and photographs for the school's annual. As a lowly sophomore I wasn't yet privileged to orbit within his stellar circle, but his work impressed me. By the time of my own graduation, two years later, mutual friends had brought us together.

Gauer and his younger brother, Norman, were the sons of a widow who operated a neighborhood candy store on Brady Street. Here, in the oversize kitchen, Vernie Gauer made her own candies on a huge marble slab which—when not covered with chocolates—served as a card table for Gauer and his bosom buddy, Herbie Williams. The two of them had invented a game called "baseball" in which ordinary playing cards were used to designate hits, runs, walks, errors and strikeouts for teams of imaginary players.

And that, dear kiddies, is how we unemployed youths amused ourselves during the Great Depression.

But there were other pastimes, and again Gauer led the way. He and Herbie Williams scrimped until they were finally able to acquire an automobile of their very own—a second-hand Model T Ford. The vehicle cost them a staggering $30.00, but it was worth every penny. Its tires were somewhat balder than Irving R. Levine, but a ten-cent tube of cement and another dime's-worth of patches were enough to repair frequent flats and blowouts; I doubt that Irving R. Levine ever got away as cheaply.

Tires weren't the only problems confronting the proud owners; the manual gearshift seemed at times to acquire a life of its own, and in order to start the car it was not only necessary to fracture one's wrist with the hand-crank but to risk breaking one's back by pushing the vehicle—preferably downhill—until the engine got the hint and took over. Once started, the trick was how to stop without killing the motor or nearby pedestrians. In the absence of reliable brakes—or any brakes at all—a passenger was required to aid the driver by opening the door and dragging one foot on the pavement to slow the car, which often attained the awesome velocity of twenty miles per hour. As optional equipment Gauer purchased a horse anchor which was tossed out the door to halt the momentum at dangerous crossroads.

Needless to say, this motoring marvel, like an elderly whore, was badly in need of a paint job. Employing all the care that the late Michelangelo lavished on the Sistine Chapel, we went at the task with brush and bucket. Carefully working on one section at a time, we finally achieved the effect we desired—a dazzle of stripes, polka dots, checks and pre–Jackson Pollack abstraction. Unable to agree on a color, we compromised on a disagreeable conglomeration of red, white, blue, green, yellow, orange and purple, with a bit of gold and silver gilt to add a touch of class.

Local citizens were duly impressed, though not necessarily favorably. In an effort to enrich the minds and hearts of rural residents, we toured the provinces. Gauer, brother Norman, Herbie Williams and I prepared for a camping trip to the faraway reaches of upstate Wisconsin. Ripping out the back seat of our pleasure vehicle, we loaded up the space with sleeping bags, camping equipment and such gourmet delights as canned baked beans, spaghetti and pancake flour. During the journey we passengers took turns sitting on our assets in the rear. This area, of course, was crammed with equipment for repairs, plus a spare tire—probably the sparest tire ever seen. We also brought along a canoe which, much to our consternation, we couldn't fit into the remaining space either in the rear or the passenger section. In the end we tied it to the roof of the car and covered it with a canvas tent which I suspect had once served as the Big Top in a flea circus.

Needless to say, the trip was an occasion. None of us started out as seasoned travelers, but we certainly qualified as such by the time we returned.

We faced a perilous journey of well over two hundred miles, but I'm proud to say we made it in just three short days. At night we camped at Depression-empty tourist sites or in open fields, making good use of our sleeping bags. The car, a bitch in heat, required frequent infusions of water for its boiling radiator. As for flat tires, I counted twenty-six of them during the time it took to reach Peshtigo and return.

Peshtigo itself had been the scene of a gigantic fire which completely destroyed the town and four million acres of timber and prairie land surrounding it, killing more than fifteen hundred people in a single day. Since that date—October 8, 1871—the community had resumed a peaceful existence, shattered only by the disaster of our arrival.

Townsfolk gaped at the car and its passengers; children were snatched up into the safety of their homes where, behind locked windows and bolted doors, grim-faced men loaded rifles and weeping women offered up prayers to the Almighty.

But the citizenry survived, and so did we. A careful scrutiny of our cash flow showed we had approximately twenty-two dollars left to maintain us in luxury during our vacation and provide the necessary fuel for a return journey. As a result we scoured the countryside and located a farmer who generously offered employment—harvesting and shucking his crop of oats at the rate of thirty cents per hour. As a bonus, he allowed us to take the sleeping bags into the denuded field for a good night's rest following our long and exhausting venture into agrobiz.

We left Peshtigo sadder, wiser and a trifle richer, then camped the next night beside a river. After a meal fit for a king—provided he liked oatmeal and candy bars—my companions retired to their sleeping bags in a tent fashioned from the canvas covering the canoe atop the car. Sated by outdoor slumber amidst swarms of mosquitoes endowed with the size and appetite of vampire bats, I elected to curl up inside the car.

During the night a thunderstorm arose, and the tent came down. I slept through it all, and when I awoke the next morning I was still in the car—which had been hit by lightning and rolled down the riverbank into the shallows. This, of course, was a blessing in disguise, because it meant we didn't have to haul the canoe there before launching. An hour later found us peacefully paddling downstream on a fishing expedition. Although no fish were caught, we were not disheartened. Abandoning our pursuit of piscatorial pleasure we returned to shore and prepared a lavish alternative breakfast of extremely flatcakes and Nabisco wafers. You may wonder how I can remember the exact menus of those meals after so many years—but if you'd eaten them, you'd know why they were unforgettable.

Of our many picturesque adventures on the homeward journey I shall not speak—you want details, go read Marco Polo.

Back on Brady Street, life went on. I had my writing to occupy the days. Gauer blossomed as a part-time cab driver. Williams finally managed to find a position, standing and swaying as third cook on a diner of the Northwestern Railroad. Other former schoolmates were less fortunate, and they tended to gravitate toward our circle. Among them were Milton Gelman, Bob Vail, Sprague Vonier and Victor Ehr; knowledgeable and intelligent, all made successful careers for themselves later in life, but during this period their outlook was bleak.

So they came to Brady Street and congregated in a tiny attic room lined with bookshelves and camera equipment. This was Gauer's private domain—the "Precision Process Laboratories." He'd come up with the designation in hopes of attracting customers for his photography, but when none were enticed, the name of the establishment was demoted to "the Lab."

He did take photographs here, with the grudging aid of a secondhand Voigtlander camera which was almost as temperamental as the car. Using outdated film and processing the negatives himself, he managed to come up with some surprisingly good pictures—the majority of which featured us in a variety of outlandish costumes and poses.*

These efforts found a repository in the *Goon History,* a running record of our daily deeds and misdeeds, further ornamented by Norman Gauer's cartoons. We'd christened our little clique the "Goons"—a term we'd picked up from the Popeye comic strip many years before the British comedy team of the same name came into existence. As Goons, we evolved a private vocabulary of our own, duly defined for posterity in a compendium called the *Goon Dictionary.* It eventually fell into desuetude, but the *History* which we began in 1934, survived, in truncated form, for decades thereafter. Its style was fantastic and flamboyant, leavened by a mordant cynicism. Emulating the Americana section of the then-popular *American Mercury* magazine, we incorporated newspaper and periodical clippings which illustrated the follies of the society in which we were incorporated, yet ignored.

All of us were avid readers—the Public Library was free—and

*None of which are reproduced in these pages. Gauer is publishing *History* material embellished with his own photography, and with this in mind, I've not sought permission to include specimens herein.

we gradually began to acquire a library of our own from the many secondhand bookstores around town. Deprived of higher education, we embarked on our own cultural crusade, discovering writers and discussing themes and disciplines gleaned from their works.

Through the efforts of another colleague, Clarence Lehr, we obtained the use of a downtown meeting place. His current girlfriend was the daughter of a local politician, and so it was that once a week we took over the Democratic Party headquarters for the meetings of a group grandiosely christened the Federated Arts Council. We spent a few dollars printing up letterheads to prove its existence, and soon we had a revolving membership of fifteen or twenty teenagers to augment our hard-core nucleus.

Each week a member presented a paper or prepared talk on a subject of mutual interest—psychology, sociology, anthropology. Anything ending in "ology" was enough to turn us on. The speaker's contribution was followed by a general discussion involving audience participation and much shouting. In time we contrived to lure some genuine authorities as guest speakers, ranging from qualified teachers to crackpot theorists without portfolio. Oddly enough, we managed to learn something from all of this activity, if only to go out and pursue our own search for enlightenment more thoroughly.

Concomitantly, we began to expand our interest in music and acquire a record library. Within a year or so we were cutting records of our own, writing, producing, directing and performing in dramas deliberately designed to delight a very special audience—ourselves.

Among the multifaceted gems we mined and polished were such jewels as *Fiddlestuffer and His Boss,* a dialogue between a morbidly masochistic employee and an employer modeled somewhat along the lines of the late Marquis de Sade. This was followed by *The Mark of the Monster,* an homage to the horror film featuring the voices of an extremely Mad Scientist, his whining Peter Lorre–like assistant, and similar stock characters.

From horror to politics was an easy step, and we took it with *God for Governor,* a dramatization of a typical campaign in which God Almighty ran as a candidate for governor of Wisconsin. Needless to say, He lost.

Some years later, following WWII, we did a mock radio newscast called *World War III.* In this one, everybody lost.

After Herbie Williams joined the railroad and became unavailable, Gauer and I wrote a novel—I *suppose* it was a novel—entitled *In the Land of the Sky-Blue Ointment.* It dealt with a group of characters cast up on a remote tropical island presided over by a rich and eccentric scientist, Dr. Nork, and visited by a variety of somewhat unusual guests: a bulimic photographer, a magician named Black Art, pious proponents of the Anti-Amusement League, the members of an opposing group called the Sexual Congress, a church official named Bishop Shapiro, and a scroungy author, one Lefty Feep. Gauer had appropriated the latter name from some long-forgotten magazine source.

Needless to say, this opus was created for our own amusement. But strangely enough, some years later I preempted Lefty Feep and reincarnated him as a Damon Runyonesque teller of tall tales for a series of twenty-three magazine stories. One of the book's episodes involving Black Art was immortalized in the pages of *Playboy* as "The Traveling Salesman." I also used the novel's setting for a tale parodying comic books, "The Strange Island of Dr. Nork." Gauer and I took turns writing sections, and my later adaptations came from sections I'd written, but the debt to my collaborator is acknowledged and apparent.

In spite of semipoverty we maintained the semblance of a social life. At sporadic intervals we obtained the run of the Gauer ménage. Here, by assessing participants the sum of one dollar or a dollar and a half, we provided our parties with alcoholic refreshment followed by a full meal of cold cuts and other delicacies. Sometimes we opted for a pony of beer, tapping the keg in the basement and sitting around it in a circle until the full seven and a half gallons were consumed. Our high school friend and associate, Tony Balestrieri, presided over the piano for dancing. Gauer had a steady girlfriend, Alice Bedard; the rest of us generally made do with whomever and whatever we could entice for such occasions. There were no sex orgies. The closest we came to them was one night when Bob Vail passed out on the sofa and some mischief-makers denuded him of his trousers while he slept, then carefully sliced open the back of his shorts. When he awoke the following morning he was more mystified than mortified, and no lasting trauma resulted from the outrage.

We also ventured into gambling. Playing poker for sums ranging from a tenth of a cent to a penny a point, with a nickel limit, we soon graduated to shooting craps on a Ping-Pong table in the basement.

One night, with all participants greedily eyeing the thirty-seven-cent pot, our play turned serious when a police officer intervened. After observing the evil activities through a basement window he entered the premises without a warrant and courageously arrested several of us as criminals. Along with others, I was taken aboard a patrol wagon and hauled downtown to jail. Once behind bars—after Gauer was denied the privilege of photographing me—my weary father was summoned to release me on twenty dollars' bail. The following Monday I was arraigned, tried, and sentenced to a two-dollar fine. Parental shame and anguish eventually abated—believe it or not, in those days, people sometimes lost their jobs because an offspring was deemed delinquent—and life went on.

But those high officials in the police department downtown never gave us back our thirty-seven cents.

So much for extracurricular activity in the Great Depression.

One more note. About this time I met a girl who claimed she'd lost her virginity. We made a thorough search but were unable to find it. And somewhere along the line I lost mine. As to the exact details of this episode I can only quote the immortal words of Carl Jung to Sigmund Freud: "My sex life is none of your fucking business."

Twelve

"**I**t may turn out after all that the weavers of fantasy are the veritable realists."

Arthur Machen said it long ago, but during the winter of 1937 I was disproving his point. He found fantasy in reality, and I compartmentalized the two. While doing my best to weave fantasy at the typewriter, I reserved my realistic approach for the outside world—an approach now made on foot. The car owned by Harold Gauer and Herbie Williams had been peddled to some lucky junk dealer for five dollars and undoubtedly resold by him for a handsome profit.

Aside from writing, the only profits I saw during the course of that winter were accumulated from our penny-ante poker games. Many of these nickel-limit orgies took place at the home of Victor Ehr or his elder brother's apartment where we high rollers usually forgathered once a week. Needless to say, particular pains were taken to avoid basement locations where cops could peer through the window.

These gambling sessions, together with biweekly meetings of the Federated Arts Council and the Fictioneers, plus a house party every two months or so, crowded my social calendar. And on once-a-week "bargain nights" I still went to what were still called the movies. At times I dated, but in a fashion which today would be called outdated.

All of this, combined with the daily stint at the typewriter, kept me thoroughly occupied, shuttling constantly between fantasy and reality. Sometimes inspiration was hindered by problems with respiration. If winter colds harassed me I either blew my nose or buried it in a library book.

I hadn't heard very much from Lovecraft after the holiday season, when I may have as usual dispatched to him a gaudy crayon-on-cardboard rendering of one of his monsters. I did learn he had seen his physician for a checkup, and was awaiting word of the results. The thought of meeting him the next summer evoked many a fantasy.

Then, on March 15, Derleth called me from Sauk City to convey the reality.

Lovecraft was dead.

THIRTEEN

It took me a while to learn the details.

Health problems had plagued Lovecraft for some months before a specialist diagnosed his advanced and inoperable intestinal cancer and chronic nephritis. He spent only five days in the hospital before his death at the age of forty-six. Apparently he had known what awaited him and accepted it.

Acceptance was a more difficult task for me. Howard Phillips Lovecraft, had been inspiration, mentor, friend. There were no words to adequately express my grief then and there are none now.

For a time I couldn't find words for my stories. Some time before, an idea had come to me for a longer effort titled *Satan's Servants*. Laid against the background of colonial New England during the time of the witch-hunts, it was definitely Lovecraftean, so much so that I had the temerity to ask if he might care to collaborate on the tale. Already ailing, he gently declined, but corrected my historical, grammatical and geographical errors. He even sent a map of New England on which he indicated possible locales for my imaginary place-names.

I'd intended to go ahead with the story on my own, but set

it aside for later consideration. Now I examined the uncompleted draft and set it aside again; *Satan's Servants,* in its final form, didn't see print until more than a decade later.

Henry Kuttner's letter came to my rescue. He and his mother invited me for a month's visit in Beverly Hills. Beverly Hills, California. Home of the movie stars. A place where nobody had to walk backwards to avoid the icy blasts. But I couldn't walk backwards to get there, either. The trip would cost a fortune—or would it?

Perhaps not. Consulting the classified ads I discovered somebody with a brand-new Chevy headed for Los Angeles in early May. He wasn't looking for anyone who might help with the actual driving; all he wanted was passengers. At twenty-five dollars apiece.

I had twenty-five dollars. As a matter of fact, I had one hundred and twenty-five dollars. My parents gave me their blessing. *Weird Tales* sent a check which would serve as an extra source of funds if needed. I finalized the deal.

Such, thank God, is the resiliency of youth. Resiliency, and stamina. During the trip there was reason to call upon both. Together with the driver and two other resilient idiots, I crossed Wisconsin, Iowa and Nebraska before enjoying a brief siesta in the back seat of the car while parked on a road shoulder just outside Cheyenne, Wyoming. Freeways didn't exist in 1937.

Once we resumed our trip the scenery grew increasingly picturesque. There seemed to be endless miles where men had not yet set foot, let alone billboards. Eventually we crossed Nevada, driving through the little town of Las Vegas, which had gained notoriety for its principal attraction—a red-light district consisting of bungalow whorehouses. Apparently my fellow passengers and the driver were on tight budgets like me, because nobody suggested a stopover. Instead we drove all night and, with dawn at our backs, descended the mountains as the sun rose over the suburbs of Los Angeles. It made a dazzling display in the smogless sky (smog, like freeways, had yet to be invented) and lighted our progress through Pasadena, Glendale and Burbank.

Somehow we discovered a pass that cut through the mountains to the south and arrived at Kuttner's second-floor apartment in a house on Canon Drive, just half a block south of Wilshire Boulevard. I was dumped off, suitcases in both hands. I rang the doorbell—presumably with my nose, since hands and arms were otherwise occupied.

During the sixty-two-hour trip I'd had a grand total of about six hours' sleep; I was tired, cramped, stiff, bleary-eyed, and, three hours later, swimming in the Pacific Ocean. So much for resiliency and idiocy combined.

Hank Kuttner had dark, curly hair, a small mustache and a large talent. He was two years my senior, living with a widowed mother and working for his uncle, Lawrence D'Orsay, whose literary agency was extremely successful. His own writing career was just beginning, and to him I was already something of a seasoned veteran. To his mother, I'm sure, I was just a twenty-year-old kid with a big mouth which seemed always open, either to emit nonsense or admit food. Nevertheless, both she and her son made me feel instantly at home.

Except that I wasn't at home and I wasn't myself. One difference was that I was no longer diffident. Hank had a girlfriend who introduced me to an attractive young redhead, presently divorced and a student at Otis Art. We spent many evenings together in what was then called the rumble seat of Kuttner's coupe and elsewhere. Among the elsewheres was old, pretourist Olvera Street, the original Chinatown, since leveled with the coming of the freeway, and the then-exotic Tia Juana. We attended a downtown burlesque show featuring Joe Yule, father of Mickey Rooney. There was a lavish party at Lawrence D'Orsay's canyon home, which boasted three acres of Shiraz roses, a huge Hispano-Suiza with silver tubing covering the hood like disemboweled intestines, and a small tram leading up from the road to the house high on the hillside above. Among those present was his young wife and a twelve-year-old son who wore a tuxedo. All very sophisticated for someone whose idea of a social gathering was six kids sitting around a pony of beer in a Milwaukee basement.

As a matter of fact, there were a lot of things about California which intrigued me: palm trees lining the major thoroughfares, the vast empty expanse between Los Angeles and Santa Monica's distant shore, the fragrance from the orchards which still flourished even when surrounded by residential development. Of course Hollywood Boulevard held its attractions, though I was surprised to find that the Hollywood Hotel was actually on Highland Avenue and an offshoot of the Brown Derby was on Vine Street. The corner of Hollywood and Vine proved to be a disappointing location even in those days; it looked better by night when I led my redheaded companion to the middle of the intersection for a bit of smooching. Naturally I thought this would leave a lifelong impression, but what I really remember today is that we did it without being killed by the traffic. Despite the Roosevelt Hotel and Grauman's Egyptian and Chinese theaters, Hollywood was still a small town with a big-city reputation.

The same could be said for Beverly Hills. Aside from a few structures around Wilshire Boulevard, the buildings in the business area were only two stories high. Virtually everyone traveled on foot, strolling past the small stores and sidewalk cafés which occupied the street floors. In those days it was possible to shop on Rodeo Drive without becoming an amputee—you could still buy things that didn't cost you an arm and a leg.

North of Sunset was where the bulk of the "movie people" lived. That's what they called themselves; nobody ever talked about the "industry." I certainly didn't, and despite my longtime love affair with films it never even crossed my mind to drive past a studio.

The closest I came to the Hollywood community was the evening Hank Kuttner escorted me across Sunset and into the realm of those palatial fifty-thousand-dollar mansions. Nestled between them were more modest dwellings, one of which was a residence of character actor Fritz Leiber.

I had seen this distinguished thespian in many films over the past few years, and once in a live theatrical performance. Heading his own Shakespearean repertory company, he came to Milwaukee and played Shylock in *The Merchant of Venice,* with his wife as Portia. Now, in Beverly Hills, I was to meet his son, Fritz Leiber, Jr., newly wedded to Jonquil Stephens.

The junior Leiber was a fantasy buff with ambitions of writing in that genre; for a short time he had corresponded with Lovecraft. When I met him that evening I found myself confronting a tall, handsome young man of twenty-six whose face and voice seemed oddly familiar. The first time I'd seen that face its complexion had been darker, but the voice was unmistakable—and, unmistakably, that of an actor trained in Shakespearean roles. And it was in such a role that I'd seen him, playing the Prince of Morocco in his father's company. Then he was billed as "Francis Lathrop."

Fritz eventually embarked on an illustrious career as a writer of fantasy and science fiction, and the friendship we formed on that May evening in 1937 endured until his death in 1992.

There were other meetings, with other results. Another Lovecraft correspondent and already established luminary in the pages of *Weird Tales* came out from Indianapolis for a vacation. While not as totally pseudonymous as "Francis Lathrop," the byline "C. L. Moore" was still deliberately misleading. Behind the "C" lurked Catherine, a charming and attractive young lady who charmed and attracted Kuttner away from his former dating companion. Catherine came complete with an accompanying girlfriend, whom I took over to form a foursome. Through the years I lost track of her, but Hank and Catherine were married and formed one of the best-known writing teams in both science fiction and fantasy.

Another encounter was with Forrest J Ackerman,* already past his first decade as a fan and collector with a special interest in movie memorabilia. I had read his contributions to amateur publications in the field, and knew he was one of the founding fathers of LASFS, the Los Angeles Science Fantasy Society.

At this time LASFS met downtown at Clifton's Cafeteria, a somewhat unusual restaurant. One of its distinctive features was a large open pool in the lobby containing a variety of live goldfish. Cognizant of the Depression, it charged no set prices, but operated on a pay-what-you-can-afford basis. I assume that those unable to pay anything had to content themselves by staying in the lobby and eating goldfish.

Ackerman may have had the goldfish concession at the time. LASFS now has its own clubhouse but no goldfish. Neither does Ackerman, a fan-turned-professional who remains active throughout the field to this day.

Before leaving California, Kuttner and I sat down with his artist friend, James Mooney. He provided illustrations for our text, which consisted of a series of stories burlesquing the styles and subject matter of various colleagues in *Weird Tales*. Provided with the necessary callipygous cover art, we titled our magazine *Plump Tales* and promptly mailed it off to Farnsworth Wright for his editorial edification. I wish I knew what has become of it today.

But at the time all I knew was that I had to leave California, returning home via Trailways bus.

When I got back from my vacation I needed a vacation. Instead it was time to go to work.

---

*Ackerman insists there is no period after the "J" in his name. Postmenopause, I suppose.

Fourteen

By this time you may be wondering just what was going on inside of this young man's head, if anything. Why was he making such a big deal out of a simple vacation trip to California? Why does it still rattle around inside an empty skull over half a century later? I share your questions; after all, people my age can't understand the young.

Perhaps memory will bridge the generation gap.

Bridging that gap was a problem even then. As a twenty-year-old airhead I was still floundering in a depressed and depressing economy. My parents were supportive, but I couldn't look to them forever. Where did I go from here? If I wanted to survive, I must turn to the typewriter and insert a blank sheet of paper. My future would depend on how I filled it.

I was beginning to realize the need of developing a style less reminiscent of Lovecraft's. And while I was at it, it would be necessary to abandon his pretense that genteel amateurs were somehow superior to money-grubbing professionals. The way things stood now, I decided it was better to be a live grubber than a dead gentleman.

Changing my style wasn't easy. I had no Rumpelstiltskin to sit down and grind out stories for me overnight while I slumbered. My only source of assistance was the minimal influence of the authors I currently read: Proust, Joyce, Maugham, Huxley, Mann, Dos Passos and Jules Romains, whose epic novel, *Men of Good Will,* continued to be published in segments. I was also partial to the work of Oswald Spengler and H. L. Mencken, but didn't think that the readers of *Weird Tales* would get off on their views or stylistic idiosyncrasies. In the end it was the purveyors of pop-lit who prevailed; years later I did pastiches of Thorne Smith, Damon Runyon, James M. Cain and others whom I'd read merely for light entertainment. As yet, nobody has ever confused my work with that of Leo Tolstoy.

When it came to confusing my work I did a pretty good job all by myself. It finally dawned on me that it might be helpful to seek other markets besides *Weird Tales.*

Amazing Stories, a science fiction magazine on the skids, landed with a dull thump in the Chicago offices of the Ziff-Davis Publishing Company. This organization's output included highly successful hobby magazines like *Popular Photography,* but it had little experience with fiction, let alone science fiction.

Why they didn't continue to let it alone, I'll never know. Whatever the reason, Messrs. Ziff and Davis were in immediate need of a new editor with a science fiction background. Somebody suggested Ralph Milne Farley as a candidate. After politely refusing the seventy-five-dollar-a-week offer, Farley recommended his fellow Fictioneer Raymond A. Palmer.

Ray was only too happy to become an editor in downtown Chicago. The problem was that along with inheriting the job at *Amazing Stories* he also inherited what had been purchased by his editorial predecessor. Upon reading the material, he decided these stories would amaze nobody. Faced with his employers' ultimatum that the magazine must appear without skipping an issue, Ray sold himself some of his own material, purchased what little was available at the moment from various writers he knew and cried out to the Fictioneers for help. But there were other hang-ups.

Several, to be exact. It seems that some staff members came up with a great idea. The science fiction magazines of that period boasted cover illustrations frequently portraying damsels being threatened by a variety of "bug-eyed monsters" who presumably had buggery in mind. *Amazing Stories,* issued in the same size and general format as *Popular Photography,* would distinguish itself from its rivals by using *photographic* covers instead.

Two of these covers had already been produced, featuring professional models in poses which had little to do with science fiction and nothing whatsoever to do with any of the yarns purchased by Ray Palmer. Supplying stories for the cover illustrations constituted an immediate problem, if not sooner. Ray sealed my doom by dumping a copy of one cover on me, and I sealed his by dumping a story on him—probably by return mail.

He should have killed the mailman. Unfortunately, the manuscript arrived safely and was published on schedule. It remains an example (along with several hundred other efforts) of my worst work.

Flushed with failure, I decided to go one step further.

My reasoning was simple, not to say half-witted. Dictating would relieve me of the typing chore and that, in turn, would afford me more time to concoct plots which would expand my output and open up new markets. After a bit of investigation I discovered it was possible to rent a one-room furnished office in downtown Milwaukee for thirty-five dollars a month. I also found a capable and competent secretary who required a salary of twenty-five dollars a week. Moving my typewriter downtown was no big deal, and with a lordly gesture I purchased a ream of paper, a package of carbons, a sheaf of manila envelopes and a lavish supply of stamps which cost me three cents apiece.

I was now in business with a vengeance, and it was not long in coming. During that first month I dictated a grand and glorious total of nine stories. One was sold to *Amazing* and one to *Weird Tales*. The combined purchase price almost exactly equaled my month's expenses—or would have, if *Weird Tales* had paid me on acceptance rather than publication. As it was, I hadn't earned a penny of income for myself and was forced to embezzle my piggy bank in order to meet the weekly payroll.

It didn't take a degree in mathematics to realize my business enterprise would never be listed in the ranks of *Fortune*'s Five Hundred. There was only one sensible thing for me to do—quit while I was behind.

Eventually my seven other efforts were sold, many of them to a new market, *Strange Stories*. But it didn't happen immediately, and the magazine only paid a half-cent a word. This was bad, but upon due reflection, so were most of the stories.

Maybe it was wise to become a part-time writer with a full-time job. Harold Gauer reached the conclusion that driving a cab was at its best a Checkered career, and we decided to seek out employment together.

Factories hired skilled labor, so we didn't join the hundreds who crowded before the entrances of local industrial plants at 6 A.M. whenever they needed to hire a dozen additional workers. The most sought-after opportunities were clerical positions in federal, state, county or city offices. But these jobs required special skills of their own. Men handled bookkeeping and accounting; women served in secretarial posts. Unfortunately Gauer and I had both flunked arithmetic in second grade and at that time sex-change operations were not yet in existence.

Gauer and I investigated the postal service. But upon receiving employment applications, we drew a blank. Actually it was the forms we drew that were blank, and remained so, because we couldn't fill them out with the necessary credentials. Apparently the ability to walk backwards in winter weather was not the sole requirement for becoming a postman, particularly when we were competing for jobs with ten thousand other guys who had the same aspirations.

Writing was the only form of self-employment we knew and as the year neared its end we hit upon an inspiration for a brave new beginning. Fired by enthusiasm—and not hired by anybody—Gauer and I decided to pool our savings for a trip to New Orleans in January, 1939. There, ensconced in a boardinghouse on Louisiana Avenue, we rented typewriters and collaborated on a "serious" novel which we hoped to sell to a commercial publisher.

The five or six weeks we spent in that city, exploring a French Quarter as yet unspoiled by tourism, was a total delight. We saw tailgate jazz bands celebrating funerals; heard then-neglected musicians perform for their own pleasure in Preservation Hall, feasted on thirty-nine-cent Poor Boy sandwiches and fifty-cent-a-dozen "raws" in the oyster bars, scoured the ancient cemeteries and the modern haunts of the Vieux Carré, where—under the tolerant eye of a corrupt administration—every bar with a green door was a gambling joint and every bar with a white door was a whorehouse. Needless to say, our meager budget precluded further investigation of either attraction.

The novel we managed to write during that period was christened *Nobody Else Laughed*. As it turned out, the title was prophetic. Nobody else did, and the book was never published.

But after returning home I sold twenty stories during the next seven months, one of which appeared in the newly launched *Unknown*. Money was trickling in at last, enough so that I could make contributions to my parents for room and board and handle other expenses on my own.

Wearing my new wool gabardine suit, I went out to Sauk City again for several visits. Derleth had built a home for himself which quickly became a local showcase. Among other features unusual at that time was a Burmese thatched roof, a black-tiled bath and a king-sized circular bed. On one trip, accompanied by the assistant to then-prominent columnist Arthur Brisbane, we spent Sunday at Taliesin, the home of architect Frank Lloyd Wright. His home was far more fantastic than Derleth's, and so was his array of guests. As to be expected, Wright was a brilliant conversationalist and a purveyor of the unexpected. That afternoon he had arranged a screening of an obscure Soviet film, *While the Czar Sleeps*, a comedy with a musical score by Prokofiev. The music is still around as a suite retitled *Lieutenant Kije.*

On another occasion I met Donald Wandrei, who had also been a member of the Lovecraft Circle. Now he and Derleth were making plans to get Lovecraft's work back into print. Unable to interest publishers, they decided to publish the books themselves. There would be two oversize volumes issued under the imprint of Arkham House. But telling the full story of this venture would require two oversize volumes in itself.

As best as I recall, these few outings represented the only breaks in my routine, and sometimes it was not only tiring but tiresome. I was happy to be meeting expenses at last and willing to work long hours turning out horror stories, but man does not live by dread alone.

During this period I discovered an unusual bar—the Wayside Inn—in a cobblestone alley just half a block south of Wisconsin Avenue in the downtown area east of the river. Despite an obscure location, this establishment had a particular attraction for many reporters from nearby newspaper offices. It also attracted me, because it was small, quiet and well run by its co-owners, Barney and Emmett Fredericks. The two brothers served as bartenders, and did so with a courtesy and generosity not common to the craft. About every fourth drink was on the house, and by the time that was consumed, I was usually deep in conversation with one or the other of my hosts. Intelligent men with a good sense of humor, both were fond of music. Before long I was bringing down ten-inch records from my own collection to play on their jukebox. *Classical* records. It was that kind of a place.

When Henry Kuttner came to town I introduced him to the

proprietors, and to Harold Gauer, who introduced him to his camera. All three of us went out to Sauk City for a day with Derleth, then to Chicago for Henry's first and (though I was unaware of it at the time) my last meeting with Farnsworth Wright.

Shortly thereafter I also introduced the proprietors to Marion Ruth Holcombe, whom I'd started courting. She was an attractive young lady whose slight and almost unnoticeable limp was due to a childhood bout with tuberculosis of the bone. Marion was a native of Weyauwega, a small town upstate; settled in Milwaukee, she lived at her married sister's home just a block away from mine. Barney and Emmett liked her, and so did I. Soon we were dating steadily and she became a part of the dazzling social whirl amidst the glamorous glitter of Brady Street and the Lab.

A great admirer of the then-popular radio team of Stoopnagle and Budd, I was emboldened to send off a spate of gag material to them for possible use. Back came an enthusiastic letter from Colonel Lemuel Q. Stoopnagle (*né* F. Chase Taylor) enclosing a check in the amount of five dollars and a request for more funnies. Visions of sugarplums dancing in my addled head, I promptly sat down and fired off a score of additional whimsies, several of which I had the pleasure of subsequently hearing over the airwaves. But I never had the pleasure of cashing an additional check.

A more direct contact with a prominent radio performer came about when Roy Atwell played a week's engagement at the Riverside, our downtown vaudeville theater. Atwell, after a long and distinguished theatrical career, had zoomed into kilocycle celebrity on the Fred Allen radio program as a monologist specializing in spoonerisms. Having imitated him in high school, using my own material, I had a ready-made "act" which I felt he might be interested in hearing. In order to reach the Great Man, I determined to appear on the same bill with him—on the theater's weekly amateur night. I did so, with the desired result; Mr. Atwell, having caught my performance, requested my presence in the star's dressing room and there promptly bought my original ten-minute monologue for ten dollars, free and clear. This represented a one-hundred-percent increase over my return from the Stoopnagle venture, but hardly guaranteed my future as a professional gag writer.

My theatrical appearance had impressed the master of cere-monies, a local radio announcer; he forthwith commissioned me to get up some material for him. I did so, to his great satisfaction and delight; however, before he got around to paying for it he left town for parts unknown. Inasmuch as I have never seen his name embla-zoned in lights since, I can only conclude that he neglected to use my material.

During the course of our meeting he brought me into con-tact with his agent, one Richard Pritchard, a brilliantined and bemustached entrepreneur with many clients on the local scene. This benevolent gentleman took a kindly interest in my career and at once secured me a number of bookings in taverns featuring "Entertainment Nitely." For a short time, then, I Entertained Nitely as solo comic, master of ceremonies and mimic, until I learned that the impresario's commission on my appearances amounted to a tidy fifty percent. Thus my ten-dollar fee dwindled to five, less carfare and the cost of the several beers and sandwiches which sustained me during the intervals between three shows per evening. Even a few bookings at banquets and lodge affairs, where the beer and sandwiches were free, did not console me; I deter-mined to retire as an active performer.

The next step was to write a full-scale act for a ventriloquist—stage name, Jimmy Murphy—a former vaudevillian who had set-tled in Milwaukee but continued to play stags, smokers, bar mitzvahs and, for all I know, brisses (at cut prices). As an old-timer in show biz, this man was a perfectionist; we spent many hours together going over every line, gag and bit of business I devised for him. By the time we finished I'd not only updated his somewhat old-fashioned act and invented a new "character" for the dummy he built according to my suggestions, but also provided him with sufficient material for two other full-length routines. Somewhere along the line his initial proposal—that I be paid a royalty for each use of my material—degenerated into an offer of a flat fee. This was acceptable to me, but unfortunately I never got the opportunity to accept it, since it was never forthcoming. He went on the road, then dropped out of sight.

Still an uncured ham, I'd developed a pretty fair imitation of the popular dialect comedian, Lou Holtz, and in 1942—after an interlude which will be dealt with elsewhere—I was offered an opportunity to collaborate with him on a book. It seems that one of the editors of the Ziff-Davis publishing company had heard my takeoff on Holtz and decided I'd be ideally suited to write a novel based on his "Sam Lapidus" character. Holtz was at that time touring as the star of a successful revue, *Priorities of 1942,* and when the show reached Milwaukee arrangements had been made for me to meet him.

My personal acquaintance with bona fide show-biz celebrities was, to put it charitably, limited. I had spent some time with a local musician and self-styled comedian and, at his insistence, had collaborated in the writing and sale of two short stories under his name; truth to tell, I'd found his egocentricity a trifle wearing and dismissed his further ambitions—which were for me to write a book to which he would contribute his byline.

But the same proposition, coming from someone of Lou Holtz's eminence in the entertainment world, enchanted me. I was somewhat disenchanted when I found Mr. Holtz to be even more enthusiastically and endlessly egocentric than my obscure musician friend; he was quite certain that his novel would be a tremendous success, quite certain that his name alone would ensure bestseller-dom, quite convinced that a sixty-percent cut of the proceeds represented the absolute minimum to which he was entitled. The only thing he was not sure of was just what this novel was to be *about*—and of course he wasn't prepared to offer any suggestions, let alone contribute to the actual writing.

Fortunately, I was able to supply the solution to this minor problem. Due to my familiarity with his repertoire*—in the course of our meetings it turned out that I knew several Sam Lapidus stories which he didn't recall—I came prepared with a brief synopsis. My basic story line was just that—a line on which to hang, in proper sequence, his well-known routines.

He warmed to the suggestion; before I'd finished reciting the plot he was already informing his charming wife that he intended to star in the motion picture version of his book. He introduced me to Willie Howard, Bert Wheeler and Hank Ladd, who appeared with him in the show, and seemed impressed when I offered knowledgeable comments on their work and careers. However, he was much happier when I directed my comments to *his* theatrical experiences. Holtz was somewhat surprised that I was aware of his San Francisco background, his entrance into show business under the sponsorship of "Ma" Janis and her daughter, Elsie, his transition from blackface comic to suave emcee, his successful engagements at the Palace, stardom in *You Said It* and other shows, his film work in *Follow the Leader* and his radio career.

I dwelt upon these matters at some length and with artful purpose because in the back of my mind I had nagging misgivings about the proposed novel. Dialect comedy was, I sensed, already on the way out, and the Sam Lapidus material needed Holtz's actual and adroit delivery to impress an audience; reduced to print, the shaggy-dog stories seemed like mongrel efforts.

After a few sessions backstage and in his hotel suite, I made my play. Why not, I suggested, abandon the novel and write, instead, an autobiography of Holtz's show business adventures? The saga of a stagestruck youngster who started his career as a coal heaver on the docks and rose to eminence as a comedy star of stage,

---

*Holtz's dresser—a mute—carried his entire stock of gags (including the "Maharajah" material he sometimes used) in a single, small black notebook.

screen and radio seemed far more interesting and entertaining; I even had a title, *I Played the Palace*. In 1942 the reading public had not yet been deluged with the life stories of every actor from Adolphe Menjou to Lassie, but I'd observed that the few such sagas available fared very well. There was a market for this material, and Holtz—who had rubbed elbows or raised them with virtually everyone of importance in the theater for the past quarter of a century—was a promising candidate for autobiography. I also pointed out that among his anecdotes about Ziegfeld, Earl Carroll, George White, Ed Wynn, Eddie Cantor, Will Rogers and Bojangles Robinson we could easily interpolate his anecdotes about Sam Lapidus and thus broaden the appeal of the opus.

But Mr. Holtz was not impressed. Such a book would require a degree of actual collaboration; he would have to mine his memory and come up with data concerning his life and times. It would be much simpler to do the novel, inasmuch as I already had a plot and would undertake all the actual writing for my forty percent of the deal. He gave me a copy of his itinerary and told me to send my chapters on to him for official approval as fast as I wrote them. And *Priorities* moved on its merry way.

Fortunately for me, I stayed put, nor did I immediately address myself to the task of setting the novel down on paper. I had reason to be grateful for my hesitancy, because in a matter of weeks, word came to me from Ziff-Davis. Someone in top management—either Mr. Ziff or Mr. Davis, or a party represented by the hyphen between their names—had suddenly decided that a novel about a character who spoke Jewish dialect was "controversial." And would I be so kind as to forget it?

Forget it I did, but I wasn't able to eradicate the haunting suspicion that if Holtz had been willing to pioneer in the field of show biz reminiscence at that time, we might just possibly have come up with a best-seller about the nostalgic days of big-time vaudeville and the Broadway of the Roaring Twenties.

Of course, by now I'd already had my indoctrination into the theatrical profession—working behind the scenes in the most glamorous, hectic, exciting and extravagant area of the land of make-believe.

I refer, of course, to politics.

FIFTEEN

In 1939 my story "The Cloak" appeared in the May issue of a new magazine called *Unknown*. This was a vampire tale with emphasis on tongue-in-cheek rather than fangs-in-throat. It marked a departure from my usual style; more importantly, it marked the arrival of James A. Doolittle.

Jim Doolittle was a young announcer on a local radio station. He wanted to move into network radio as an actor, and set up an audition for himself in Chicago. Like many in the profession, Jim could read words but couldn't write them. As luck would have it, among the words he'd recently read were those of my story.

One fine spring day he appeared at the apartment and made me an offer I couldn't refuse. Like all the previous offers during the past few years, it involved writing something in return for promises of future payment, and the reason I couldn't refuse it was that I was too stupid to learn from experience.

I wrote him a brief dramatic monologue in which the speaker was finally revealed as John Wilkes Booth. As of today I've no recollection of whether Jim actually got an audition. I do remember that he remained an announcer at Station WISN. Introduced to Harold Gauer, he was enchanted by our activities at the Lab on Brady Street. Already a family man, he was free to make only sporadic appearances and by summer's end he was making an appearance elsewhere.

For a week Jim occupied the announcer's booth for WISN at the Wisconsin State Fair. Shortly thereafter he came to me with a strange story.

Jim's father was the manager of the prestigious Milwaukee Athletic Club. Divorced and remarried, the elder Doolittle had no close ties to his three sons, although there was no reason for this fact to be generally known. Certainly it was not known by the young assistant city attorney who approached Jim during his announcing stint. Very likely the young attorney believed that through Jim he could make useful contacts with important club members.

To put it in a nutshell, the youthful assistant city attorney told him he wanted to run for mayor of Milwaukee in next year's election—and would Doolittle help manage his campaign? A nutshell is where this belonged, but it didn't stay there. Jim immediately accepted the invitation.

Now he had a small problem. Suppose the guy was really serious? Doolittle had opened his mouth and he wanted us to help him get his foot out of it.

Jim had come to me primarily because I was a writer. I suggested teaming up with Harold Gauer. With Jim acting as production manager and front man to deal with the press, why couldn't Gauer and I stay behind the scenes to write the candidate's speeches, originate the advertising, supply photography for it? Among the three of us we could take over the creation of the entire campaign.

Doolittle picked up the phone and called to arrange a meeting with the potential candidate that very evening. Despite their somewhat tenuous relationship, Doolittle's father allowed him the use of the Athletic Club's ballroom for rehearsals of what Jim hoped might become a band with himself as leader. It was during that night's session that our meeting was to take place.

The earth didn't tremble when that event occurred, but the walls did as Jim's aggregation of unemployed (and probably unemployable) musicians perpetrated what they presumably believed to be a number called "Tiger Rag." As the band went into its tiger-holding pattern, Jim introduced us to Carl Zeidler.

Carl Frederick Zeidler was a tall, blond, handsome young man with piercing blue eyes, an engaging smile, and a firm handshake born of long practice. Conservative in dress, he had a pleasant voice which, we learned, was frequently raised in song. Approaching his thirty-second birthday, he had none of the attributes then associated with the local breed of politicians.

Gauer and I liked what we saw.

We told him what we had in mind and he seemed enthusiastic. Zeidler invited us to visit him at City Hall a few days later.

By this time Gauer and I had formulated a few specific notions. Mayoral campaigns had little color or glamour to recommend them. They were generally held in neighborhood meeting halls around the city where the candidate exhorted small audiences of local followers. A primary election in March resolved which two candidates would face each other at the final election early in April. Traditionally the planning for these activities began around January first or thereafter.

Carl Zeidler would have to make the obligatory orations in the usual meeting halls. The difference would lie in the stunts and gimmicks we intended to dream up which would distinguish his gatherings from those of rival candidates. In addition, the speeches we planned wouldn't be written for the audience in attendance. They would be designed to command newspaper stories read by eligible voters throughout the entire city.

As for beginning work on the campaign after January first, forget it. We wanted to start *now*.

Zeidler's response was immediate and enthusiastic. "Great! You'll be my brain trust."

His reference was to a term currently used to describe presidential advisers, and we found it a flattering comparison.

Praise pays no bills.

We discussed salaries. Jim aimed high; with a wife and children to support he was emboldened to demand seventy-five dollars weekly. As bachelors, Gauer and I were content with sixty-seven-fifty apiece. The sum total, two hundred dollars a week, was what it would cost Carl Zeidler to trust our brains.

He met the proposal with immediate approval. In fact he suggested our salaries be retroactive to the first of September. His campaign backers would be starting to raise funds shortly. Meanwhile we required an office; for this he referred us to one of his friends and supporters.

Milton R. Polland presided over an insurance agency in the John Mariner Building two blocks from City Hall. About Zeidler's age, he was amiable and agreeable. He found us space there, and the Northwestern Furniture Company provided desks, chairs and file cabinets; the typewriters were our own.

Polland presented us to George W. Ernst and other members of the agency as his personal friends. We were, he told them, a couple of young magazine writers down on their luck. Only part of this was true, but the explanation was a necessary one, and not just because Carl Zeidler had yet to publicly declare his candidacy.

Today it's common knowledge that most political figures employ speech writers, even gag writers to supply one-liners. Their strategists and so-called "spin doctors" appear on talk shows to discuss how they have masterminded a campaign. In 1939 the situation was different. President Roosevelt was known to have help in speech writing from eminent playwright Robert E. Sherwood and to consult his "brain trust" for input. Nonetheless, it was generally believed that the majority of politicians originated their own ideas and wrote their own words. It was thought the public would lose respect for anyone haunted by a ghostwriter.

Carl Zeidler's position was even more precarious. Revealing that his campaign would be planned by two amateur spooks aged twenty-two and twenty-five seemed inadvisable. And as his advisers, we must remain Carl's dirty little secret.

Carl had other secrets, too, which were slow in coming. So were our weekly salaries. It soon became apparent that the financial committee remained unformed and no contributions had been taken in. The only thing Gauer and I could count on was that we had been taken in ourselves.

Jim Doolittle had taken leave. With no campaign cash flow to keep himself and his family afloat he had paddled off to Wausau, in northern Wisconsin, and a new announcing post at Station WSAU. Once the funds streamed in he would return to sail through the campaign. Meanwhile Gauer and I were up the creek without a Doolittle.

Rather than sink, we decided to swim. Our first task was to collect biographical material on the would-be candidate, get the details of his public record and qualifications. And, incidentally, learn just what had inspired him to seek the mayor's job in the first place.

"Paul Bergen told me to run," Carl confided.

"Bergen?"

"One of my best friends," Carl said. "He works for the city."

"In City Hall?"

"Not exactly. He's a truck driver."

If Carl had been advised to run for mayor by friends like truck driver Bergen and insurance agents Polland and Ernst, they must have had good reason to believe in his potential.

We visited Polland and Ernst to question them directly. They told us that Carl was widely known for his community activities, held memberships in many civic organizations and had spoken before most of the others. His speaking and singing talents were remarkable.

"But what about his background?" we asked.

This too, in their opinion, could be a great asset. Carl's father was a barber; the family, though of German descent, lived on the South Side amidst a predominantly Polish population. Over three-quarters of Milwaukee's voters were either Poles or Germans, so what more background did Carl need? But just in case this didn't satisfy us we should remember that Carl had two brothers. One of them was a monk in a monastery, which ought to secure the religious vote. The other was a county surveyor, which should appeal to the scientific-minded when they marked their ballots. The fact that this brother, Frank, was also an ardent supporter of the present mayor might even be a bonus; it could add drama to the campaign, like in all those movies where the good brother and the bad brother fight it out and the better-looking one ends up with the girl.

Carl was doubtless the better looking of the two, but we reminded his friends that this would be an election rather than a beauty contest. To that end we were interested in details regarding his public record.

"Public record? But you already know about that. He's an assistant city attorney." This from Polland.

"Is that all? He's never run for any other office?"

"No. He was appointed."

"What about his job? Did he handle any important prosecutions? Has he come up with any ideas for new laws or better ways of enforcing old ones?"

"I couldn't say offhand," Ernst was on hand to say. "Maybe you ought to ask him about that yourselves."

We did better than that. Gauer and I violated the privacy of the Zeidler household and raped it of several cartons of memorabilia, including every published item mentioning Carl's name, supplied by his clipping service.

Back at the office we weeded out snapshots, luncheon menus, place cards and male-chorus programs. Going through the actual news clippings we discovered that Carl's name seldom received more than a passing mention in reports of meetings or functions at which he spoke, sang, presided, represented the city attorney's office. Although Carl was constantly available for banquets, picnics, barbecues, memorial services and spelling bees, we located nothing which indicated his activities were either noteworthy or newsworthy.

We read the half-dozen prepared speeches he had used on special occasions. Carl's material had been derived, frequently and without attribution, from "inspirational" texts of the late Theodore Roosevelt and the early Douglas Fairbanks, before the latter had abandoned his all-American image in favor of costume films.

Discouraged but not defeated, Gauer and I located Carl yet once again. Perhaps his public appearances hadn't been all that important, and maybe his ideas weren't all that original, but everybody we consulted agreed on one point: Carl Zeidler was a great public speaker. Here we weren't willing to take someone else's word. We preferred to hear Carl's words, coming from his own lips. We took Carl up to the Lab, thrust one of his speeches into his hand, and turned on a borrowed machine.

We were not turned on by what we heard.

Carl wasn't a bad speaker, but he certainly was no spellbinder. He had a pleasant enough voice, the problem being he didn't know how to use it. He didn't know the value of a pause. When he wanted to emphasize a point, he spoke loudly. And it was evident, even in delivering a speech he had used before, he didn't always recognize a point when he sat on it.

We had known from the start that we had absolutely no experience in politics. And now we were beginning to find out that our candidate had no experience either. As sixth—and least—assistant city attorney, he had done little except what was chronicled in those insignificant news clippings. He had friends, but no personal following, no political affiliations and certainly no political organization. And, we now had reason to suspect, no source of financing. All he had were these two dummies, Gauer and Bloch, with their idiotic notion that it was possible to do the impossible and beat the unbeatable Mayor Hoan.

Daniel Webster Hoan was a fiery Irishman who had risen to power when the Socialist Party won the election back in 1910. It was then, at the age of twenty-nine, that he entered the city attorney's office, not as sixth assistant but as the city attorney himself. In 1916 he was elected mayor of Milwaukee. Now, twenty-three years later, he was still in office. Once regarded as a maverick, he had become nationally known as "the dean of American mayors" and served as president of the Council of American Mayors. At fifty-eight he was just as feisty and fiery as ever, armed with years of experience.

Over those years he'd been appointing department heads in City Hall and organizing ward workers outside of it. Although Milwaukee elections were held on a nonpartisan basis, Hoan had allied the Socialists with Wisconsin's then-powerful Progressive Party in the Farmer-Labor-Progressive Federation.

All of which sounds pretty unexciting, and it was—except for the fact that Hoan had an expertly constructed and efficiently run political machine which steamrollered all opposition. Republicans, Democrats and *The Milwaukee Journal* were powerless against him. Milwaukeeans continued to reelect Dan Hoan for five consecutive terms. Now he would be reelected for his sixth.

Or would he?

Aside from fault-finding and nit-picking, Gauer and I had responded to Carl's friendliness and enthusiasm. He had what has since become known as charisma, and we both sensed a potential here. If we could convey that quality in words, pictures and media events we would give the voters a new kind of candidate.

We had done our homework on previous mayoral campaigns all the way back to 1916. Microfilms were not available; under the pretext we were seeking information to write a book, we invaded local newspaper morgues. These were the offices where the actual papers were preserved, in huge leather-bound volumes. Their weight ruptured us, their dust blinded us, their dullness bored us. But we made discoveries.

Hoan's previous opponents, judging from reports of their speeches and activities, were colorless figures. Although many of them had held public office, none had a record of outstanding accomplishments. They seemed to have spent money like water, but since the repeal of Prohibition, much of it had been spent on beer. Their ward workers favored meetings held in taverns and rallies where liquid refreshment compensated for dry speeches.

Never had they sought to broaden the base of their political appeal, and few of them realized the importance of doing so.

But we did.

Despite his weaknesses, Carl had two areas of potential strength. He was young, and he was handsome. In those prehistoric, pretelevision times such qualifications were regarded as unnecessary. But fifty percent of the potential voters were women. Presumably some of them voted the way their husbands advised; a lot of them didn't bother to vote at all. It was, Gauer and I concluded, a wonderful opportunity for Carl. This good-looking young bachelor would naturally attract women's attention—and if we could provide him with campaign material designed to address their needs as working women, wives and mothers, we'd get votes which Hoan had ignored.

Carl's youth was another plus. One of the chief reasons Gauer and I were so eager to jump into this risky venture was that we had nowhere else to go. In that respect we were typical of tens of thousands of young Milwaukeeans. Mayor Hoan's opponents never addressed themselves to young people bedeviled by the Depression. Nor did Hoan himself.

Hoan had once campaigned with a youthful image and youthful vigor. During his early years in office he had surrounded himself with young appointees and followers. But now he and his supporters were entering late middle age; in the eyes of our generation they were already elderly men.

More important was the fact that the local Socialist Party had grown complacent. Hadn't every election proved they were unbeatable? Their smugness would be our ally too.

For all these reasons, Gauer and I believed Carl could make a good showing in the coming race. And at the end of September we had an additional incentive.

By then, Carl Zeidler owed us five hundred dollars.

Sixteen

During October our back pay accumulated, but only on paper. By mid-November we had received a promissory note and a grand total in cash of fifty dollars apiece. Now, between us we were owed $1,325, a sum then roughly equivalent to the national debt.

At the time we fumed, frustrated by empty assurances which did nothing to fill our pockets. The so-called finance committee was frustrated too, because Carl had not yet publicly announced his intentions.

Operating under wraps, the best Carl could do was sanction the formation of a secret Booster Club—a group to help in the forthcoming campaign. With few exceptions, the Booster Club consisted of scrapings from the political pork barrel. Struggling young attorneys, discredited ward heelers, self-styled "leaders" of various racial minorities—all they had in common was a desperate desire for self-advancement. We anticipated a potential clash, and when the battle lines were drawn, how could we insure our victory?

We had one secret weapon. Carl owed us all that money. Until or unless he paid us off, the debt hung like a Damoclean sword over his head. With the January starting date for the campaign only six weeks away, Carl was still hedging. Announcing his candidacy meant quitting his job, and after that there would be no turning back. He was still a young man, and maybe if he waited another four years . . .

But we were young men too, and we weren't about to wait four years for what he owed us.

Working seven days a week, Gauer and I had assembled a complete campaign, from blotters to billboards. We had laid out and written copy for newspaper ads in both the big dailies and the weekly neighborhood papers. This material was coordinated with the content of a dozen speeches, which in turn were built around themes that we intended to exploit at campaign rallies. And if their content wouldn't make news, the gimmicks we invented to accompany the talks would do the job for us—and, more importantly, for him.

There was just one more thing we'd forgotten to mention. In order to distinguish him from all the other candidates, we proposed the preparation of a special piece of advertising in booklet form.

Carl frowned. "What's so new about that? Lots of candidates put out pamphlets."

"Not with pictures on every page," Gauer said. "Pictures of you talking to voters, pointing out city problems, all kinds of informal poses the way they do it in *Life* magazine."

"It's going to* cost money," Carl said.

We agreed. But we also pointed out that there was no better way of familiarizing the electorate with his face, unless he could become a movie star overnight.

The reference to movies made Carl wince. Someone who

---

*Please note that Carl did not say "gonna." Television, and television newscasters, had yet to upgrade spoken English.

suspected the ambitions hidden behind his hectic schedule of speaking activity had already dubbed him "the Shirley Temple of Milwaukee politics."

But it wasn't our intention to push him into something he had doubts about. Since one picture is worth a thousand words, why didn't he let us take some photos?

On Thanksgiving Day most Milwaukeeans enjoyed the fun of preparing for a turkey dinner. Ignoring this fowl play, Gauer and I gathered photographic equipment together. We dumped it into the rumble seat of Carl Zeidler's roadster and took off with him for the downtown area. Here, for the benefit of the camera, Zeidler conversed with a group of idle cab drivers, then with the pump jockey at a filling station. Now we had our shots of the candidate talking to the man on the street.

Next stop, City Hall, deserted for the holiday. In Carl's office we posed him seated behind his desk, surrounded by piles of law books. Then we headed for the West Side home of Paul Bergen and his family, where Mrs. Bergen and the two kids huddled around the kitchen table with Carl, presumably discussing the problems of housewives and homeowners.

Returning to the Lab, Gauer seated Carl under the lights like a suspect facing interrogation, and violated his civil rights by aiming directly at him with a loaded camera. Thus portrait shots were taken, after which Gauer subjected the film to indecent exposure.

The results of these criminal activities pleased us both. Whether they would impress anyone else remained to be seen.

Marion Holcombe and Alice Bedard were both (if you'll pardon the expression) privy to our situation, interfering as it did with the usual pattern of dating. Knowing the facts, they could also understand how social life was curtailed by a limited budget.

Milt Polland, now officially the unofficial head of the campaign's finance committee, came banging on our door. But Polland brought no payment, and our mouths dropped open when he told us we were being evicted from our office. It sounded like highway robbery to us; first we'd been deprived of our dollars and now they were taking away our quarters.

The best Milt could offer us in exchange was a vacant storage space on another floor of the building. Left with no alternative, we lugged files, furniture and typewriters to the empty storage room. What Milt had neglected to tell us was that the room was not entirely empty. Lining the four walls were piles of cartons rising ceilingward, hundreds of open boxes, all with the same contents. Toilet paper.

So much for progress. After more than three months of full-time work, Gauer and I had nothing tangible to show for our efforts except for fifty dollars apiece and an opportunity to continue creating a mayoral campaign in a roomful of toilet tissue.

Without a doubt, Milt Polland had presented us with a liability. But almost immediately after our banishment to the realm of bathroom supplies, an asset knocked on the door.

Somehow, because of our move, the Morison Advertising Agency learned that there were a couple of real live writers in the building. An emissary from their office approached with a proposition. They were in need of someone to turn out fifteen-minute radio dramas for an unusual client, the St. Charles Boys' Home. This Catholic charity institution was located, I vaguely remember, in Illinois. The scripts, meant to be broadcast over a wide area, were to present fictitious case histories of how youths got into trouble, then got out again with the aid of the Home's guidance. All of which would be designed to lead up to a pitch for contributions.

This was not Gauer's specialty but I quickly agreed to provide the necessary tearjerkers for thirty-five dollars per jerk. The fact that I'd never written a radio script before didn't faze me, and apparently what I wrote didn't faze the Morison Agency moguls. To compensate for the absence of ecclesiastical information or inspiration, I wore a St. Christopher medal while scriptwriting. The playlets subsequently ran as written, and in my great good sense I retained no copies of them.

By now the holiday season was approaching, and so was the hour of decision which must precede the opening of the campaign. But our booklet material was effective, at least as far as Carl Zeidler was concerned. When we showed it to him his reaction was so extreme that we could only congratulate ourselves on the fact that our surroundings offered an immediate source of toilet tissue if necessary.

"That settles it!" he said.

"You really like the booklet idea?" I said.

"It's perfect! I don't care if we print anything else, just as long as this is put out."

Gauer frowned. "You won't get by with just this booklet. You'll need display advertising—blotters, handcards, window posters, billboards. Later on there's newspaper ads and radio time—"

"I know," Carl cut in impatiently. "But maybe we won't need it. Don't forget, I'll be making the rounds every day. After I resign we'll form a Zeidler for Mayor Club and have them set up meetings for me all over town."

Not too gently, we pointed out that he would be one of five candidates opposing Dan Hoan in the primary. In order to win the nomination, according to figures gleaned from previous campaigns, it would be necessary for Carl to get fifty thousand votes.

If the yet-to-be-formed Zeidler for Mayor Club set up ten meetings a day between now and the primary—an impossible feat to begin with—Carl would end up making roughly nine hundred speeches. Most of them would take place in the back rooms of bars and small halls, with daytime audiences of ten to twenty people. As a generous gesture we assumed Carl could attract the latter number to eight hundred of his talks. And if the other hundred were given at ward meetings nightly, he might have an average attendance of fifty.

Carl nodded, his face flushed with enthusiasm. "See, what did I tell you? We don't need all that other stuff—"

Gauer shook his head. "After nine hundred speeches we end up with a dead candidate—and exactly twenty-one thousand votes."

Carl whipped out his pen and did a little figuring. When he looked up again there were no roses in his cheeks.

"That's why your campaign has to be different," Gauer said. "If you want to get out and meet people, that's your business. The only speeches you need are the ones we're preparing for the formal rallies. Which reminds me—have you given any more thought to the points you want to emphasize in your platform?"

Carl frowned. "I've been too busy lately. Couldn't we just use some of that stuff from the booklet?"

Incredible. We had a candidate with no money, no organized support, no political experience, no record—and no platform.

Okay, so be it. We'd come up with a platform, and maybe construct a gallows on it just in case. Meanwhile other matters took priority.

Carl must resign at the last possible moment, probably the end of December. And the announcement of his candidacy would not take place until a week after his resignation, at his very first public rally. This way he could get extra publicity: one news story on his sudden mysterious resignation, a second one on the announcement at the meeting.

Carl was perplexed. "But how can I get people to come to a rally when I'm not a candidate yet?"

"We've figured out an idea," I told him.

Or something like that. To be perfectly frank it's difficult to do anything other than convey the general tone of dialogue which took place over half a century ago. Perhaps there are some autobiographers whose eidetic memories enable them to quote such conversations verbatim. All I can do at this late date is attempt to make these incredibilities credible and unscrew the inscrutable.

Why didn't we forget any ideas, just steal some toilet paper from our so-called office and go home, after extracting the promise from our overdue promissory note?

As any proctologist can tell you, hindsight is easy. Looking back at what we had done over the years, it's not difficult to discern our ends. It would appear today that we had, in various ways, anticipated the activities of young people in generations yet to come.

Our so-called *Goon History* was more diarrhea than diary—a constant voiding of complaints and dissatisfactions. Alcohol and tobacco were our substitutes for other forms of substance abuse, and in the absence of any gangs to join, we had created our own with the now-defunct Federated Arts Council. All we lacked were beards and mustaches, but in those days such hirsuteness was only associated with Civil War veterans, all of whom were dead.

We weren't, but it was difficult to get the adult world to take notice of the fact. True, my byline had appeared in print with my published stories, but most of the readers didn't know whether I was eighteen or eighty. Gauer, three years older than me, was equally lacking in identity.

For better or worse, in becoming a part of the Zeidler campaign we were becoming a part of the adult world which—God only knows why—we so desperately wanted to enter. Although unsuccessful in getting paid for our services, we could still call ourselves the masterminds of a political campaign. What proctologists would call us is perhaps another matter.

Scatological references aside, let's return to the little room in which toilet paper was stored, along with Carl Zeidler's campaign speeches. Carl himself returned to it a few days later, accompanied by Milt Polland, and we exchanged blows. Now Milt delivered a stunning counterpunch. As fund-raiser he hoped to get enough money for the start of the campaign as we'd planned it. But in order to do so, Gauer and I must accept deferral of our salary payments in hopes of winning the primary election, in which case we would be compensated in full, with an added bonus. Meanwhile we'd have to content ourselves with a token salary of thirty dollars a week apiece.

Reeling under the impact of this low blow, it was difficult to keep from crying foul. Instead, we sparred with our opponents, jabbing them with the news that Jim Doolittle had no intention of returning to Milwaukee. In his absence, it would be necessary to have someone out in front to take over the job of dealing with salesmen and solicitors, make the arrangements for meeting halls, monitor printers and engravers, set up distribution of flyers, posters and window cards, choose billboard locations, contract for newspaper ads and radio time, hand out speech copies and stories to the press. Outside of that, what he did in his spare time was his own business. But it would help if he was a personable, intelligent, sober adult who had a working knowledge of advertising, publicity, and the rituals of Tantric Buddhism.

Milt Polland thought he had a solution to our problem in the person of one Max Pollack, an advertising man who also managed a downtown office building and shopping center, the Plankinton Arcade. Milt brought Mr. Pollack to audition for Carl and us. Actually, aware of the immensity of our demands, we had to audition for him.

At first glance, Max Pollack was a short, plump, mustached, elderly man, probably close to forty. He was quiet, soft-spoken, courteous and restrained. Perhaps his lack of enthusiasm was due to the fact that friend Milt hadn't clued him in about working with two slightly overaged juvenile delinquents. But after we told him what we had in mind, he was transformed into a much younger, highly excitable man given to broad gestures and a broad grin.

By the time the meeting broke up, Mr. Pollack had become Max.

Within a few days, out of respect for his talents, he had become Max the Ax.

There were others whom we christened in less friendly fashion—namely (but not to be named here) the members of Carl's newly assembled steering committee for the coming campaign. Just before the holidays they steered themselves into the Elks Club for a dinner meeting to discuss what one of this erudite group called campaign "stragedy."

Milt told them a Zeidler for Mayor Club was presently being assembled, with Paul Bergen as chairman and George Ernst as secretary. Headquarters would open, unofficially, on January first in the Plankinton Arcade.

The group listened impatiently as Carl outlined needs for printing, distribution, promotion and advertising. These items were greeted with unanimous disapproval. Why waste money on advertising? Cash should go to pay workers in the ward organizations or fund ethnic support groups. It turned out that by some strange coincidence all the members of this steering committee were either ward organizers or self-proclaimed leaders of ethnic groups.

Milt Polland tried to duck the issue by answering earlier queries about Zeidler's resignation and announcement. It had already been decided; Carl would resign on Tuesday, January 2, and announce his candidacy on Saturday, January 6.

Objections rose loudly here in the private dining room, alarming other Elks Club members and rattling their antlers. The one thing everyone agreed on was that holding the opening rally on Saturday, January 6, was a crazy idea. Nobody in their right mind would forsake Saturday night's tavern-going in order to attend a political campaign meeting. Nevertheless, Polland told them that was the way it was going to be. Carl would resign on Tuesday as planned. When he called in the reporters he'd even have a prepared *script* on his desk, reminding him just what to do and say. The tease was that he'd give no explanation. His actual words would be, "Boys, I cannot answer today. But I'm invited to speak at a meeting at the South Side Armory next Saturday night and that's where I will tell my story." This would generate a news item in itself and stimulate interest in Carl's plans.

Just to make sure, Milt displayed the copy of a postcard to be mailed out to a list of six thousand members in various organizations Carl had joined over the years. The postal pitch invited recipients to come to the Saturday night meeting and hear WHY CARL ZEIDLER RESIGNED AS ASSISTANT CITY ATTORNEY. Expecting some kind of exposé, they'd find themselves attending the opening rally of the Zeidler campaign.

More outcries greeted this revelation. The South Side Armory was one of the largest public meeting halls in town. If Carl really intended to commit political suicide, why not do the hara-kiri in more intimate surroundings instead of a huge empty hall which would only reveal his lack of public support?

Neither Carl nor Milt had an answer to that question. All they had was us, and we were admonished to get to our feet. We told them why we had selected the South Side Armory and gave them a hint of what would happen there.

The thirteen members of the steering committee didn't like what they heard. And they certainly didn't like us. Since when were we telling the candidate what to do?

For the past four months, we said.

That information didn't please them either. As for our dumb ideas about the coming rally, Carl would end up being laughed out of town, if not run out on a rail.

The lines were drawn. Gauer and I, plus Max Pollack, on one side; the steering committee on the other. Which left Carl Zeidler standing in the middle, on Milt's shoulders.

But not for long. At eight P.M. on Saturday evening, January 6, he was standing at the microphone on the stage of the South Side Armory as the Zeidler campaign began.

SEVENTEEN

$\mathcal{T}$he South Side Armory had been designed for the National Guard. Lacking their presence, it resembled an empty shell when viewed from the stage at the far end.

Max Pollack, Gauer and I were the sole viewers on the cold winter afternoon of January 6, 1940. This was not a pleasant sight for eyes bleary from a week of frantic activity. At the moment we awaited the arrival of a commercial decorator who would dress the stage according to our instructions. Next came the crew to set up folding chairs, lug an elongated speakers' table onstage (even though few of our speakers were actually elongated), with additional chairs for the committee and the press table below. As all this was going on the three-piece orchestra arrived, plus a trio of young ladies with accordions, and then the entire Male Symphonic Chorus, conducted by Alfred Hiles Bergen, Paul's brother.

As the orchestra rehearsed, the accordionists rehearsed with it, the chorus rehearsed separately but simultaneously, the commercial decorator shouted orders to his assistants, the armory custodian screamed at the setup crew, the electrician yelled at helpers lugging in microphones, amplifiers and lighting equipment.

The only remaining task was to await the arrival of the neophyte candidate and suggest he read over his speech before making it.

To ease Carl's burden we had already underscored words and passages demanding particular emphasis and indicated pauses for (we hoped to God) applause. And once again we emphasized the importance of the First Commandment: *Thou shalt not sing.*

"Not even *God Bless America?*" Thus spake Carl, in a last-ditch attempt to sneak into the domain of singer Kate Smith.

"Look, we're using an orchestra. We hired girl accordionists who sing and also have cleavage. And we've got a whole furshlugginer male chorus yet. That's enough music. You handle the words."

A uniformed police officer came backstage, part of the squad detailed for crowd control.

But where was the crowd?

Suddenly there was a clatter of footsteps up front.

Yes, here they were! But on closer inspection the intruders bore little resemblance to an audience; they might more easily have been mistaken for the infernal hordes of the demon King Katschei in *The Firebird.* In other words, the campaign committee had arrived. Dignitaries and indignitaries started pawing for their name badges and bickering over the order of their onstage seating arrangements.

When they settled down at last there was ominous silence. The orchestra ceased orchestrating. The accordionists acted accordionly. For all one heard from the male chorus, they might as well have been emasculated.

The same held true for Max, Gauer and me. Had we made the wrong call? Were the elder statesmen on the committee proven right in their misgivings? Was it wise of us to venture so far up the creek without a compass, or even a periscope?

Max signaled to our friend Jose Mayol, whose violin bow did double duty when he conducted his mighty three-piece orchestra. Accompanied by the accordionists they began to play. I no longer recall what selection was performed, but I suspect it was not an excerpt from *The Firebird*. Nor did it matter, for within moments the music was drowned out by the sound of voices and footsteps, the scraping of chairs.

We peeked through the backdrop again.

Within the space of minutes over a thousand people swarmed in to occupy every seat and whatever standing room was available in the rear. Excited by all they had not wrought, the committee galloped onstage too soon; as a result the symphonic males never uttered a single chorus.

But the rest of the program went as planned. "Glamour girls" in evening gowns passed out campaign booklets and the new double postcards we had prepared—one half being a pitch to the effect that Carl's platform would be written by the voters themselves, the other half consisting of a questionnaire about issues to be filled out and mailed back to the candidate. The houselights dimmed, the stage brightened, accordionists sang. Stanley Jarz introduced his fellow committee members as though he was reading off a necrology. Someone named Czarnicki stumbled in and out of a short introductory speech which, by some strange coincidence, we had written for him.

Now the orchestra played a fanfare, the electrician turned on the spotlights, the largest American flag in captivity was lowered before the backdrop and Carl Zeidler was on. As his speech ended, Gauer and I yanked strings backstage and a net opened from the Armory ceiling to release a thousand balloons.

Looking back on all this today, it may be difficult for television audiences to realize how innovative these touches were a half-century ago. Local political rallies were singularly uninspired. There were no glamour girls, and usually nothing to pass out except the more inebriated members of the audience. Candidates didn't seem to realize that politics was show biz. They didn't dim the houselights, use spots; such now-familiar visual effects as the American flag backing and the cascade of balloons were then novelties. I doubt they were even employed in presidential campaigns or speeches; to the best of my knowledge Lincoln didn't inflate a single balloon at the Gettysburg Address.

At the time all this was new to the crowd at the South Side Armory, and so was the candidate and his style of speaking. Did it go over? We waited for the Sunday newspapers the way playwrights wait for first-night reviews. And the headlines read:

ZEIDLER OPENS CAMPAIGN FOR MAYOR'S SEAT: HOAN HIS FOE
ZEIDLER ENTERS MAYORAL RACE: BELABORS HOAN
SHOW STARTS ZEIDLER DRIVE
ZEIDLER DRIVE BRINGS PROMISE OF COLORFUL CAMPAIGN
CITY DUE FOR SHOW

We had only begun to fight.

Since his next speech dealt with problems at City Hall, we had a plywood replica of that structure built in miniature. With Max's enthusiastic aid we located the other props necessary for Carl's performance. When he talked about City Hall, one of the glamour girls wheeled it onstage. As he spoke about lack of progress and general neglect, he produced a feather duster and dusted the decaying edifice (the "dust" consisted of flour sprinkled on the model). When he spoke of "lifting the lid" on laxity and neglect in City Hall he proceeded to lift the lid from the model. Whereupon paper moths, activated by rubber bands, were released to "fly." Reaching into the replica, Carl drew out rolled-up representations of city plans which had been pigeonholed in city departments for years.

The campaign committee muttered, "Circus," but their remarks were not quoted in the press. Zeidler's were.

And we made sure that journalists would have plenty to quote from in the weeks to come. Carl made a speech presenting his platform, consisting of seven planks which had been hammered together by nonunion carpenters Gauer and Bloch. When he did the obligatory tax speech he indicated box after box labeled with the names of unnecessary levies being discussed, piled them one on top of the other and then smashed down the "Leaning Tower of Taxes" with his fist.

Our golden boy was cooperating to get the media attention we had aimed at, and for that we gave him full credit. Unfortunately, we could not give him cash. Even more unfortunate, from our point of view, was that he couldn't give *us* cash, either. Paul Bergen and Milt Polland had become our allies now that they saw the results of the strategy we had proposed. But their capacity as fund-raisers was exhausted and the campaign was running on empty.

Promises—and promissory notes—fell around us like the February snows. On occasion we escaped both blizzards and snow jobs by retreating to the Wayside Inn with Alice Bedard and Marion Holcombe. Along with the genial proprietors of this establishment, these two young ladies were among the few privileged to know what we were up to. Or, as time progressed, what we were down to.

Now we had our own office in the Plankinton Arcade, on the opposite side of the building that housed the campaign headquarters, to secure privacy. But by this time we were less concerned about our security than we were about the campaign's insecurity.

The rival candidates were micturating money like water. Richard Lehmann apparently expected to reduce taxes through diarrhea, for he was pledged to eliminate waste. Otto Werkmeister, perennial antitax candidate, showed stereopticon slides at his meetings which illustrated his criticism and excited nobody. Evidently he decided to take a cue from Zeidler, telling reporters he was hiring a press agent—a long-distance runner from Beverly Hills in sunny California. God only knows what the candidate had in mind, but what the long-distance runner had in mind was easier to determine. Shortly after checking into a local hotel he was arrested and thrown into the slammer after "examining" a couple of young females for secretarial positions. Werkmeister went back to his slides. A trio of minor candidates known to history only as Schultz, Selz and Blair, had about as much chance of election as the Three Stooges.

Carl's chief rival was wealthy realtor Earl Lillydahl, with his fifty thousand signatures on petitions and his slogan, *"50,000 Milwaukeeans Can't Be Wrong."* He had money for billboards, tons of campaign literature, mailing pieces, lapel buttons, and all the other items we lacked. He also printed up enormous posters featuring his portrait for display in every tavern and empty store window in town.

In a subtle hint to Carl regarding our own need of such advertising, Gauer and I filched one of these posters and smuggled it into the backseat of Carl's roadster. At the same time we acquired a second copy which, in the dead of night, we glued to Milt Polland's front door. Loyal supporter Polland was thus set up for an early-morning phone call asking him why he displayed a Lillydahl poster at his own home. Max Pollack got into the act by displaying a phony press release, announcing Carl's withdrawal from the race due to lack of funds.

We couldn't match this. And the worst was yet to come.

On Monday, February 19, the Honorable Daniel Webster Hoan would make his entry into the race with a traditional opening rally at Bahn Frei Hall. Naturally, none of the other candidates would waste time or money holding rallies of their own on the same night that the mayor and his slate of Socialist candidates would combine forces in a show of strength.

This, of course, was exactly why we intended to defy reason with a rally for Carl.

A week before the Hoan rally, Gauer and I sat down with Max Pollack. We fumed and fretted. What to do? Suddenly the idea hit all three of us simultaneously.

Carl answers Hoan!

The rest was complicated, but simple. Simple enough for Carl to understand when he bounced into our private sanctum on the following day.

"Yeah, that's a great idea, answering Hoan, but how am I going to do it?"

We told him.

Hoan speaks at Bahn Frei Hall. Sitting in the audience, Gauer takes notes. He gives the notes to an assistant, who keeps a lobby pay phone open and connected with Jefferson Hall where Carl is speaking at the same time. There is a telephone onstage with Carl, hooked up to another phone underneath the stage. Crouching beside this phone is me. I get Hoan's words from Gauer's assistant, invent impromptu answers and then ring up Carl as he speaks onstage. Carl picks up the phone, listens both to Hoan's quotation and my reply. Then he addresses the audience. "Do you know what the Mayor just said a minute ago down at Bahn Frei Hall?" He quotes Hoan and then, without a pause, continues with, "Now let me tell you, Mr. Mayor—"

Which is exactly the way we did it. With the aid of Carl's self-appointed bodyguard, Bob Winkle, Gauer managed to sneak into the Socialist lair undetected, commandeer the communications system and deliver the necessary information to me underneath the stage as above my head Carl was explaining about his direct line to the Hoan rally.

It went over with the audience and with the press. More importantly, it accomplished what we had been aiming at from the very start, establishing Carl Zeidler as Hoan's direct opponent. It also seemed to stimulate the cash flow. By some coincidence money was now coming in for billboards and a few other items. An anonymous benefactor donated funds for a radio speech. And Carl's performance might, we hoped, cancel out another performance on his part which we learned about through the newspapers.

The headline told the story: STYLE SHOW HEARS LOVE SONGS BY A CANDIDATE.

Carl had kept busy in a daily round of pressing the flesh, and if this was good therapy for him we had no objections. But at his campaign rallies he didn't sing a note, and we took every possible precaution, save actual castration, to prevent him from doing any local vocals as he toured on his own. But now he'd indulged in tonsillectual treason.

By accident he'd learned of a card party attended by six hundred women and brashly made his way backstage to suggest delivering a few remarks. But before he could take advantage of this opportunity he got caught with a group of fashion models moving onto the stage. Appearing on the platform arm in arm with a girl wearing a bridal costume, he took advantage of the musical accompaniment to sing "I Love You Truly." With encores.

Our chief bogeyman remained Earl Lillydahl. We weren't afraid of his efforts; it was his exchequer that concerned us. He kept bombarding the media to spread his name around and we were anticipating a last-minute barrage. And our team had run out of money. That being the case, we decided on a generous gesture. We turned the final meeting over to the campaign committee. Now at last they had a chance to demonstrate their political prowess.

For several months we'd importuned for a campaign newspaper. As expected, Hoan and his slate had one; rival candidate Richard Lehmann also distributed his news sheet citywide. Carl, Milt and Paul Bergen weren't daunted. It was a foregone conclusion Hoan would emerge as one of the two finalists. Like the rest of his stodgy campaign, Lehmann's effort, *Voter's Guide,* was hardly a threat. So why worry?

On the Friday night before our own last rally, they found out why.

It was then that Max Pollack rushed in, carrying a large bucket filled with an information leak. Our big-money competitor, Earl D. ("50,000 Milwaukeeans Can't Be Wrong!") Lillydahl, had placed ads in Monday's daily papers. And he was distributing, citywide, a tabloid newspaper of his own!

By tomorrow it would be the common property of Milwaukee's electorate. Tonight it was the common source of consternation for Carl, Milt and Paul. There was no point reminding them we'd proposed a similar project months ago and predicted some sort of last-minute salvo from the Lillydahl camp. And if we did so, they wouldn't hear us. Our voices would be drowned out by their concerted cries: "We gotta have a newspaper too!"

Speaking softly, Max reminded them that this was late Friday night and Tuesday was election day. He also mentioned that printers don't work Saturdays or Sundays, and unless such a paper was distributed early Monday morning it wouldn't be received in time to have any effect. He then brought up another minor detail—there was not so much as a dime with which to pay for printing and distribution. And, oh yes, another small problem. There was nothing to print or distribute anyhow. After our proposal was rejected, not one word had ever been written for such a newspaper.

So what happened?

Max, Gauer and I performed our usual chores at the rally that night. Then we returned to headquarters and wrote the newspaper. Max decided a smaller format printed on glossy paper would look better than what the other candidates put out. He did two layouts simultaneously and cued boxes, columns and half-columns with headlines. Gauer and I wrote stories to fit the spaces exactly.

At four A.M. we handed over a set of completed copy and layout to a waiting Paul Bergen. He sped off into the countryside, delivering the material to a small out-of-town printer who agreed to work throughout the weekend and furnish 100,000 copies for Monday morning distribution.

As for the final rally, this was the campaign committee's problem, not ours. Their big idea was to turn out the entire organization of ward workers in a huge display of strength, parading up Wisconsin Avenue to the site of the rally. This was to take place at the Eagles Ballroom, which had been cleared of dancing birds for the occasion.

All Saturday afternoon the members of the Zeidler for Mayor Club busied themselves preparing cardboard signs to carry in the giant spectacle to come. And promptly at seven P.M. the mighty cavalcade was under way—all thirty-five cars of it. The ballroom remained almost empty. This was probably a blessing in disguise; there were few attendees to witness what the campaign committee had overwrought.

Sunday we fretted about the next radio talk, the brief one to be given the following night in a roundup featuring all the candidates. We worried also about whether or not the newspaper would actually arrive for distribution in time.

Contrary to all expectations 100,000 newspapers went into the hands of distributors promptly on Monday morning. Gauer and I joined Carl, Milt, Paul Bergen and George Ernst at the Athletic Club for a steam bath and dinner. While the others hastened off to the radio station, we went off to hear the special program on which all the candidates were given five minutes to air or fumigate their views. The order in which they appeared would be determined by draw.

Otto Werkmeister apparently was aiming for the religious vote. He said, in effect, that he hoped God might take a few minutes off from blessing America and help him be a good mayor. Minor candidate Selz indicated little other than that he wanted votes. Communist Fred Basset Blair didn't sound all that optimistic but he too wanted votes. So did the county coroner "Doc" Schultz and antitax candidate Lehmann.

The next performance came from Earl Lillydahl, who dampened the microphone with actual tears. "I love Milwaukee. Elect me. Why, I couldn't walk down the street and hold my head up if I did anything wrong as mayor."

He was followed by Dan Hoan. His Honor didn't cry or

describe what he might do if he became a streetwalker. All he wanted was to have himself and the entire Federation ticket elected.

Much to our relief, Carl was the final speaker and he read the words well. "I'm not pleading with you at the last minute, like a criminal before a jury. I can't tell you in four minutes what it's going to take me four years to accomplish."

There was nothing left to do now but wait for tomorrow.

Carl voted, then drove out of town to avoid the press and the pressure. Gauer and I voted and went to Max Pollack's office in the evening, before the polls closed. There were, of course, no computers during Cro-Magnon days, which meant votes had to be hand-counted. At headquarters the campaign committee and the volunteers gridlocked before a blackboard which had been set up to record results.

We didn't go there. A call summoned us to a private dining room at the Schroeder Hotel where Milt Polland, George Ernst and their wives had already gathered, together with the Bergen family. Carl showed up. So did a liquor cart. Both were welcomed. During the community songfest that followed, the drinks poured out and the returns poured in.

Mayor Hoan racked up 75,000 votes, which was about 15,000 more than had been generally expected.

A funny thing happened to Earl Lillydahl's 50,000 voters on their way to the polls—only 18,000 of them actually showed up.

The other contenders got far less. The only notable exception was Carl F. Zeidler.

He received a total of 50,316 votes.

EIGHTEEN

All at once it wasn't funny anymore.

As dawn came it began to dawn on us that this situation might have serious consequences. Electing a candidate for mayor of the twelfth largest city in the United States posed not just problems but responsibilities.

We liked Carl. He was warm, enthusiastic, hard-working, and far removed from the arrogant, pompous posture of most professional politicians. But did these qualities qualify him as the potential head of city government? Could we honestly compare him to a man with the experience and public record of Dan Hoan?

These considerations were important, but it would be the height of hypocrisy to pretend that self-interest didn't enter into the picture. For six months the two of us had worked night and day with no time off for good behavior and little to show for our labors except broken promises of payment. The only result was that now we had a success on our hands—and on our conscience.

Since rival candidates had received fewer votes than generally anticipated and Hoan had received a good deal more, it seemed unlikely that Carl would be able to buck the odds against him. And if he didn't, there were still greater odds against us ever being paid for all we'd done. But if he did, what would be the payoff for Milwaukee?

Nesting in the office on the day after the primary election we found ourselves sitting on a possible solution, one we had partially hatched way back in the early days of the campaign. It was then that we had put out those double postcards urging the citizenry to help write Carl's platform. Needless to say, we received few replies of any note, and in the end we had to do our own carpentry. Now, looking through the platform, we began to realize that the seven planks made considerable sense.

What was wrong with the idea of establishing a City Plan for Milwaukee, or setting up a working organization to promote an influx of new industry into the community? As a city economically dependent on heavy industry which employed union workers, a Labor Mediation Board might well help to avert strikes and disputes through open arbitration. And for the many thousands of unemployed in our age group, calling a top-level conference to map out training programs and mount possible job opportunities could be far more than a token gesture. Consolidating the Harbor Commission with the Department of Public Works was the fifth plank and cutting salaries of overpaid department heads was the sixth; together they would help carry out the inevitable seventh, which promised a reduction of taxes.

There was nothing particularly brilliant about these concepts, but they did not require any particular brilliance to execute, and they would work.

So would we. And we called a council of war to discuss our proposals.

What Gauer and I cared for, and insisted upon now, was a private office where we could meet with Carl and without interruption.

Carl was only beginning to realize that in twenty short days a final election would decide whether or not Milwaukee would have a new mayor. We reminded him that, based on previous final election figures, it would probably be necessary to come up with around 110,000 votes in order to beat Dan Hoan. And in six months Carl had managed to capture just 50,000. Question: With less than three weeks to go, where was he going to come up with another 60,000 votes?

We thought we had a few answers.

The first one was to save time, energy and as yet nonexistent funds by chopping off a full seven days from the campaign. Neither Gauer nor I held a degree in theology, but we had both read the calendar and noted that Easter would be observed a week from Sunday. Tomorrow we would send a press release announcing that out of respect, Carl Zeidler would refrain from political campaigning during Holy Week. That would give us a chance to gird our loins for the final drive, or furnish them with trusses in the event nobody came up with money to implement our plans. It would also put the Hoan forces on the spot. If they didn't go along with Carl's pious resolve they might be flouting the predominantly Catholic and Lutheran electorate. And if they did, all they were saying in effect was, "Me too".

As for the campaign to follow, we recommended there be only one final public rally. Whatever money was available should be spent on a revised booklet, plus as many radio talks as the budget would allow. Radio speeches would be duly reported upon in the press if Carl had anything to say worth reporting. It was our job now to provide him with serious material.

Everybody nodded, but there was a hint of disappointment. No more gimmicks?

Well, perhaps one. Carl Zeidler was going to challenge Mayor Hoan to a public debate.

It sounds tame and old-fashioned in today's atmosphere of televised presidential photo-opportunities masquerading as debates. But in 1940 this was an idea which had scarcely seen the light of day since the Lincoln-Douglas clashes more than eighty years earlier.

"Great!" Carl shouted. Then his voice dropped to a noticeably lower level. "But what if he accepts?"

"Don't worry, he won't," we assured him. "Hoan is too smart to accept the open debate you'll propose. What he probably won't realize is that refusal puts him on the defensive. Which is where we want him."

"Then what happens?" Carl asked.

"By this time you'll get people talking, and some of Hoan's own advisers will start wondering if backing off makes it look as if the mayor has something to hide. So you create dissension in his own ranks and build extra support in yours. Saturday, you go on the air to announce you'll do no campaigning during Holy Week. Then you give Hoan a double whammy with the debate challenge."

Everyone at the table nodded, including Carl. "Sounds good to me," he said. "Let's do it."

The next morning we set up shop in room 317 of the Maryland Hotel. Our first job was to write Carl's radio talk. The program was set for the following night, as we insisted, in order for write-ups to hit the Sunday papers. We were off and running and foaming at the mouth.

Our rabid reaction came when we learned that the $150 for the broadcast had been publicly donated by none other than the ultrareactionary governor of Wisconsin, Julius P. Heil. The last thing we wanted was a tie-in between Carl and the Industrial Establishment.

Although not yet reported in the press, this news spread quickly in political circles. It might have had a bearing on what happened that night at a meeting arranged for all of the candidates for public office pitted against Hoan's elected officials. The idea— not ours, to be sure—was to unite them in a nonpartisan ticket headed by Carl. But one by one they chickened out.

So perhaps Governor Heil had made a greater contribution than he realized. At least we were spared the added burden of more would-be advisers who claimed to speak for pressure groups while talking through their hats.

This left Carl free to talk on the air Saturday night, and the Sunday papers responded as we'd hoped. MAYOR GETS CHALLENGE TO DEBATES BY ZEIDLER, and ZEIDLER WANTS TRUCE WITH HOAN ON NAME-CALLING, and MAYOR TO STUDY TALK, DECIDE ON ANSWER.

The Holy Week truce also scored signal success. But on Tuesday the papers reported Governor Heil's $150 donation and the Socialist newspaper proclaimed HEIL CONTRIBUTION KISS OF DEATH.

That was about as sexy as the campaign ever got. Before it could steam up any more there was a welcome diversion—Hoan's answer to the debate challenge. As we'd anticipated, Hoan branded the plan "vaudeville," but at the same time agreed to meet on a subject of his own choosing: "Resolved: That no city of a population of 500,000 or more in the United States has better or as good government in its administrative branches as the city of Milwaukee since 1916."

Delighted by the clumsy wording, we were even more over-joyed by the obvious bias it betrayed. This we pointed out to Carl, at the same time providing him with a letter which regretted the mayor's insistence on choosing a subject of his own. Was it "vaudeville" to debate the issues fully and clearly, to discuss unemployment, the decentralization of business and homes, the lack of a solution to traffic and zoning problems, etc., etc.? What was wrong with having debate topics selected by the Parent-Teachers Association, the City Club, the Wisconsin Federation of German-American Societies, the Pulaski Council, the Junior Chamber of Commerce, the Allied Veterans Council of Milwaukee County? Plus a reiterated challenge.

That evening there was a knock on the door of our hotel hideaway. The unexpected visitor identified himself as a Mr. R. O.

Wipperman, a "tax analyst" who would like to aid Carl's campaign by putting together a "statistical newspaper."

In actuality, as we soon deduced, this aging gentleman was a professional lobbyist from the state capital whose presence had been foisted upon us by unseen and unnamed campaign contributors. He'd managed to get through to Carl and the big question now was whether he'd be granted an opportunity to get through to the voting public. There would be only one route.

"Over our dead bodies," we told Carl at our next meeting.

We reminded him that financial backers were strangely absent during the primary campaign. But now that Carl had scored his unexpected victory they were hoping to use him as a mouthpiece for their reactionary and antilabor propaganda. Instead of trying to bribe Carl openly they'd probably propose a package deal: just enough money to maintain headquarters, bring out some literature, and finance the final rally and radio talks, on top of which they were contributing the services of Mr. Wipperman and his "statistics." At least that was our assessment. And we were perfectly willing to let Carl, Wipperman and the finance committee have their way, provided we could also assess them for immediate payment in full of our back salaries and bonus. Until or unless that happened Mr. Wipperman would be welcome as a guest but his material wouldn't be used in Carl's speeches.

It was an instant replay of an ultimatum we'd delivered in the primary and it had the same effect. Carl agreed.

He had little reason to regret his decision when the *Milwaukee Journal* broke precedent by running a front-page editorial landing on Carl's side in the debate dispute. It even offered a question of its own: HAS MILWAUKEE THE BEST GOVERNMENT IT COULD HAVE, AND IF NOT, HOW COULD THAT GOVERNMENT BE IMPROVED?

We couldn't have asked for more—except, perhaps, some of that salary money. Instead Paul Bergen offered fifty dollars a week apiece, back bonuses soon and another bonus if the final election was won. Meanwhile, just to pass the time, why didn't we write another campaign newspaper?

Damned if we didn't. And damned if we did, because we were in the same position as Carl; it was just too late to back out now.

Or not quite that late. Working with Max on the first newspaper for the primary had taken us until four A.M. This time we got it finished around two A.M.

Wipperman, despite his antecedents, was a pleasant lunch or dinner companion. From time to time he offered "facts" for our use in speeches which we politely declined. The Whip, as we christened him, never lashed back.

Mention should be made of a generous gesture on the part of Carl's brother. Frank Zeidler was an ardent supporter of Dan Hoan. But he voluntarily announced that under the circumstances he would not take part in the mayor's election campaign.*

As for Gauer and me, we were off to see the Wizard, and the Yellow Brick Road was beginning to feel a little less bumpy. Carl put in an appearance at our hotel room daily, money was flowing at last to pay for our expenditures—although not our promised back salaries and bonus. Carl's ward workers, about as useful to us as dandruff, were out of our hair. Aided by secretary Virginia Smith, a former schoolmate, we turned out radio speeches with multiple copies for press release. Good Friday passed, then Easter loomed.

On Sunday afternoon we called Milt Polland, Paul Bergen, Max and the Whip to join us at the hotel room for an impromptu poker game as we waited for our candidate. When he arrived we

---

*This good deed did not go unrewarded. Fate dispenses strange surprises, and not too many years later Frank Zeidler himself became mayor of Milwaukee. Our longtime friend and companion Sprague Vonier served as his press secretary. Small world.

presented him with another letter to Dan Hoan, urging him to accept the debate topic proposed by the *Milwaukee Journal.*

Carl shook his head. It was too late to make arrangements. With the expected exception of Max Pollack, the others agreed. Obviously, like Carl himself, they were afraid of what might happen if our little David engaged in face-to-face combat with the gigantic Goliath of Milwaukee politics.

This reaction had been anticipated. We hauled out a file of material about city mismanagement, favoritism in contract awards and other embarrassments to the administration which we'd assembled and held in reserve. If Carl raised these issues during the debate, Hoan would be hard-put to come up with impromptu explanations. And instead of communicating with our candidate by telephone, we would sit at Carl's platform table and huddle with him regarding replies whenever his opponent was speaking. The bottom line was that we still didn't believe the mayor would accept the challenge. But either way, Carl had to sign the letter. And he did.

Monday brought us into the final full week of the campaign, and it kept getting fuller. We wrote a broadcast speech for Carl's former rival, coroner Schultz, appropriately filled with dead issues. Somebody volunteered to speak on the Polish radio station and we provided words for him to translate just before air time. Meanwhile there was always Carl's schedule to consider. Our radio material had been designed not just for listeners but for newspaper readers. And over the week they had plenty to squint at:

ZEIDLER RENEWS DEBATE CHALLENGE

NEW CALL FOR DEBATE DECLINED

(As we expected, and much to Carl's relief)

MILWAUKEE DEBT FUND HISTORY HURLED AT HOAN

INDUSTRY FLEES HIGH TAX RATE, ZEIDLER SAYS

WATER RATE INCREASE BLAMED ON SOCIALISTS

And more of same. Much more. We stressed the platform plank about creating a Labor Mediation Board, but used none of the Whip's propaganda.

His unseen employers wouldn't accept defeat. Without our knowledge or consent they sneaked off and bought radio time on Station WEMP. Here the Whip personally delivered the message which we had refused to let Carl slide past his tonsils. The Whip's talk was so dry that the humidity level in the studio dropped seventeen degrees. And next day, when the silver-tongued orator and his bosses scanned the local papers for write-ups, not a word was printed—not even in the weather reports.

Max had his own project. Contemptuous of the feeble effort put forth by the Zeidler for Mayor Club in organizing the last rally before primary election, he intended to show how much more could be accomplished by just one man who knew what he was doing. And, if that wasn't enough, he'd throw in a parade, too.

We applauded his efforts and bent our own to writing Carl's speech for this final rally.

Max's parade hit Wisconsin Avenue on Saturday night and ended at his own purlieu, the Plankinton Arcade. Instead of a thirty-five-car funeral procession, Max's version was led by the American Legion band and followed by marchers carrying red flares. The professionally decorated motorcade featured a donated open roadster with ex-truck driver Paul Bergen as chauffeur and ex-sixth assistant city attorney Carl F. Zeidler as its passenger. There was no problem attracting an audience for such a spectacle, nor for the rally on the second-floor rotunda of the arcade.

Sunday and Monday were downers. While the press had given us the publicity we had aimed for, there were no editorial endorsements. Except, of course, for the Socialist paper's inevitable pledge of allegiance to Dan Hoan. And despite the kid gloves we'd worn when handling labor questions, the unions announced their support of the mayor. Meanwhile, word from informed sources—

our friends Barney and Emmett at the Wayside Inn—set the professional gamblers' betting odds at six to one against Carl.

Tuesday was Election Day. There was a quiet dinner with Max; then Carl showed up with Mr. Fredricson, his old music teacher. Noting that his former pupil was uptight he suggested that Carl lie down on the bed while he told him some funny stories.

Somehow the stories didn't seem all that funny, and neither did the situation. Carl kept assuring Max and us that no matter what happened we had his undying gratitude. We were afraid he'd deliver a full-length speech and, with his music teacher present, end by singing *God Bless America*.

Instead we scooted over to another hotel, the Medford. Its Bamboo Room had been rented for the Zeidler for Mayor Club. Stuffing down a buffet of cold cuts, they milled around the big blackboard on which election results would be chalked up, and waded into the free beer. As elitist members of the Dom Perignon and Pepsi crowd, we had our own private hidequarters upstairs, where we joined Milt Polland, Paul Bergen, George Ernst and the ever-dangling Whip.

Nobody had ever heard of exit polls, mathematical projections based on one percent of the returns, or scientific predictions made by photogenic blond newscasters. That night in the private room we huddled around the radio and scribbled down figures as they came in. Slowly.

It had taken seven months to get this far, but these last few hours seemed an even longer stretch. Somewhere past midnight the final results were announced.

Carl Zeidler would be the next mayor of Milwaukee. He had defeated Hoan by more than twelve thousand votes.

NINETEEN

What followed is a blur.

Carl went downstairs to be mobbed and photographed. We were later told that, free of his bonds at last, he actually did sing *God Bless America*.

When he returned to us he was trailed by none other than Governer Heil and his buddies, Colonel Wabiesjewski and Sam Smith. Congratulations and drinks poured forth. The Gov and the Whip went home; detectives Cronce, Wysocki, Werble and Jeffries took over to guard the halls. The phone rang. Telegrams arrived by messenger, not through the mail. Carl went to bed. Milt, Ernst, Gauer and I started up a poker game with some of the detectives, finally retiring to rooms across the hall.

After short naps we rose for an early breakfast, then wrote a speech to be broadcast at noon directly from Carl's home.

Everybody showed up for that audio opportunity, including the Whip. Somebody stole his hat. Reporters crawled out of the woodwork and an Associated Press crew persuaded Carl to pose for a picture with a violin. As he did so I mumbled, "Zeidler fiddles while Hoan burns." Carl broke up and repeated the remark at top volume. It duly appeared in magazine reports—needless to say, without attribution.

Believe it or not, we went back to the office to write another radio speech for the evening, which we delivered to the station and thrust into Carl's hot little hands just moments before he went on the air.

Tomorrow would be my twenty-third birthday, but who cared?

Columbia Broadcasting arranged a nationwide hookup for Sunday, and guess who was going to write Carl's speech?

By that time, and in the few days that followed, Gauer and I were finally forced to confront the truth: Carl had won, but we had lost.

Submerged in a swirl of reporters and preening for photographers, he was on his own, without monitoring from Max or orders from us. The results were predictable.

Newspapers nationwide reported HOW ZEIDLER WON, SINGING IN MILWAUKEE. His vocal efforts were deprecated by *Time* magazine. *Newsweek* explained that the "crooning mayor" had triumphed by singing solos at "dozens of funerals." *Life* was honest enough to admit that nobody knew just why Milwaukee had elected Zeidler, but ran a full-page photo of Carl seated at the piano with his mouth open. The *Washington Post* said, "Time takes its toll even of gratitude."

We had reason to agree.

As expected, Paul Bergen would become the mayor's secretary, with Wallace Maciejewski as his assistant—a concession to voters on the South Side. Presumably—and deservedly—Messrs. Polland and Ernst might enjoy some future benefits from their City Hall connections.

Ours had been severed. Soon a newspaper article attributed Carl's success to his youthful campaign, in which young people like Stanley Jarz, thirty-nine, and Paul Cramp, forty-four, joined with "slightly older men" such as George Weiler and R. O. Wipperman to win the election. Among those not present in the write-up were us. Nor were we invited to the subsequent "victory banquet."

Who needs skeletons at a feast? And while one of our speeches had christened City Hall "The House of Mystery" there was no mystery as to why our ghosts would not walk its corridors.

The only real mystery was how we had ever been foolish enough to expect any other outcome. Our campaign efforts couldn't substitute for the college degrees and employment records that would qualify us for civil service jobs or appointments. And if the new mayor tried to buck regulations by placing us in some sort of salaried position, questions would arise which could only lead to embarrassing answers. Our very presence was now discomfitting to the conquering hero who had won the hearts of a great city with his golden hair and golden voice.

While we suffered in our anonymity, Carl became the victim of his own celebrity. At the time, unnoticed and unpaid, our resentment clouded our comprehension. Today it's easier to see the parallel.

Gauer and I had entered the campaign as outsiders desperately seeking a way into the adult world. We mistook temporary success for permanent acceptance and for a moment it looked as though our dreams had come true. We didn't realize it but this was very much the same case with Carl Zeidler. Already accepted as an adult, he was still an outsider as far as the upper echelons of society were concerned. Speaking and singing attracted inconsequential attention, but he yearned for true recognition by the people who counted—the movers and shakers in the private dining rooms of the Athletic Club. Now, thanks to his unexpected election, he'd proven his abilities to the powers behind the throne, the voting public, and himself. He had come to believe his own publicity.

In that respect he was no different from the vast majority of those who achieve overnight success in any field. Stars of stage, screen, television, novae in rock or jock heaven—all seem dazzled by their aura. As a sudden luminary, Carl found himself fawned upon and flattered by the very authority figures he'd always hoped to impress. The sixth assistant city attorney was now on a first-name basis with everyone of consequence socially, financially or politically, including the governor of Wisconsin.

In retrospect Carl's reaction was natural enough under the circumstances. But then it was hard for us to handle, along with the realization that there would be no guarantee he'd follow through on his own to carry out the pledges we'd constructed as planks for his platform.

Adding assumed insult to fancied injury was the fact that we had not been paid our back wages, to say nothing of the bonus. Truth to tell, we said quite a bit about our bonus. We never saw a dime of it, although several months later we settled for half of the salary amount owed us. Milt Polland promptly borrowed my half from me.

One of the things we gained from our experience, besides a much-needed modicum of humility, was the enduring friendship of barkeepers Barney and Emmett. Having followed our politicking with great interest, they became convinced Hoan would be overthrown. When the professional gamblers put out their odds of six to one against Carl, the proprietors of the Wayside Inn bet every penny they could lay their hands on. As a result they made far more on the Zeidler campaign than we did.

Our ancillary benefits were few. The two of us turned our hands and typewriters to a full-length (and full-credit) account of our recent experience, but this labor of self-love got nowhere. Gauer's article, "Photography Wins an Election," did reach the pages of *Popular Photography,* but as is the case with a bad negative, nothing developed. My only use of an electioneering background was in the short story "A Sorcerer Runs for Sheriff," which I would hardly nominate for a Pulitzer Prize. It is a matter of some amusement that I had already and unknowingly made my literary contribution to politics quite some time before. At least I like to think so.

If Carl Zeidler had not asked Jim Doolittle to manage his campaign, Doolittle would never have contacted me about it. And the only reason Doolittle knew me to begin with was because he'd read my yarn in *Unknown*.

Rattling this chain of circumstances, one may stretch it a bit further. If I had not written a little vampire story called "The Cloak," Carl Zeidler might never have become mayor of Milwaukee.

TWENTY

1

It was time to leave the fantasy of politics and return to the reality of the typewriter.

The transition wasn't easy and during the next two years my output was limited. But somehow I managed to fill the time. Inevitably there would be involvement in other campaigns. Re-electing popular district attorney Herbert J. Steffes required little more than arranging for him to be photographed with Jay Jostyn, then reigning as radio's "Mr. District Attorney." Gauer and I did turns with various other candidates but, mercifully, their backgrounds merit less attention than Zeidler's. Enough to say we won a few, lost a few, and never felt prompted to devote ourselves wholeheartedly to any political project. At least not after five P.M.

In the evenings I saw Marion Holcombe.

Henry Kuttner had come to town earlier on to be photographed with *Weird Tales* editors and myself in Chicago. Now he returned, but the latter experience couldn't be repeated. *Weird Tales* had been sold, its offices removed to New York, and the fast-ailing Farnsworth Wright soon resigned.

That summer I met the new editor, Dorothy McIlwraith, and

her associate, Lamont Buchanon. Together with Victor Ehr's brother Henry and Bob Vail, I headed east for a vacation trip in the passenger seat of an open red convertible. At least it was open after a storm blew the top off on the road to Niagara Falls. I had already visited Washington, suffered heat prostration in Baltimore and slept on a torture rack in the YMCA. But at no time did I abandon the basic components of my travel attire—a yachting cap and a pair of black knee-high riding boots. To this day I credit the flimsy cap for the heat prostration and the tight boots for resultant varicosity. It's hard to say how this outfit impressed the people in the *Weird Tales* office at Rockefeller Center, but subsequently they kept on buying my submissions. A while back I'd acquired representation by Julius Schwartz, a former fan who served a term as literary agent before being paroled to *DC Comics* as the editor of *Superman*. He guided me through the city and, by subway, all the way out to the grounds of the World's Fair. I gazed through the entrance, turned around, and took the subway back downtown. This epitomizes my state of mind during those years of transition; I kept doing the wrong things at the right time or the right things at the wrong time.

On October 2, 1940, Marion Ruth Holcombe and I were married. The afternoon ceremony was performed before a justice of the peace, and neither of us had our families present, although they approved the match. At the time economics served to dictate the need for simplicity, but today I think it was a mistake not to have gone through the usual rituals for our parents' benefit even though neither Marion nor I practiced any religious observance. All we wanted to do was be wed and get out on our own.

Marion had been living with a married sister and her brood of children; I, of course, had stayed with my folks. But now they planned a move to another apartment and my sister was ready to begin her teaching career. It was high time I left the next.

The new roosting place was a one-room furnished apartment on Hartford Avenue, only a half mile away from 1825 East Lafayette Place, my parents' new address. Again due to economic circumstances, we spent our honeymoon on a Murphy bed.

Just how Marion and I expected our tiny quarters to serve for both domestic and social activities remains unclear, to say nothing of unrealistic. But to also use a portion of that one little room as office space for my daily writing schedule was downright insanity.

Marion proved to be a good housekeeper and a good cook, but there wasn't very much house for her to keep, and it began to seem that there might not be very much to cook. Within a year the money I'd made from politics plus the increment from current writing dwindled down to almost nothing. And we dwindled down to another one-room refuge—back with my parents. They were fond of Marion and made us both feel welcome, but I was ashamed to realize my failure.

Gauer and I were commuting, chauffeured by car owners, to the Racine headquarters of the Amlie For Congress campaign. Tom Amlie, a former congressman, was a mature and keenly intelligent man blessed with a sense of humor and cursed by a social conscience. He had been nominated for an important government post by President Roosevelt, only to be rejected after hearings which stigmatized him as a "liberal." Now he was seeking a return to elected office and sought our services. His candor and honesty were far more attractive to us than what little recompense he was prepared to offer. But this time we took our gamble with an assurance that if Tom won we would accompany him to Washington.

He didn't win. His Republican opponent managed to strike fear into the hearts of conservative voters—not a difficult feat in the period prior to our entry into WWII, when propaganda frequently was indistinguishable from paranoia. Needless to say, there was the usual clash with campaign workers and the usual trickle of molasses in place of the necessary cash flow.

All we retained from the campaign was Tom Amlie's gratitude. As a token of same, he suggested Gauer and I take a trip to

Washington. Tom would arrange the loan of a friend's serviceable Chevrolet and provide us with introductions to various dignitaries. In spite of his political reverses he still had contacts in the capital; he would write ahead to some and give us letters of introduction to others. Washington, already playing host to a host of New Deal government agencies, now spread the welcome mat for a variety of additional bureaucracies vaguely involved in what was called the "defense effort." Surely our writing abilities could be employed in one of these fledgling operations without our having to risk the incivilities of civil service.

It sounded like a reasonable possibility and after due deliberation, we decided to gamble two weeks of our time for the undertaking. I use the term advisedly, for it soon became apparent that we needed the services of a mortician.

Instead of heading for the nearest funeral home, Gauer and I holed up in a boardinghouse and then started to meander through the labyrinth of Washington streets and the minor mazes of its government offices. We had an interview at the Library of Congress, but nobody offered us a library card, let alone positions as librarians. We visited the OSS, a recently formed organization with specific functions as yet unclear even to its chief, Colonel "Wild Bill" Donovan. Any functions we might be capable of performing also remained unclear to him. Our next stop was at the office of a new young congressman who was impressed by some of Tom Amlie's views on agrarian reform. But Lyndon B. Johnson was apparently not impressed by us.

Most of our other appointments were doomed to failure because the agencies involved were still subject to screening by civil service. We might just as well have been back in Milwaukee, applying for positions as garbage collectors.

Now it was indeed time to call in a funeral director, but we didn't have enough money left for embalming. Instead we pooled our small change to buy gas for the homeward journey.

Tom Amlie had urged us to remain; he was in Washington

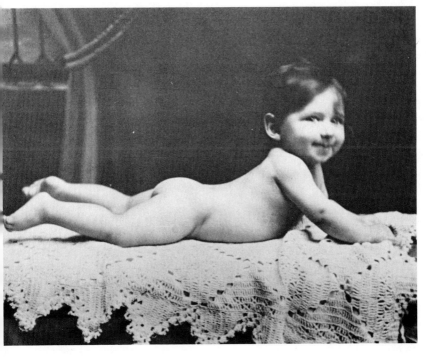

Is this the future author of *Psycho*?

With sister Winifred, 1921. Behind us are our parents, not ventriloquists.

1927. Portrait of the Artist as a Young Man. I haven't worn that necktie for years.

Mother, Dad, and sister Winifred in 1940. I miss the way it was then.

With August Derleth, 1946. He'd published my first short story collection a year earlier and it looks as if both of us were still traumatized by the experience.

Domestic photo, 1945, just before moving to larger quarters. Sally is almost two, Marion is enjoying motherhood, and I have a lamp growing out of my head.

With Arthur C. Clarke at the 1953 Midwescon. He was just heading for fame and fortune: I had already begun my decline.

Weekly guest panelist on TV show *It's a Draw*. In 1954 Carolyn Lawrence was an exceptionally attractive lady, Arthur Fiedler was the famed conductor of the Boston Pops, and I was a guy whose last name was misspelled.

now on the same mission. Shortly afterwards Gauer joined him there and tried his luck again. This time he landed a responsible position with the National Youth Administration and stayed there until its dissolution.

As for me, I voted against leaving Marion behind and decided it was time to return to the typewriter. My first priority was to get us back into a place of our own and relieve the family of any further imposition. During the long stretch of political involvement I'd managed to squeeze in or squeeze out only a few stories, and now had a plethora of plots. As a starter I turned out a novelette, *Hell on Earth,* which was twice as long as any previous story submissions, then quickly moved on to augment my income. When the new year got under way we were ready to follow suit.

But by now there was a minor complication which, for want of a better term, is known as World War II.

It was a conflict in which I did not participate, and in retrospect it would be hypocrisy for me to express my regret. Marion's situation and dependency upon me for support kept me out of the ranks. Very probably this saved my sanity, if not my life.

It was then I turned my attention once again to *Amazing Stories* and its companion magazine, *Fantastic Adventures.* Both were part of the Ziff-Davis publishing empire and seemed exempt from the exigencies of rationing. Heretofore it had been editor Ray Palmer who importuned me to submit material. Now it was my turn to become a regular contributor under both my own name and my pseudonym, Tarleton Fiske.

One of the first things I perpetrated was a yarn about a racetrack habitué named Lefty Feep. The nomenclature came from Gauer's use of it in the alleged novel we'd written for our own amazement years before; he in turn had derived it from a long-forgotten magazine source. The style of the present-tense narration by its petty-gambler and petty-larcenist hero was openly borrowed from the then-popular Damon Runyon. It occurred to me that using current slang and "tough guy" terminology would add comic incongruity to fantasy. I'd already written one such story for *Unknown* after it had been retitled *Unknown Worlds*. A sequel ended up in *Weird Tales* when *Unknown Worlds* lost its paper chase in the war years of rationing.

Neither of these stories had named the narrator, and while I did so for the first time with my *Fantastic Adventures* effort I had no premonition that this would be the start of a series. But after I sent in the story Ray Palmer immediately requested a sequel. Apparently the magazine's readership was satisfied, because over the remainder of the decade twenty-three of Lefty Feep's adventures saw print. All I ever saw was the same penny a word I received when the saga started.

This was no incentive for me to create more series, and as I brought my craft to bombard other markets, the Feep tales constituted a loose canon at best. (I added a final story in 1987, when John Stanley published a collection titled *Lost in Time and Space with Lefty Feep*.)

But during the forties I sold a great number of nonseries efforts to the Ziff-Davis publications as more magazines were added to their schedule. Over the latter years of the decade I combined a weekend visit to Chicago relatives with a poker game at Palmer's residence. On occasion I'd also pay my respects at the office. Thus, over desks or the poker table I met fellow writers who, like William P. McGivern, became lifelong friends. Howard Browne, himself a contributor, was the associate editor and took over Palmer's job when he left. Other staff members who came and went included Louis H. Sampliner, Paul Fairman and William R. Hamling. When Bill departed, it was to publish magazines of his own, including *Imagination, Imaginative Tales,* and *Rogue*. I contributed to all three and for a year and a half wrote a monthly column in the latter which Bill titled "Basic Bloch." Another new acquaintance was Frank M. Robinson, then a lowly office boy, who later rose to the heights as a science fiction writer and coauthor of a book which became part of the film *The Towering Inferno*.

As mentioned, I enjoyed a friendly relationship with these people, except when they sat across from me at the poker table. Oddly enough, over all those years I never met Mr. Ziff or Mr. Davis. Perhaps neither of them played poker.

With the advent of 1942, however, poker—even penny ante—was not a practical priority. What little funds I accumulated went into moving and setting up a new household on Brady Street for Marion and myself.

I had nothing against the location, which was just a block away from where Gauer lived until his mother remarried and closed her candy store. Nor could I really fault our second-floor apartment, which seemed cramped only when we tried to close the door. It was situated at the rear of the building, one of four such cubicles designed by the architect who built the Black Hole of Calcutta. Downstairs was occupied by an Italian deli, which is why we seldom left the windows open.

Still I can't say that Brady Street could ever be mistaken for the Champs Élysées. A streetcar line ran past the entrance to our quarters and when the trolleys weren't clanging we could rely on the booming of the church bell from St. Hedwig's just a half-block away. Interspersed with this, our echo-chamber hallway conveyed the clamor of constant combat from a front apartment occupied by a petty hoodlum and his bimbo. Gauer, who was later to move into the flat directly opposite ours, amused himself by taping the sounds emitted by this pair joined in unholy matrimony and playing the results at full volume on a machine placed outside his door.

I must say that Marion was very patient about all this and didn't complain, so our conversations were never recorded. But it wasn't necessary for us to discuss the difficulties we confronted. While revenue from writing increased it still didn't cover mounting expenditures, which sometimes escalated to as much as fifty dollars a week. Part of the problem was medical; Marion's right hip was giving her trouble, and the doctors weren't giving her either a diagnosis or a prognosis. This was a development neither of us had anticipated when we married, and we didn't know what to expect now. Only one thing was certain. In the face of financial and physical crisis, a secure and substantial source of steady income must be found immediately.

As usual, I came up with a solution.

I went to work for the Gustav Marx Advertising Agency for six months, at a salary of exactly nothing per week.

TWENTY-ONE

For years I had suffered in silence. But now, with the approach of 1942, I added a sound track. And at a buffet session following a meeting of the Milwaukee Fictioneers, I voiced a few personal complaints.

The way I saw it—myopically, from behind thick lenses—my problem seemed insoluble. I had been a professional fiction writer for almost eight years, written for radio, ghosted speeches, prepared proposals and briefings, turned out copy and layouts for newspaper ads, posters, billboards and booklets and was rapidly reaching the point of learning how to change a typewriter ribbon. But there was no likelihood of a livelihood in my particular area of fiction or in political campaigns. What I needed was a steady income. It seemed to me that my background was suitable for a job in advertising or public relations; trouble was, it didn't seem that way to anyone else. On the applications I filled out, the spaces following "College" and "Previous Employment" were as empty as my chances of being hired.

As I trampled on the vintage where my gripes of wrath were stored, one of the Fictioneers seemed to have gotten a squirt in the eye. The next day he phoned and invited me to pay a visit to his office.

Located in an ancient building at 125 East Wells Street, its downstairs entrance was flanked on one side by a sporting-goods shop. On the other was a store presumably catering to the victims of sports mishaps; it featured crutches, wheelchairs, neck braces and similar gifts for the man who has everything. During the holiday season its front window displayed—I swear to God—a Christmas tree decorated with eye patches and trusses.

The Gustav Marx Agency, located on the third floor, was equally distinctive. It consisted of a commodious reception area-cum-storage space occupied by a single broken-down couch, a huge open inner office, a smaller adjoining room, a red-haired secretary named Dunnie and proprietor Gustav Marx.

Gus was what in those days used to be called a character, a description he himself would be the first to acknowledge or even furnish for your attention. To this day I have no idea how he ever became a member of the Milwaukee Fictioneers. Of course advertising is a form of fiction, but aside from copy, I never saw him write anything else. An infrequent attendee at meetings, he seldom entered into the workshop discussions and up to now I'd had little reason to take special note of him.

Married, father of a son and two daughters, Gus was a short, stocky man in his late forties. He'd started out in newspaper advertising, then left to serve as office manager, layout artist, copywriter, account executive and president of a one-man agency which specialized in handling anything and everything. Apparently he handled everything well, because he'd been in business for twenty years. Secretary Dunnie—Vera Dunn to strangers—was a fairly recent addition to the firm, indicative of its growing prosperity.

From time to time, however, Gus had taken on extra help, young men who, like me, wanted regular employment in advertising. Gus told them up front he needed no help.

He was a loner and a highly unorthodox member of his profession. As an account executive, he never solicited accounts; all business came from clients who knew him by reputation and sought him out. He had no written contracts with clients. In planning an advertising campaign he studied the market and allocated the budget according to his own analysis of the situation. The clients had no say-so in this. Gus told them that all he had to offer was his judgment and experience; if they or their wives intended to dictate policy, it would be cheaper for them just to hire a stenographer.

When Gus explained his modus operandi to aspiring employees he also pointed out that they would be unable to follow his example in the creation of the ads themselves. His layouts for newspapers, magazines, flyers, indoor or outdoor display were usually prepared without the benefit of any professional assistance. A free-lance commercial artist would be hired later if actual illustration was required; the same held true when photography was involved. Printers and typographers might be consulted, but only when necessary. As for copywriting, forget it. His style, ranging from highly technical prose for an electronics laboratory client to lowly verse for less prestigious customers, was always individual and never successfully imitated.

What Gus offered was an opportunity to look over his shoulder and learn the step-by-step creation of an ad starting with a call to a client and ending with the finished product, as well as the mechanics of office routine, dealing with salesmen, suppliers, newspaper and magazine advertising departments, printers, engravers, typographers, and direct-mail outfits. There would be exposure to the nuts and bolts involved in setting up everything from streetcar ads to radio commercials.

It was a long dark tunnel, but at the end was a bright future. One would emerge with a legitimate record of six months' employment in the Gustav Marx Advertising Agency and go on to the prospect of a job with another outfit. If one was willing to devote the proper amount of time and attention he could learn enough to qualify him as a salaried employee elsewhere. There would be no salary during his stay at the Marx Agency.

Gus told me that the system worked, and so did my predecessors; all three of them had found a place in the field after their apprenticeship and one of them had opened a small agency of his own.

The only doubts I had concerned my ability to survive and sustain Marion for six months or more without income. Gus made a suggestion. Why didn't I plan on continuing my own writing while working with him? The smaller office was occupied by file cabinets and a drawing board. There would be plenty of room for a chair and a table on which to support the typewriter which might in turn support me. Since I already did have some basic experience in advertising, it probably wouldn't be necessary for me to spend much time watching Gus call on a client, talk to a typesetter, or write a costume jewelry ad for *Women's Wear Daily*.

I thanked Gus for the kind offer and told him I'd think it over. Then I went home to Marion and talked it over. She could see the potential, but like me, she noted the conspicuous gap left by the absence of income. Unlike me, however, she had faith I could manage to fill that gap during my stay at the agency. If that proved impractical, I could still work in the evenings or over weekends at home. Her confidence reassured me; in turn I assured Marion that come what may, she would never hear my typewriter pounding at home if I accepted Gus's proposal.

Accept it I did, and kept my word to Marion as well. Once established in my niche, the typewriter pounded readily and steadily at the office. During the six months after I arrived I wrote—and sold—twenty stories. Somewhere along the line I also managed to pick up bits and pieces of information regarding Gus's clients, their advertising programs, and something of his techniques.

At least I think I did, because by the end of that period I was writing most of the copy for all of the accounts and nobody knew the difference.

Nobody but Gus, that is. When the time came for me to make my departure he asked if I would like to stay and keep writing my own work when not accompanying him to see clients or writing copy for them. As a starter, he offered me two hundred dollars a month.

During my tenure at the agency I had ample opportunity to develop a variety of writing styles. Having started with pseudo-Lovecraft, imitation Thorne Smith, ersatz Damon Runyon and synthetic Carl Zeidler, it was no great trick to pick up the techniques Gus Marx applied to his copy. The challenge lay in learning about the merchandise itself and the market for which it was intended.

Over the years we had a wide variety of clients. I wrote copy for virtually every wholesale distributor of major appliances throughout the state, extolling the virtues of stoves, refrigerators, washers, dryers, phonographs, radios and—eventually—televisions. I did ads for model railroad kits, high-fashion furriers, women's shoes, men's clothing, furniture stores, record dealers, a camera exchange, downtown restaurants, a savings and loan, a cosmetics manufacturer, an electronics firm turning out top-secret material for the armed forces, an optometrist, a lumber company, a jewelry firm and Wisconsin's largest coal company. I also wrote briefs, prospectuses, direct mail, speeches for clients, mail-order catalogs and program notes for music concerts presented by a client in Spokane.

The results appeared in local newspapers and throughout the state in national magazines; some of it polluted the airwaves. But in my spare time I continued to get my own stories into print. None were designed to pose much of a threat to Ernest Hemingway, but they did help to pay our bills.

I wrote only one item which I later had reason to regret. In the fall of 1942 *Weird Tales* asked me to furnish them with an autobiographical sketch to be used in their monthly correspondence column. What I wrote appeared in the November issue, refuting any possible linkage between myself and the monsters I wrote about. Included in my protestations was the following passage: "Deep down underneath it all I have the heart of a small boy. I keep it in a jar on my desk."

Readers singled out the statement for comment, so some while later I used it again when a similar need arose with another magazine. There the matter rested, or so I thought.

I thought wrong. For fifty years this simple statement of fact has been quoted time and again, in magazines, books and over the air—usually without attribution.

Actually, he who steals my jar steals trash, and he who steals my heart will have feminine competition. I also object to instances in which I am credited with the remark. These generally occur on a public platform. Seated at a banquet table I listen to the applause as the toastmaster extols the virtues, triumphs and achievements of each preceding speaker. Finally it's my turn to be introduced. And the toastmaster says, "Here is a man who has the heart of a small boy . . ."

That's all I get, a two-sentence medical report.

There were other medical reports in the latter part of 1942, reports which could not be taken so lightly. Marion was beginning to have problems with her leg. Her doctor couldn't arrive at a diagnosis; nor could the orthopedist whom we consulted for a second opinion. As the year ended, the physicians suggested she enter the hospital for observation to find out if there was a possibility that tuberculosis might have been reactivated.

It was a sad holiday for us. With the coming of the new year we were separated by a two-hour trip via public transport. She underwent a series of tests which seemed to go on forever. Neither one of us knew what to expect. There was no effective treatment for TB of the bone. A progressive deterioration was sometimes temporarily halted by surgery. In this situation all we could do was wait to get the report.

Finally the word came. Marion didn't have tuberculosis.

She was pregnant.

TWENTY-TWO

The bright spot of 1943 was the birth of a daughter we named Sally.

For a time there was some doubt as to whether or not she'd be born at all. According to medical findings, women with previous histories of tuberculosis were in danger of reactivating the disease in pregnancy. But Marion wanted motherhood and was prepared to take the risk.

Because the birth would be cesarean we could select the date in advance. Learning that there was no reason to be concerned if the delivery was slightly premature, we decided the baby should be born on July 28, which was my mother's birthday.

One of the reasons for this decision was the growing decline in my mother's health. When my sister married Franklyn Marcus and they took a West Side apartment on Blue Mound Road, my parents moved next door. By now my father's condition precluded working. The daily trips to and from work on the East Side weren't easy for my mother, but it was evident that there was more to her problem than fatigue alone.

Both she and my father were delighted at the prospect of

becoming grandparents. In spite of the stress of pregnancy, Marion was enthusiastically expectant. As for me, I gave birth to another twenty stories that year, to help meet additional expenditures, both medical and paternal.

Sally was born precisely on schedule, and shortly thereafter I got my first glimpse of her. To me she looked somewhat infantile. Marion assured me that in time she would probably outgrow it. There had been no complications during delivery, and in less than a week we were together at 1018 East Brady Street. As I recall, all three of us came home by taxi, Marion having overruled my suggestion of sending Sally along later by parcel post.

Now we had a crib, diapers, formula, and no further need of a wind-up alarm clock. Watching Sally grow proved an unexpected source of pleasure.

But there wasn't much else that was pleasant during 1943. Within months my mother underwent exploratory surgery, followed by a second operation for rectal cancer. She recuperated at home, but by holiday time there was no doubt as to the prognosis.

A number of friends were in uniform. Emmett Fredericks, coproprietor of the Wayside Inn, died on an island somewhere in what was ironically known as the Pacific war theater while attempting to rescue a wounded comrade.

Carl Zeidler had enlisted too. Although we received a congratulatory telegram at our wedding, I'd seen little of the mayor during his stay in office. Not that he'd become invisible; the newspapers carried constant accounts of his activities. As Gauer and I had feared, none of the program proposed during his campaign was carried out. He began to say things which attracted unfavorable comment and criticism. Accepting the gift of a new car from one of the Big Three automobile manufacturers proved unwise, and he hastily returned it. Rectifying some of his other actions or retracting public statements wasn't all that easy, and his personal popularity waned.

It rose again when he enlisted with the rank of lieutenant

174 / Robert Bloch

commander, in charge of a gunnery crew aboard a vessel in the
Merchant Marine. He came home on a ten-day leave which was
abruptly canceled by an immediate recall to duty. A short time
afterwards the ship to which he had been assigned disappeared,
presumably as the result of a submarine attack. What begins as
comedy frequently ends in tragedy.

For quite a while, ever since Carl's enlistment, the acting
mayor had been John L. Bohn, president of the Common Council.
Now, with the advent of spring elections, he decided to run for
office. Milt Polland suggested his campaign retain our services.

Gauer and I were tempted for several reasons, not the least
of which was a combination of vanity and inability to profit from
experience.

Over the past several years our involvement in the Zeidler
campaign had become known to a number of people. We got
feedback from various sources, and the general consensus leaned
heavily toward the opinions—or lack of opinions—expressed by
outside journalists at the time of Carl's upset victory. That is to say,
he won because he was tall, blond and handsome, and sang *God
Bless America*.

Now we had an opportunity to demonstrate otherwise. John
L. Bohn was Carl's antithesis. Short, bald and hardly handsome,
this elderly gentleman couldn't even carry a tune. A member of the
City Council for more than twenty years, he had a record so
spotless as to be almost invisible. The secret of his success seemed
to be defined in just one word—longevity. If we could add a touch
of color to this man and his campaign it would swell our contention and inflate our self-esteem.

The latter was due for puncturing, and soon. In my spare
time from agency duties I joined Gauer in mapping out the strategy
and requirements for Bohn's primary campaign and drafted some
speeches which served to emphasize his experience, wisdom and
absence of any known criminal record. Our candidate was the kind
of man who always wore a dark suit, a white shirt, and a tie which

nobody could describe from memory. We tailored his public image accordingly, and he was pleased by what we trumped up. His election seemed to be in the cards.

But there was a joker in the pack. Bohn's financial supporters supplied him with a campaign manager and director of public relations. This was a former newspaper editor who had lost his position but retained his take-charge attitude. Naturally he began undermining our influence whenever and wherever possible. Since Gauer and I were not working full-time together in an office, our direct contact with Bohn was minimal and we were soon at a disadvantage.

The joker became a wild card. By the time he arrived on the scene it was too late for him to alter the basic structure or the initial literature of the campaign, but the characterization of the candidate in our speeches became a Bohn of contention. Before the primary was over we cashed in our chips and quit the game.

Gauer had been wooed by John Seramur, former police officer and Carl's bodyguard, who now sought to oppose Bohn with the aid of our old friend Max Pollack. I wanted no part of this. My mother was sinking rapidly and after finishing a day's work at the agency I frequently went out to see her before returning home in the evening and taking up the responsibilities awaiting me there.

The most I could do was agree to meet with Gauer, Max and their candidate for an assessment of the situation in a free moment over the weekend. The date was set for noon on Saturday, February 12. I was at home that morning, mulling over the coming meeting while helping Marion with a few household chores. Then the phone rang and I learned that my mother, whom I'd last seen two evenings before, had died.

During her terminal phase my sister and brother-in-law had moved her into their own apartment while my father continued to occupy the one next door. Consequently he was unaware of my mother's death and it fell to me to break the news.

Consoling Marion as best I could, I took a cab out to the

West Side. Seeing my mother was less traumatizing than the task of telling my father that she was gone. Nor was my grief subsequently lessened at the funeral service.

In attendance, along with relatives from out of town, were many members of my mother's *other* family—the people she'd known and served during her years as a social worker. She'd watched children grow into middle-aged pillars of the community, first met the elderly in the audience when they were teenage immigrants newly arrived from Europe. And there were other teenagers present today, youngsters who shared the activities she supervised at the center.

In spite of her disregard of formal religious observance my mother had indicated she wanted a rabbi to conduct the funeral service, a decision with which my highly orthodox brother-in-law concurred. As a result he summoned the community's foremost rabbinical leader. This balding, bespectacled, pompous and poker-faced man duly arrived and delivered his all-purpose routine remarks without a single suggestion that he had any personal knowledge of my mother and her work over a period of almost forty years.

The person he was talking about—or occasionally referred to in the midst of his almost televangelical pitch—certainly wasn't my mother as I knew her, or as she was known to and loved by those gathered together at her last rites. Oddly enough, as I sat through this meaningless, impersonal ceremony it was the little things I remembered. Violet Simplicity, her favorite cologne, with the single flower floating in the green fragrance. Her voice, raised in song, as she prepared our family meals in the kitchen. The ruby-studded pin in the shape of an anchor which she had worn for as long as I could recall, and which she wore now to her grave. And of course the most elusive yet most enduring recollection of all—the memory of her smile.

But life goes on, and we go with it. During the months that followed, my father moved to Chicago and the apartment shared by his sister, Aunt Lil, and her cousin Bea. Soon my brother-in-law and sister followed and took up residence a few blocks away. I went down to visit whenever possible; right now Sally and her mother both required attention.

Sally grew rapidly and healthily but Marion gradually began to exhibit possible symptoms of what I'd feared: a recurrence of the tubercular condition. Doctors were consulted, examinations were made, and their diagnosis ruled out TB. For a time there was talk of osteomyelitis, a medical buzzword which covered a variety of conditions. Marion was advised to do less walking and have a further orthopedic buildup of her right shoe. It was not the happiest of times.

Meanwhile work at the agency continued, though due to wartime shortages many clients switched to what was then called "institutional advertising." In some cases this seemed appropriate, not only for the products involved but also the clients themselves; I felt that a number of them should definitely be institutionalized.

We did work for a great many people with whom business relations escalated into friendship. It was Gus's custom to brown-bag or purchase a fast-food luncheon to be served at the office several days during the week. Friends were invited, along with artists, sales representatives and other service personnel. At times they were joined by favored clients.

While I had smelled the lions and made a hasty departure from the political arena, Gauer was still involved. Employed in managerial duties in Milt Polland's insurance office, he free-lanced in some campaign work, and from time to time I joined him for a Saturday social visit with some aspirant to office. Thus I found myself meeting a congressional candidate Gauer serviced, a widower who shared a home with his daughter on Milwaukee's West Side. He offered cold beer and warm hospitality to us both— surprising and generous gestures, considering that they came from none other than our old Zeidler campaign archenemy, Dan Hoan.

Milwaukee was changing as the war began to wind down.

Blind Jake still stood in front of the downtown Boston Store, wearing his big black bearskin coat and chanting his endless litany of "Beeman's Pepsin Chewing Gum" to potential purchasers. Riding the streetcars was loudmouthed anti-Semite Dan Smith, who happened to be Jewish. On the South Side, a lady known as "Dirty Helen" still presided over a bar where she hurled obscene insults at delighted customers. But the city itself was in transit, and so was I.

Fall found me busy on yet another project of my own. Once again it came about at the instigation of James Doolittle. You may remember that back in 1939 it was Jim Doolittle who took on the role of Moses to lead Gauer and me out of the wilderness and into the Promised Land of politics. Although we found no overflow of milk and honey, and even though the cash flow had been limited, there was still reason to accept Doolittle as the poor man's Charlton Heston.

Thus, when he mapped out a way to break into the magic world of radioland, I was prepared to go the route.

At that time "Lights Out" was a successful anthology series of horror shows. How it managed to stay on the air without the services of Jim as an actor or myself as a writer was a mystery, but now he was prepared to offer a solution. His idea was roughly equivalent to the one he'd first approached me with five years earlier. The equivalent consisted of his auditioning, and the rough part was that I would write him a free script. The only difference lay in the fact that both he and my script would be given a hearing by the powers that be at "Lights Out."

It took me less than a week to come up with a few suitable pages, but suddenly, within that brief period of time, the powers that be had stopped being. To our surprise and dismay, the show was canceled.

Jim thought we could do better, and we did. He brought together Chicago agent Berle Adams and a radio sports announcer named John Neblett who covered major football games and also had a program of his own. They listened to us and liked the idea.

As a result they went into partnership to produce a series of thirty-nine shows to be sold through syndication. It was decided to start with a fifteen-minute length rather than a half hour. This would save production costs and increase the sales potential to smaller local stations which couldn't afford across-the-board purchase of longer programs. Syndication would avoid cutting a network in on ownership and prevent their control of the show itself. Once Berle Adams bankrolled the project, Neblett would produce and distribute. Jim, using the stage name Craig Dennis, would do leads and narration. All that was required of me was the writing.

My payment was a matter of choice. I could either opt for ten percent of the profits or settle for a flat fee in advance. Marion and I talked it over.

A percentage of the profits meant nothing if there were no profits. And even if a profit was made, it would have to be divided among Jim Doolittle, Berle Adams, John Neblett and me, with a hefty chunk to the sales personnel who handled the distribution end of the deal. On the other hand, seventy-five dollars a script in real money tended to add up when multiplied by thirty-nine. And if the first series of episodes prospered I had the option of renegotiating the next time around. Meanwhile, the addition of almost three thousand dollars to our annual income would help us move to better living quarters and furnish them, as well. After concluding our arithmetic, this was the deal I went for.

If I'd gone into higher mathematics perhaps I would have figured out that with each of the thirty-nine shows averaging a little over ten pages in length, I was committing myself to writing over four hundred pages of radio script—a complete series—for a total payment of $2,925.

Moreover, I was expected to deliver all thirty-nine of those finished shows within the coming three months. In other words I must write three scripts a week for the next thirteen weeks in addition to handling my regular full-time job at the Marx Agency.

On top of that, once this entire task was successfully completed, I was also obliged to spend the following weeks overseeing the actual production of the show. This meant that at least two days of each week I would leave the office at five o'clock, catch a train for Chicago, grab a bite to eat and rush over to the former Columbia Broadcasting Studios in the Wrigley Building. There the programs were first rehearsed and then recorded on huge 33-⅓ RPM transcription discs, which, strangely enough, played back from the inside of the record rather than starting at the outside. Since it was necessary to complete at least three shows at each session, work could continue until midnight, after which I'd crash at John Neblett's pad, rise early, take the train back to Milwaukee, then go directly to the office for another full day of work.

Somewhat to my surprise the easiest part of these illogical logistics was writing the scripts. Since the majority were adaptations of my own stories from *Weird Tales* it was a simple matter to arrange a tie-in. The magazine agreed to run a full-page ad in every issue in return for a mention in the introductions to each show. Actually, some of the stories had appeared in other publications and a few were originals I came up with as I worked. But all of them seemed appropriate for a series called "Stay Tuned for Terror."

The only real difficulty in the adaptation was the problem of condensation. A story which required half an hour's reading time in printed form had to be aired within just twelve minutes. It was like trying to squeeze seven ounces of toothpaste back into a three-ounce tube.

Since I retained no copies of the scripts and never obtained recordings on those unwieldy and unplayable transcription platters, it's difficult to recall which stories worked. All I remember is that we did. Doing shows back to back at each recording session there was no time to be anything but good, a fact to which I was not indifferent.

Our director was Howard Keegan, who had previously

served in that capacity on "Lights Out" itself. In addition to Jim Doolittle, aka Craig Dennis, the regular cast included his younger brother Donald, network leading lady Angeline Orr and veteran character actor Wilms Herbert, who also did some of the female voices because he was bivocal.

It was a versatile and talented cast, and their professionally paced performances improved my pedestrian scripts. Further improvements were added by a sound engineer and a sound-effects man, who combined forces to create aural illusions particularly necessary in a show of this character, or lack thereof. Our music was provided by a portable organ, known in the business as a "God box" because of its frequently funereal accompaniment to soap operas. Luckily, the organist knew the classical excerpts I indicated for use and could improvise on his own. Also vital to the success of these sessions was John Neblett, who produced, and Berle Adams, who wrote checks.

After run-throughs—during which music and sound effects were rehearsed, and the show itself was properly timed—the real job began. Johnny Neblett, Howard Keegan, the sound engineer and I retired to the glassed-in recording booth at the rear of the studio. The organist went into our theme, borrowed from old-time Universal monster movies which had borrowed it from Tchaikovsky's *Swan Lake.* During what followed I had the privilege of making suggestions to the director without having to join the union. If the show went well, we moved on to the second one. Often we managed to sneak in a third. Around midnight, after blood pressure rose and blood-sugar level fell, we finished the cutting session and cut out for a late dinner.

It was a strenuous schedule, but I survived, and so did the family. Marion was buoyed by the prospect of moving into new and improved surroundings and Sally was honing her walking and talking skills. Neither Gus Marx nor any of his clients complained about the quality of current copywriting, so it must be assumed my work and their judgment were no worse than usual.

Completed on schedule, the series went on sale that spring and on the air that summer. I never received a listing of play dates, but know the show aired in various outlets across the country and in Hawaii as well as over the stations of the Canadian Broadcasting Network. We heard the program on WMAQ, Chicago. I think it was a modest success. At least they started talking about making another thirty-nine shows and Mercury Records approached Berle Adams about doing an album.

Then, as if on cue, but without any sound effects or musical stinger from the God box, the roof fell in.

Berle Adams's principal client, Louis Jordan, demanded his full-time attention on tour, and Mercury Records sold out. Some advance sales for the fall season came in but there would be no payment until a month or more after delivery. The show just wasn't worth the gamble and it went on hold.

Nothing happened, and continued to happen all the rest of the year, except that Johnny Neblett and Angeline Orr were married. He continued his sports reporting, piloting his own plane to and from football games across the country. All too soon thereafter he died in a crash during one of these flights. Any further hopes for the show crashed with him.

I mourned his tragic passing and continue to do so to this day. As for "Stay Tuned for Terror," its demise left me with many pleasant recollections and few lasting regrets.

Besides, as 1945 began, I was already involved in the coming publication of my first book.

TWENTY-THREE

arion was not an avid reader of my work. We seldom if ever talked about it at home and neither she nor other members of my family commented about stories which appeared in print.

Come to think of it, I was not in the habit of discussing these efforts with close friends, my employer, or even the Fictioneers. For that matter, little was mentioned when I saw Ray Palmer or other editors. On social occasions, admitting that one wrote for the pulps was like telling people you were into necrophilia; both led to a dead end.

Sometime in 1944 the *Milwaukee Journal* ran another article about my dreadful secret, this time featuring an outdated photograph taken by Harold Gauer on outdated film. The shot pictured me as a monster and the story itself was something of a monstrosity, but both served to illustrate a point. Aside from a few casual comments from friends there was no discernible reaction. After a decade as a professional writer, nobody was particularly interested, either in my work or me.

Except for August Derleth.

Following Lovecraft's death in 1937, he and fellow writer Donald Wandrei tried to market a collection of HPL's short stories, with no success. In the end they resolved to do the job themselves. Under the imprint of Arkham House, a publishing firm founded for this purpose, they brought out a huge volume containing some of Lovecraft's best output. Because of its size, the limited edition was advertised at five dollars, but could be obtained by advance mail-order for $3.50.

Despite their frequently professed admiration for Lovecraft's fiction, few of his fans were willing to put their money where their mouth was. Certainly not at those exorbitant prices. The twelve hundred-odd copies of *The Outsider and Others* took years to sell out. Undaunted, Derleth and Wandrei tried again with *Beyond the Wall of Sleep*, a companion compendium which contained much of Lovecraft's ouevre that was left over. And when Wandrei left for military service, Derleth continued at the helm of Arkham House, steering into uncharted waters. He innovated the policy of publishing volumes of short stories by other writers, starting with himself, then *Weird Tales* contributors Wandrei, Frank Belknap Long, Clark Ashton Smith and Henry S. Whitehead.

Now it was my turn. He suggested I go over the one hundred-plus published stories and select a score for collection. It wasn't easy for me to find twenty titles I felt would bear reprint in a genuine hardcover book which might be sold in real bookstores to actual customers. In the end I wrote an additional story—"One Way to Mars"—which brought the wordage up to Derleth's requirements for proper length. After all, this two-thousand-copy edition was going to cost its readers three dollars, and they couldn't be expected to pay more than a penny a page for the privilege of ownership. My reward would consist of a grand total of six hundred dollars in royalties, a portion of which came in the form of a retarded advance. The rest of this stupendous sum would take years to arrive, and the contract Derleth offered gave Arkham

House fifty percent of any reprint rights to the volume in perpetuity, or longer, whichever came first.

Since at that time nobody else was printing, let alone reprinting, this sort of material, I had no compunctions about such an agreement. Although mildly anemic, I would have willingly signed it in blood.

One of the stories selected for inclusion was "The Opener of the Way." I chose this for the title of the collection itself, because I hoped it might be prophetic of the future in opening the way for other books to come.

Before it appeared, late in 1945, I already had a book of sorts, a dreadful, slim paperback collection put out in England. "Sea-Kissed," a retitling of the story I'd done with Henry Kuttner, was reprinted along with three other stories. It featured what was for those times a daring nude photo on the cover hinting at porno goodies which rooked readers but were not to be found inside.

No such problem, if any, confronted purchasers of *The Opener of the Way*. The book came out, received good reviews, and served as another milestone on the road to oblivion. Still, it pleased my father, to whom it was dedicated, and gave my efforts a certain legitimacy amongst older friends and relatives who had not yet abandoned reading for radio.

It also resulted in a salary increase at the Marx Agency; Gus was beginning to rely more heavily on my presence. Besides which there was another and sadder reason.

Vera Dunn, our orange-haired "Dunnie," had forsaken secretarial duties for domesticity. Happily married and in her seventh month of pregnancy, both Dunnie and the child she carried were instantaneously electrocuted while she was vacuuming a rug. The manufacturers of the vacuum cleaner indignantly denied that such a thing was possible, but this didn't halt the funeral or a long-continuing grief over the loss of a truly lovely lady.

Over the years that followed we had a number of other secretaries, good, bad, and indifferent. Unfortunately, as time went on, more and more of them were indifferent. The rising generation had fewer skills and more coffee breaks.

Meantime the war ended and I suggested to Gus, in view of rising prices and demand for our services, that the time had come to inform all our clients the Marx Agency was doubling its basic retainer fees. I pointed out to him, with the aid of higher mathematics, that even if he lost a few customers he'd still probably come out ahead because of the increased income from those remaining. Besides, the clients who might object wouldn't be worth keeping if they proved to be that stingy. After talking it over, Gus took a deep breath and started calling. The upshot was that not a single client objected. And as peacetime business boomed, most of them increased their advertising budgets to a point where the agency's income more than doubled.

This phenomenon had other consequences.

First of all Marion, Sally and I moved from Brady Street to the much more desirable East Side environs of Maryland Avenue. True, we were still living upstairs in the second-floor rear flat of a two-story frame house which its owner had drawn and quartered. But now we had a living room, a capacious kitchen, and two bedrooms. The furniture, though largely and necessarily second-hand, was of good quality, and the place itself had been expertly redecorated and repainted—by us.

Secondly, the Marx Agency itself moved to a bigger and better location. Gus now parked his Packard alongside the American State Bank Building on North Water Street, where we had a suite remodeled according to our own plan. The vast outer office was the secretary's domain, bordered by a semicircular counter twenty feet long. The space below it stored all our filing material, with enough room left over for Gus to park a second Packard if he bought one. At the moment the possible purchase price went into further remodeling. There was a private office for Gus, a private office for me, an office designed for commercial artists who might do layouts while on the premises. And there was a big conference room which was actually used for the traditional luncheon sessions. Our Wells Street quarters had been on the third floor; our new quarters were on the fifth. So much for upward mobility.

And so much for irony. The space we occupied had once housed the offices where my friends and I held the meetings of our Federated Arts Council ten years before.

Both old and new clients seemed impressed by the new offices; they talked less about expenses and more about expansion. Over the next few years the agency's income soared and my own salary elevated; when kites rise, so do their tails.

Remarkably, we still maintained Gus's long-established rule of strict honesty in our dealings. We refused to misrepresent the merchandise in our ads, or write copy designed for "bait-and-switch" sales tactics. Unlike many of the larger outfits in town, we rejected the time-honored custom of dishonorable double-billing. Manufacturers and distributors often contracted to pay fifty percent of a retailer's costs for advertising their products. The retailer generally retained an advertising agency to purchase space and radio time at lower prices, then provide a fake bill at higher rates. This second bill would be presented to the manufacturer or distributor. The practice was well known, even to its supposed victims, who winked indulgently and covered the extra outlay by raising wholesale prices on the product. The retailers then raised *their* prices. So in the end nobody really got hurt except the consumer. And the advertising agency involved in this transaction made extra money by billing the client fifteen percent of the fake costs.

Gus refused to go along with this chicanery, and strange as it may seem, his clients respected him for it. I would imagine they were more honest than the average.

It's true that not all our clients were aboveboard. Our cosmetics-factory client showed us the lipstick he supplied to a dozen different companies, ranging from exclusive firms to the local five-and-dime stores. The most expensive brands and the cheapest all came from the same barrel; the only difference was in the packaging of the tube. Sometimes a drop of perfume might be added to lend a distinctive touch, but it didn't make the process smell any better to me. Our pharmaceutical wholesaler sold us unlabeled bottles of a hundred aspirin tablets for seven cents. The bottles cost more than their contents, and he still made money on the deal. Once labels were affixed, prices rose accordingly, but that was the customer's headache. An optometrist client made a twelve-hundred-percent profit on sales of frames and lenses. His luxurious office was a site for sore eyes.

At home I was subdued for a brief interval, when Dr. Samuel Higgins reached into my mouth and tore out my tonsils. This excision was performed under local anesthetic while I was seated in a chair with the surgical instruments resting in a bowl on my lap. The tonsils proved to be embedded and the operation took so much time the anesthetic wore off. This oral castration was followed by a magical night in Lutheran Hospital. The surgery cost fifty dollars, and the use of the operating facility, the nurse in attendance, and the overnight stay cost me an additional fourteen. All things considered, I suppose it was worth it.

There were other medical fees during the latter half of the decade. Marion's leg problem was gradually intensifying, and so was the mystification of the physicians we consulted. What it amounted to was an annual flare-up of fever and swelling in the affected area that led to hospitalization for a week or more, during which time she was usually treated with the newest antibiotics available. As a result the symptoms subsided and we were back to square one.

Square one was not all too restricted a space in the postwar years. Victor Ehr went off to Chamber of Commerce posts in Louisiana, and Milton Gelman took his bride to New York, where he went from publishing to agenting, then writing for live television. But Sprague Vonier came back from service to marry Mary Jo, and Bob Vail returned with his wife, Angie. Mary Jo's sister Emma married photographer Norbert Janowiak and they joined the ranks; so did Polland's secretary Bernice and her artist husband, Forrest Flower. Together with Gauer, Alice Bedard and a dozen other friends, they turned square one into a social circle.

Memory is a storehouse with many rooms. Some of the doors open easily at the slightest touch; others stubbornly resist my entry. And when I do enter I'm frequently surprised to find many of these rooms are smaller and their contents less important than I recalled while others are much larger than I had imagined them to be. Some of them are still richly furnished; some seem bare or utterly empty. Passing now along the corridor leading to the end of the decade, I glance quickly through doorways.

There were the weekend trips to Chicago to visit my father, aunts and Winifred. Jonquil and Fritz Leiber lived on the South Side now with their young son, Justin; I often spent the evening and the night at their home. Pleasant memories.

Max Pollack died suddenly and unexpectedly while still in his forties. Another good friend gone. Barney Fredericks moved the Wayside Inn a few blocks to a location on North Water Street, where business flourished.

During this period Marion decided to go into business herself. For a time our oversized, high-ceilinged kitchen was filled with bird cages containing a rainbow of fifty budgerigars. Birds were sold but more kept hatching and the process of care and feeding became a burden. Any possible profit was lost in upkeep, and when Marion finally disposed of the aviary she contented herself with a pet cockatiel.

These years sped by in a blur of working, socializing, visiting doctors or hospitals, running back and forth on out-of-town trips, writing or cleaning up after the anonymous cockatiel.* Somewhere along the line we managed to find a few odd moments in which to bring up a daughter.

---

*The cockatiel is anonymous because I am attempting to avoid name-dropping. Apparently, however, there is no way to avoid bird-dropping.

Marion was a fond and devoted mother; she nursed Sally through a sudden and serious bout of rheumatic fever and defended her from the onslaught of the neighbor kids. She also saw to it that Sally had a closetful of toys, and created a variety of character dolls dressed in their national costumes. My function consisted of bringing nightly glasses of water to the bedroom and improvising a story which would continue until the glass had been emptied sip by sip.

Lacking a car, I frequently spent time during weekends or vacation periods transporting Sally to downtown stores, theaters, museums, the zoo, playgrounds, beaches and various public parks. We flew over to Michigan and returned by boat, entrained for Chicago and bussed back.

Once or twice a year I'd get up to visit Marion's parents and relatives in Weyauwega. Two of her married sisters made their homes in Milwaukee; her brother Leslie and his wife lived across the street from us. These family members provided us with transportation—long, slow, unairconditioned—on crowded interstate highways. Squeezed into cars, together with their own offspring, we traveled like so many sardines, but without benefit of tomato or mustard sauce. And lacking a can opener at the end of the ordeal we had to get out ourselves.

Television was already beginning to rear its ugly head, or vice-versa. In the Marx Agency we were buying the first live remote broadcast on a local channel; it was, believe it or not, a polo match. I was concocting commercials for a weekly public nuisance called "Keen Teens." That it had any winning appeal to youthful audiences is debatable, but there is not the slightest doubt that it would, as an offense against society, lose every appeal all the way to the Supreme Court. Even so, the agency lost no time getting into the new medium.

It was then, in the late forties, and his late fifties, that Gus Marx volunteered his intention of leaving fifty percent of the agency to me as an unrequested bequest. I was surprised and touched, plus greatly pleased and reassured about the future. Uncertain of what might lie ahead we'd already arranged with our physician's nurse, Ida Binder, that she and her recent bridegroom would assume custody of Sally in the event we received free publicity in the obituary section. Thanks to Ida, and now thanks to Gus, we felt the future was secure.

The quality of life had certainly improved since the start of the decade. Morticians became funeral directors, garbage collectors were elevated to new status as sanitary engineers, and having a tooth pulled was now oral surgery. Of course there had been a few minor irritations, such as WWII, the Cold War, and the fact that comic strips were smaller, but there was comparatively little cause for complaint.

I was now able to indulge in pipe smoking, just like those writers in the movies. My tastes gravitated toward curved-stem models holding perfumed, specially cured tobacco. Today I suspect some of the tobacco was only partially cured or, at best, in a state of remission. Eventually the pipes gave me a sore mouth, so in the interests of good health I discarded the collection and resumed smoking cigarettes.

Before the century had turned fortyish, there were times when I satisfied my craving for tobacco in an unsatisfactory manner with the aid of dime-brand cigarettes—Marvels, Wings or Twenty Grands. The latter came in a pack emblazoned with a portrait of the real Twenty Grand, a famous Derby winner. After smoking Twenty Grand cigarettes you could understand why they were named after a horse.

Now, snuggling into the lap of luxury, I could on occasion indulge myself with Balkan Sobranies, which cost thirty-five cents just for a pack of ten. In some ways these tasted just as bad as Twenty Grands, but they were black, with silver filter tips. Upon entering a crowded room with a Balkan Sobranie dangling from my lips, I could imagine the comments. *Don't look now, but who is the distinguished gentleman over there, the one smoking that black cigarette?* Instead, the most common remark probably was *Jesus H. Christ, get a load of that creep with the faggoty fag!* Not to worry; wasn't I the future coproprietor of a flourishing advertising agency?

My increased feelings of security were not founded merely on Gus Marx's words, but on his deeds. Raising my salary to a hundred dollars a week indicated satisfaction with services rendered. And Gus's vote of confidence in my ability to handle any phase of the operation now came in the form of his lengthy vacations. Once or twice a year he would take a two-week trip, usually in the company of a friend and client, fun-loving Charlie Bass. Since Charlie frequently found his fun in places like Bolivia, many of Gus's excursions were to points south: Meanwhile he relied on me to keep the home fires—and the Balkan Sobranies—burning. I was almost as pleased with this demonstration of his trust as I was with his promise of future rewards.

Before the decade's demise Harold Gauer and I made one more brief involuntary venture into the field of politics. It came about at the instigation of Milt Polland, and consisted of a meeting in a suite at the Schroeder Hotel. This time the candidate he wanted us to counsel was Senator Robert M. La Follette, Jr.

La Follette was a famous name in Wisconsin's political history. The head of the clan and father of the present senator had himself served in that capacity, and also as governor of Wisconsin and the Progressive Party's candidate for president in 1924. "Young Bob" had been his father's secretary until the latter's death in 1925 and replaced him in the Senate, where he remained in office for over twenty years. Still in his forties, he was generally regarded as one of the most illustrious and influential senatorial leaders and had recently been selected Man of the Year by *Time* magazine.

Now he was back from Washington to campaign for reelection in the state's primaries. It was a foregone conclusion that Wisconsin would continue its policy of sending Republicans to the

U.S. Senate, so the winner of the Republican primary race was automatically assured of a win over a Democratic opponent in the final election.

Such assurance was doubled when one had the La Follette name, the La Follette political organization, and the personal record of accomplishments racked up by Young Bob. Expert opinion had it that he was unbeatable.

Naturally, we disagreed. And Milt Polland, while not necessarily sharing our concern, was an insurance man; if the candidate followed our advice it might just give him the extra protection to insure his victory. The bottom line was that the meeting cost nothing except an hour or so of the candidate's time, and whatever the outcome he would suffer no possible harm by listening to us.

Or so Milt Polland thought. What he'd forgotten was that Senator Robert M. La Follette, Jr., R Wis., like every Man of the Year since the beginning of *Time*, lacked a puncture-proof ego. What we had to say within the first few minutes of our meeting constituted a severe wound to the senator's vanity.

We told him we knew about his customary strategy, but that times had changed. In previous campaigns he'd return to Wisconsin for one-stop token appearances in a few key cities, then vanish until the primary election was over. The vast majority of voters in smaller communities or rural areas saw him only as a smudged face peering from an ad in the local newspaper and heard him only in a canned radio broadcast. When combined with the efforts of the party organization and the magical appeal of the La Follette name, this had always sufficed.

Now, we maintained, that wouldn't be enough. During the past six years of war and its aftermath, a whole new generation of young voters had emerged. To them the La Follette name was not magical, merely too goddamn hard to spell. The exploits of Young Bob's father and brother were ancient history, and to be blunt about it, these new voters hardly recognized a man in his late forties as "Young Bob." Listening to a prerecorded recital of campaign pledges was not going to establish a bond with the formidable number of eligible voters under the age of thirty. It was much easier for them to identify with someone closer to their own generation. True, La Follette's rival in the primary was small-town and small-time, but he was young, and a WWII veteran to boot. It was all very well for La Follette to contrast his imposing past achievements with the almost nonexistent public record of his opponent, but the trick was to do it in person, not in absentia. Let fledgling voters feel that they already had a man in office who cared enough about them and their welfare to speak to them face to face. Let his presence also speak, providing contrast between quiet, dignified authority and the loud, brash, cocky self-assertion of his challenger.

Senator La Follette listened attentively, thanked us courteously, then went away to do exactly what we told him not to do. After a couple of public appearances in the largest communities he sped back to Washington, and the rest of his primary campaign consisted mainly of boilerplate newspaper ads and acetate-record radio transcriptions. I still wish that he had believed us when we said that a week or so spent in public appearances throughout the state could make all the difference.

As it was, he lost the primary election by the narrowest of margins.

If he'd heeded our warnings, it might well have changed history. Because his victorious opponent was a man named Joe McCarthy.

During the decade, in addition to ghostwriting, radio scripting, copywriting and spraying graffiti on Mount Rushmore, I contributed about one hundred stories to various magazines. Perhaps the best-known was "Yours Truly, Jack the Ripper," which saw publication in the July 1943 issue of *Weird Tales*.

There was nothing particularly unusual about this story's composition, probably the last of my output prior to joining the

Marx Agency. It was just one more product of the secondhand typewriter mounted on the secondhand card table in a corner of our one-room apartment, as well as a product of my interest in those whose lives were overshadowed by the looming of their own legends.

The real-life Ripper had captured the imagination of millions, but he himself had never been caught, or even accurately identified. Over the more than half-century which had elapsed since Jack the Ripper carved a name for himself, he had been commemorated time and again in factual and fictional accounts of his efforts to disorganize prostitution—and five individual prostitutes—in London's Whitechapel. He had also cut a figure on both stage and screen.

One of the oddities connected with this mysterious murderer was that *he* had christened himself, in a letter to a news agency signed "Yours truly Jack the Ripper." This interesting little detail, although often recounted, had implications which others seemed to have overlooked. I was fascinated by the phrasing the murderer used for self-identification and, upon due reflection, realized that these five words could constitute both the title and the plot of a short story. Bringing the Ripper into modern time and using an American city as a new setting for his successfully unsuccessful operations required the addition of a supernatural rationale which I had no difficulty supplying. And which others since then, I might add, have had no difficulty borrowing for their own.

But in 1943 my idea was fresh, and after stealing the usual penny a word for it, I received a thirty-day sentence on various newsstands. As usual, aside from a few comments in the letter column of *Weird Tales,* the story went unnoticed.

Then fate—or dumb luck—took a hand. Agent Julie Schwartz sold the yarn for an additional twenty-five dollars to editor A. L. Furman's *The Mystery Companion.* I was quite excited by this, my first appearance in a hardcover anthology. Then the piece was bought for dramatization on a CBS radio show, "The

Kate Smith Hour." The playlet starred Laird Cregar, who by some coincidence was about to be seen on-screen as Jack the Ripper in *The Lodger*. Since then my little story has continued to lead a charmed life in print, and on radio and television, for a total of fifty revivals thus far. I have also been obliged to reincarnate the Ripper in everything from an episode of "Star Trek" to a full-length novel of my own. Over the years Jack and I would become blood brothers.*

At the time, however, it was earthshaking enough just to have had a story published in a book and broadcast nationwide on a popular radio show. The aftershocks were a long time in coming; nobody popped up immediately to purchase more reprint or radio rights for other efforts of mine, and the next new story I wrote sold for the same old penny a word.

In 1945, as detailed earlier, I added an entire book to my list of credits, but when you got right down to it—and few people did—*The Opener of the Way* was only a collection of previously published short stories. The next step, obviously, involved writing a brand-new full-length novel.

It was a step I wasn't consciously prepared to take. My few earlier experiments in the form, collaborating with friend Gauer, had not produced satisfactory results. Moreover, while switching from advertising copy to short stories and back again seemed to work out, writing a novel in brief segments of borrowed time would be a much more difficult task. Another minor consideration was the fact that I hadn't the faintest idea of a plot or characters to write about. Best to leave well enough alone.

And leave it alone I did, contenting myself with expanding duties of regular employment, extension of short-story writing into

---

*As a result, over the years I've been asked my opinion of the Ripper's true identity. After much study and consideration, I now firmly believe that Jack the Ripper was actually Queen Victoria.

the mystery field and having lunch at Toy's Restaurant with August Derleth whenever he came into town.

But there was more to life than just work and chop suey. Once in a great while, when domestic duties or privileges didn't interfere, I would take a few hours off on a Sunday afternoon to get in a bit of physical exercise. Mine was a rather pedestrian approach; I walked. One afternoon in the summer of 1946, as I strolled beside the Milwaukee River, the entire plot of a novel channeled into my stream of consciousness. Not to write at home was a rule of long standing, but I returned to sit down and do an outline for the book which became *The Scarf.*

I had the anticipated difficulties working on a novel at the office, but writing about criminal activity in the first person was easy. What this proves, I am not prepared to say, except to state that all you'll get from jumping at the obvious conclusion is a broken leg. *The Scarf* is not the story of my life. Its protagonist is an author, and a serial killer. I admit to being an author, but I have never written a serial.

My character is seduced by his high school English teacher. This never happened to me. I recall that real-life English instructor Frieda Reynolds was a nice maiden lady pushing sixty to my sixteen. She evoked no rush of desire in me, and her idea of a hot date was Alfred, Lord Tennyson.

Hollywood is one of the principal locales of the novel, but at the time I wrote it all I knew about the community firsthand was what I had learned on that brief vacation back in 1937. Nor had I ever lived in Minneapolis or New York, or lived with (let alone killed off) any of the ladies in my opus.

There is a psychiatrist in the novel, and another one in "Yours Truly, Jack the Ripper," and Freud only knows how many more scattered throughout my published work—but I have never undergone any form of psychotherapy. On the few social occasions I have met shrinks I shrank from discussing any aspect of their profession, just as they have shrunk from discussing mine. My frequent use of analysts and psychiatrists in fiction is a result of observing their status in fact. As elsewhere noted, I believe the psychotherapist has largely replaced the clergyman as the authority figure and keeper of the mysteries in modern society. And the terminology of the therapist is more familiar to today's readers than the language of the Bible. Authors and dramatists used to draw special attention to a heroic or villainous figure merely by reversing his collar. I frequently employ the same ploy without using the customary costumery.

It is odd that my closest contact with psychotherapy came about as a direct result of writing *The Scarf*. Once in print, the novel was favorably reviewed by the late Dr. Fredric Wertham in the pages of a psychiatric journal. This in turn provoked the interest of Dr. Edmund Bergler, who wrote asking response to a questionnaire dealing with the creative process. A while later he voiced his conclusions based on answers received from members of my profession. It was his theory that all authors were neurotic.

I found myself somewhat upset by this judgment, until I learned that Dr. Bergler himself was the author of eleven books.

Writing my first novel involved a learning experience almost equal to attending kindergarten. In the course of this neurotic behavior I was forced to make several erotic decisions. It was my belief that detailed accounts of sexual activity are gratuitous unless they reveal something new about the characters involved. If the hitherto domineering hero surprises us because he's into bondage, there's a legitimate reason for a scene which reveals the tie-in, or -up.

But most writers then and now seem to lack that rationale. In their steambath approach, the hero is generally just the same macho guy he was when he still had his clothes on. All we learn is that he and his partner have the usual great sex.

I suggest a writer who is habitually graphic in his porn may be sending a message to the readers that he is quite a lover-boy himself—or would like to be. And both his and his characters' use of four-letter words cloaks an ignorance of the *mot juste.*

Insofar as characterization is concerned, there are other actions and words which, according to our psychiatric friends, might be even more revelatory. Yet writers seldom follow their hero or heroine into the bathroom for explicit excretory scenes which might tell us something about their anal-retentive proclivities and all that other good stuff an analysand gets from his analyst. I don't recommend the genitourinary approach but I daresay it is as legitimate as the one almost exclusively employed at present.

Another resolution I arrived at was to avoid other detailed descriptions which do not make a story point or advance the story line. This particularly holds true in the area of weaponry and ballistics. Technical data about the use of guns and ammo may delight members of the NRA but do little else except emphasize the writer's expertise. And who needs it, after he's already used the same approach to tell the reader how knowledgeable he is about sex? If you've got foreplay, then forget the gunplay; let's not be greedy.

Another reason I vowed not to describe weaponry is because of my personal ignorance. The only machines I've ever been able to understand are the electric chair and the guillotine. The former can be used for frying potatoes if you place them on your lap, and the latter can be used for slicing same, but there are easier methods; besides, fried potatoes aren't good for you. I may not know much about mechanics, but I'm not a dummy when it comes to questions of health. For that reason you will never catch me within miles of either an electric chair or a guillotine.

All of which has little to do with *The Scarf.* I myself had less to do with it than anticipated. Since Julius Schwartz was primarily an agent in the science fiction and fantasy magazine field, I was advised to offer my novel through another representative. The firm recommended to me was A. & S. Lyons, Inc., one of the largest literary agencies in the country. They read my manuscript and speedily sold it to Dial Press, where it would be published as their first novel in the field of mystery-suspense. Although postwar paper and binding left much to be desired, they provided the book with cover artwork which won an award for jacket design. The contents generally found favor with the reviewers and a second edition was promptly put in print. A sale to one of the fast-developing paperback markets soon followed.

At last I had an identity in newspaper advertisements and book reviews throughout the country, from the local press to *The New Yorker*. I could now look upon myself as a legitimate author with a well-received novel to my credit, under contract to a reputable publisher, and represented by a major literary agency.

But while I was gazing at myself so favorably and fondly, I made the mistake of blinking, and in that moment everything changed. Suddenly, my supportive editor at Dial quit to get married.* The mighty roar of A. & S. Lyons faded to a pitiful whimper as the great agency suddenly expired. Thus it was that when somebody out in darkest Hollywood produced a modest film titled *The Scarf,* about a serial killer who strangled his female victims, I had no editor or agent to support me in protesting or contesting this dubious coincidence. And by the time I sketched out my plans for a second novel I didn't even have a publisher anymore. Margot Johnson, a survivor of the A. & S. Lyons catastrophe, undertook to represent me but Dial bounced my proposal and she couldn't sell it anywhere else. It looked as though I were fated to join the ranks of one-book authors, along with Casanova and Adolf Hitler.

After thirteen years as a professional writer I'd produced over a hundred and fifty short stories and novelettes, published a collection and a novel, written radio series and rattled my typewriter in

---

*Both quitting and marriage were quaint but common twin customs for young ladies in those days.

the fields of politics, advertising and public relations. For sheer diversity of output perhaps I could have pointed at my record with pardonable pride.

But there was little point in pointing, because nobody was watching.

This was by no means a unique distinction. Members of the Milwaukee Fictioneers and its rival group, Allied Authors, remained largely ignored in their hometown. When Fredric Brown and William Campbell Gault won the Mystery Writers of America's awards for first novels the matter was duly noted by the local media, but after that their names were placed in the revolving file. My friend Fred also got mentioned when a short story and a novel sold to films, but his chief claim to fame—and his proudest moment—came when he received an invitation to the exclusive Walrus Club masquerade ball, an annual highlight of Milwaukee's social season. He had his picture taken in costume for use on the dust jacket of his next book. A proofreader for *The Milwaukee Journal,* Fred wrote clever and inventive science fiction and detective stories, eventually becoming a prolific and popular novelist in the field of mystery fiction. Years later I had the privilege of editing and introducing a volume of his short stories, and today he enjoys a well-deserved posthumous reputation. But at the time both he and Bill Gault created no stir when they left town to pursue their destinies.

Meanwhile, it appeared that my own career was suffering from rigor mortis. By contrast, members of my peer group were now engaged in flourishing occupations. Milton Gelman became a talent agent and budding television writer in New York; Victor Ehr was a powerhouse of Louisiana's Chamber of Commerce. Bob Vail had joined an advertising agency. Sprague Vonier wound up as program manager of WTMJ-TV. The latter two joined forces to emulate Gauer and myself by electing protégé Henry W. Maier Mayor of Milwaukee, a tenure he enjoyed until retirement. Harold

Gauer had also found a permanent niche as Midwest Regional Director of CARE.*

As for me, all I could say at the moment was thank God for *Weird Tales* and the other fantasy or science fiction magazines.

And thank God for science fiction fandom.

---

*There are many others important to my life who are not adequately represented in these pages. And if you're looking for your name and haven't found it, remember that this is an autobiography, not a phone book.

Twenty-four

"**F**andom is a way of life."

So went the saying once current in the pulp magazine era, and for a time it seemed to contain an element of truth. The reference was to science fiction fandom, which was undergoing an expansion matched by the genre itself.

Tracing science fiction fandom back to its origins is like trying to find the first rat responsible for carrying bubonic plague. It's my guess that in the beginning fans were merely individual readers who gradually made contact with counterparts through the letter columns of the periodicals which catered to their tastes, or lack thereof. In a few major metropolitan areas this led to personal contact; when two fans met they frequently became friends, and when three fans got together they started a club. Soon fandom discovered the mimeograph—a prehistoric ancestor of the copier and the computer printer in use today. The result was the fanzine.

Early examples of these amateur publications were generally skimpy, smudged, and almost impossible to read when lining the bottom of a bird cage. Nonetheless they served as a means of self-expression and communication and were indirectly responsible for preserving fandom as an entity. At first fanzines dealt almost entirely with science fiction in print or its comparatively infrequent presentations on film or radio. Such interests naturally expanded to include producers, directors and actors associated with the genre, as well as publishers, magazine editors, and writers.*

I had read or at times contributed to fanzines since the mid-thirties, and upon becoming a professional writer I began to receive communications from readers with aspirations of their own. One such was Milwaukee resident Earl Pierce, Jr.; I encouraged his successful submission of stories to *Weird Tales*. Through the mail came letters from youthful fans like Charles Beaumont and Robert Silverberg, who went on to better things. A slow learner, I stayed in fandom and continued to contribute articles, essays and occasional fiction to fanzines. Thus far two book collections of this material have been published, but at one time such a possibility seemed unthinkable—or, even worse, unprofitable. In 1956 I wrote and sold "A Way of Life," set against an imaginary future in which science fiction fandom ruled the world after a global disaster of another sort had occurred. But even then fandom was a microcosm—in terms of numbers, a mere pimple upon the body politic.

As early as 1939, New York fans, organized into several clubs modeled along the lines of the legitimate Mafia, banded together for the first science fiction convention. A year later Chicago followed suit, and Denver hosted its own event in 1941. WWII interrupted annual continuity, but the idea of a national or so-called World Science Fiction Convention persisted.

In 1946 the tradition was resumed with the Pacificon in Los Angeles, and at the prompting of various West Coast correspon-

---

*Penologists sadly observe that many of today's most vicious adult criminals began their careers as mere juvenile delinquents. Similarly, most science fiction writers and editors started out as fans.

dents, I decided to attend. Outside of a brief wartime visit to Minneapolis where I met fellow writers Clifford D. Simak and Carl Jacobi, I'd not had a travel vacation since 1939. Marion, hesitant about flying and the problem of leaving Sally in someone else's care, decided not to go.

As it happened, a plane strike began when I landed in Chicago, and I reached Los Angeles by train. On my arrival at the station I was surprised by thirteen fans, exactly ten percent of the total convention attendance. The affair itself was held, kicking and struggling, across the street from MacArthur Park on the second floor of the Park View Manor. Guests of honor were writer A. E. van Vogt and his wife, E. Mayne Hull. I'd met local fans Forrest Ackerman and Walter Daugherty in 1937, but not the writer attendees. One of them was Illinois resident Wilson A. Tucker, whose byline has appeared on numerous mystery and science fiction novels, though he is best known to fandom as Bob Tucker. At subsequent conventions we have frequently exchanged name tags, with interesting results. Another colleague was Leigh Brackett, who, in addition to writing science fiction, married science fictioneer Edmond Hamilton, and shared script credit with William Faulkner on *The Big Sleep*. A third was youthful and exuberant fan-turned-pro Ray Bradbury. I often wonder what became of him.

The convention itself was a casual affair, highlighted by speeches and panel discussions featuring professionals and prominent fans. For gourmets there was a banquet which lingers in my memory as something best forgotten. A masquerade party offered the dazzling, kaleidoscopic vision of at least five people in costume, including two females who were partially out of theirs. An auction of rare books, manuscripts and artwork resulted in heated bidding; one gets some idea of the excitement by noting that I purchased an artist's original for a staggering four dollars in cash.

It was probably my reputation as the last of the big-time spenders that won me an invitation to appear at the 1948 convention in Toronto. Bob Tucker was the fan guest of honor and I suspect he may have had something to do with it, because my work was scarcely known outside of the United States, and I couldn't even speak Canadian. But there I was, the youngest writer to be the professional guest of honor at a World Science Fiction Convention. As far as I know, the record still stands. And Toronto was the first truly international event of its kind. Despite the flattering nature of these circumstances, the memories I cherish revolve around fans and fellow writers.

Tucker and Ackerman were familiar presences, but this was my first meeting with science fiction historian Sam Moskowitz and author David H. Keller, M.D. A practicing psychiatrist and sexologist (though I'm not sure just how much practicing he'd done for the latter role), he had written "The Revolt of the Pedestrians." Since this was the very first science fiction story to attract my attention back in 1928, I had special reason to follow his subsequent work and looked forward to some interesting conversations. Unfortunately the good doctor proved to be more of a monologist than a conversationalist. During the course of the convention's somewhat haphazard programming he would jump to his feet and deliver a disquisition at the drop of a hat. In fact his wife, Celia Keller, carried a hat around with her for just that purpose. A combination of spokesperson, guardian angel and director of public relations, she made more of an impression on me than the talented writer himself.

Aside from the Kellers and another physician-turned-fan, Dr. C. L. Barrett, everyone made a habit of being young in those days, and science fiction conventions were youthful affairs.

The warm hospitality of Canadian fans remained memorable. Over the next few years circumstances prevented any consideration of convention attendance, but when New Orleans captured the bid for 1951 I urged Marion to join me there. I thought she'd enjoy sight-seeing in the company of the Chamber of Commerce executive Victor Ehr, our old friend from Milwaukee whom Gauer and I had both visited and vacationed with previously. At the gathering itself would be a number of people she already knew, including guest of honor Fritz Leiber, Fredric Brown and the ubiquitous Tucker. Best of all, she could travel comfortably by train. In order to avoid neglecting her during our stay I resolutely refused requests to take part in the convention program.

This didn't stave off the inevitable. Once we arrived at the hotel I was unexpectedly confronted by the convention committee, which in turn was confronting an unexpected problem. For the first time in history, Hollywood had recognized the potential of science fiction fandom. Paramount would screen George Pal's production of *When Worlds Collide* in the hotel's main meeting hall. Not to be outdone, Twentieth Century-Fox was rushing a print of *The Day the Earth Stood Still* for an exclusive midnight premiere at the biggest theater on Canal Street. Since both studios were sending representatives (or at least people to carry the cans of film) it was important these efforts received the widest possible promotion and publicity. What could be more natural than having a stranger from a distant city take over the responsibilities of press conferences and coverage without any previous notice?

I had several answers to that question, none of them particularly civil, but I ended up with the job anyway. In addition I found myself ad-libbing a speech at the banquet. Fortunately these activities didn't curtail our excursions with Victor Ehr and his bride or prevent socializing with conventioneers.

Slowly but surely I was beginning to meet some of the people in my profession and supplement their names with mugshots in my memory.*

In 1952 the convention was held in nearby Chicago. Marion

---

*One of the consequences of the Dianetics-oriented New Orleans convention was an attempt to pursue this then-new craze lauded by editor John W. Campbell. I spent 100 + hours experimenting with the recommended methodology after returning home, and then abandoned any further efforts without noticeable results; I'm still waiting.

elected to skip it, but I looked forward to another informal weekend and agreed only to one program appearance with a speech demanding scarcely more effort than the sort of thing I used to do back in high school. It was going to be a much-needed R&R occasion.

Unfortunately, a number of other people shared this expectation, and it seemed as though close to a thousand of them converged on the Hotel Morrison, including a dazzling array of writers, artists, editors and publishers. In the absence of tight security, even a few agents got in.

American fandom played host to a fan from abroad. The guest, from Northern Ireland, was fanzine editor and writer Walter A. Willis. Over the weekend he met more famous fans and prominent pros than you can shake a stick at, which is one way of dealing with them.

Lacking a stick in his luggage, Willis shook hands with convention chairperson Julian May and her husband Ted Dikty, eminent editors John W. Campbell and Anthony Boucher, publishers Kyle, Greenberg and Korshak, and literally scores of writers.

I met them too, and began lasting friendships with many. At future conventions I would get a guided tour through Henry Ford's Dearborn from John Campbell and visit the haunts of the Cleveland Torso Slayer with Tony Boucher. Alongside Lester del Ray, Frederick Pohl, George O. Smith, Jack Williamson, Poul Anderson, Gordon Dickson and Judy Merril, I sprawled on the floor of Campbell's suite, listening to Ted Sturgeon play his guitar. Bette and Philip José Farmer showed up; so did Ruth and Richard Matheson, on their honeymoon. I met Evelyn Gold, wife of editor Horace Gold, but ever the victim of bad timing, our friendship was to end years later just before she won more than thirteen million dollars in a lottery.

Apparently no one had dreamed that the hitherto modest convention would suddenly assume corridor-crowding and elevator-jamming proportions, with standing room only in both the meeting halls and the public toilets. The realization that science fiction had become a class act was exciting.

Having delivered my little talk, I settled back to enjoy a weekend. Once again it was the convention committee that unsettled me. The unexpectedly large attendance had resulted in a sell-out banquet scheduled for the following evening, and its program had been augmented. Since the latter was entrusted to the capable hands (and lips) of toastmaster and author Murray Leinster, there was nothing to worry about except for one small detail.

Murray Leinster was not going to show up.

I spent a sleepless day working on the necessary preparations and when evening came I did my best to keep the audience awake. It proved rewarding to present the guest of honor; Hugo Gernsback was known as "the father of Science Fiction," along with less flattering descriptions I omitted in my introduction. I then pointed out the editors I would be most willing to submit to, all of whom were female. Also on the platform was well-known science writer Willy Ley, who earlier in the program had insisted there was no proof anyone had ever seen a genuine flying saucer. I now remedied this lack by letting fly with a saucer at Willy. So much for science.

Not too long after the convention had ended, the hotel was torn down. Sometimes I think the critics go a little too far.

TWENTY-FIVE

Conventions provided me with support and encouragement from fans, and during the early part of the new decade I needed all I could get. So did my father, now living with his sister and cousin in Chicago. Both of the ladies worked, and while my own sister and brother-in-law were not far away, Dad had few visitors and little to occupy himself with during the day. I made some contribution to his upkeep and went down to visit him regularly. What I saw was disturbing.

He was now confined to a wheelchair without hope of recovery, nor had he ever recovered from the shock of my mother's death. Most of his close relatives and friends were already gone, and the empty hours must have been agony to endure. Adding to the problem was an accelerating physical decline; he was incontinent and paralysis made him a deadweight, which became increasingly difficult to deal with when he fell after trying to rise from his wheelchair. Lil and Bea couldn't handle him. My sister had a small child to raise. So did Marion and I, and Marion's own condition made it impossible for her to cope with the demands of lifting and daily care involved. Finally the Chicagoans arrived at a decision.

There was too much danger involved in leaving Dad in the apartment alone and unattended, too many physical problems just getting him in and out of bed. Their only alternative was to place him in a nearby nursing home.

It had been my painful duty to inform my father of my mother's death. Now everyone again agreed that I must be the one to break more bad news. Accordingly I was summoned from Milwaukee to tell him.

He accepted the situation with his customary courage. But when I came down to visit him in the nursing facility a few weeks later, he was deeply and understandably depressed. Aware of what my own reaction would be in a similar situation I was not surprised that soon thereafter he just turned his face to the wall and died. Frankly, considering the circumstances, my grief was tempered with relief.

Such had been the case with my mother's passing, and the parallel did not end there. The funeral which followed was, if anything, even less fitting than hers; the graveside service, conducted by a total stranger, surely didn't describe the father I knew. His had been a life touched by tragedy and deprivation. A proud man, he had postponed marriage until the age of thirty-two in order to adequately support the woman he loved and the children he longed for. It must have been a terrible blow when, little more than a decade later, he found himself without a future and forced to rely upon his wife as the family's main source of support. A brave man, he endured the loss of his career, his home, his physical abilities; the death of my mother was the final blow.

Not a word of this was mentioned in the sermon, and there was no reference to the patient, caring, soft-spoken, witty gentleman who had gallantly confronted misfortune during his sixty-seven years and found happiness in far too few.

A rainstorm had flooded the storage section of the basement in Dad's apartment building, and the water destroyed most of the family mementos. Dad's books, letters, photographs—all were lost. There was nothing left now except what was preserved in memory.

I returned to Chicago over the next few years to see my nephew Peter and niece Barbara on the South Side and my aunt Gertrude, who was still at City Hall, and even made a North Side pilgrimage to seek out the spots I remembered from earliest childhood in an effort to alleviate the pangs of recollection.

During 1951 and 1952 I wrote very little fiction, aside from a few short stories and an unsuccessful effort at a novel, which was published in abbreviated form by *Blue Book* magazine. One of the short stories was a pastiche titled "The Man Who Collected Poe," in which I deliberately inserted sentences taken directly from *The Fall of the House of Usher*, combining them with my own just to see if anybody would notice. One of the few who did was Professor Thomas Ollve Mabbott, of Hunter College, who was putting together a collection of Poe stories for publication. In the course of his research he encountered Poe's final and unfinished tale, "The Lighthouse," and wrote to me, suggesting that I might complete it.

The notion of posthumous collaboration with Edgar Allan Poe was irresistible, particularly since in the event of a sale I wouldn't have to split the fee with him. It proved quite a challenge to pick up the story where Poe had left off and continue it in such a manner that the reader wouldn't detect any change of style. Poe was considerably more difficult to imitate or emulate than Lovecraft.

I kept at it until the result was reasonably seamless, and "The Lighthouse" found first publication in *Fantastic*. On the whole, however, writing provided little escape from the vicissitudes of the day.

My chief source of distraction now lay in the gregariousness of science fiction conventions. The annual Worldcons had been augmented by other affairs; one such was the Midwescon which, in 1953, took place at Indian Lake, Ohio. Hosted by Dr. C. L.

Barrett, Lou Tabakow, Don Ford, and other regional residents, this informal gathering attracted both midwestern fans and pros. It was here that I first encountered noted futurist Harlan Ellison, aged eighteen, and British author Arthur C. Clarke, aged thirty-five. At the time, Harlan was still a fan, Arthur had scored a triumphant success with his nonfictional *The Exploration of Space,* and I was just me. Although probably the most unlikely trio since The Three Stooges, we have remained friends ever since.

In the years that followed, the Midwescon relocated, first to Bellefontaine, then to mysterious, exotic Cincinnati. I frequently hitchhiked back as far as Chicago with Jeanie and Doc Smith, usually stopping on route to visit with their daughter Verna Trestrail and her family in Indiana. In science fiction circles Edward E. Smith, Ph.D., was both lauded as a writer and loved as a human being, with good reason. He was perhaps the most modest and unpretentious author I ever met, and one of the kindest.

On other occasions I rode shotgun for Bob Tucker; once we left the convention to visit Mammoth Cave, but made a wrong turn and ended up at Niagara Falls. I was disappointed because there were no bats.

I returned to the Worldcon scene with the 1953 convention in Philadelphia, where I served as toastmaster and had my first meeting with Isaac Asimov. This was long before he wrote *The Bible* or many other of his well-known works. I also encountered one of my future agents, Harry Altshuler. As usual, the convention was an opportunity to make a splash as a big frog in a little pond. But back home I returned to reality; once again a small frog, it was all I could do just to avoid croaking.

Twenty-six

By 1953 I had been sitting in the pay toilet of advertising for eleven years—and I was beginning to see the handwriting on the wall.

The Gustav Marx Advertising Agency had changed, but I wasn't changing with it. The raise in client fees I'd urged on Gus following WWII had inevitably resulted in a quest for more important accounts, which in turn demanded more effort and attention. During the postwar years many new agencies headed by younger men had sprung up in the growing metropolitan area. Now competition was intense, and the arrival of television brought additional complications.

Marx's son Byron had joined us, bringing the youthful zest for promotion and the ambition to expand into the national advertising scene. At first Gus resisted, but inevitably he came to realize that there was no survival value in stasis. He must embrace what he'd always rejected: singing commercials, promotional sales-campaign films, and the new forms of television flackery. Just as we'd subcontracted artwork in the past, we must now subcontract the writing of music and lyrics, animated cartoons, and the packaging of filmed commercials. Like most agencies, we were gradually being transformed from creators to wholesalers. Amidst the competition, emphasis shifted from writing to selling. Gus was increasingly interested in enjoying the newfound leisure of life on a four-acre miniature estate in the country. But his son was a born salesman, and his talent for filmmaking was exactly right for the time. Byron was generally known as "Duke," though the nickname was inexact; actually, he was the crown prince and heir apparent. It was now obvious that Gus's promises that I'd inherit fifty percent of the agency when he passed on would never be fulfilled. Which only goes to show that nobody can tell what the future holds, but we all know what's in the pasture.

Staying on as a copywriter was a dead end. Unless I became an account executive there was no future here. But I lacked the qualifications, the gregariousness and competitive spirit required for aggressive selling. And the nursing of big-money clients entailed the capacity to suffer fools gladly: play golf with them, provide booze and broads. That was the account exec's traditional role in the big agencies, and since Byron eschewed it in favor of concentrating on sales, it was the only function left for me. With my family situation this was manifestly impractical, even if I elected to go that route, which I emphatically did not.

The family situation brought matters to a head. After thirteen years of constant consultation with medical specialists—including the best orthopedists available—Marion's condition continued to deteriorate. Her intermittent high fevers and drainage from the fissure in her leg was now an increasing problem. It began to look as though the time would arrive when walking itself might become impossible. Sally Ann, at ten, was restricted in her activities because of the situation at home.

I had no illusions about our financial setup. Even if I found a copywriting job at another agency the same limitations would prevail, and medical costs would continue to eat up our income.

The alternative was to take the plunge back into the murky waters of full-time writing and hope for the best.

Gradually I evolved the notion of moving to Weyauwega. It was Marion's hometown; her parents and a married sister lived there, and she had over a score of relatives scattered throughout the immediate countryside. If her health worsened, at least she'd be surrounded by family and friends. Sally would have the freedom of small-town life, plus access to the horses she loved, and I'd be able to write in peace and quiet.

Marion wasn't sold on the idea; after all, we had many close friends in Milwaukee and the attendant benefits of metropolitan pleasures. But what good were friends if she couldn't get out to see them, and what good were shows one couldn't attend or shopping trips one couldn't make?

In the end, we decided upon the move. After scouting around, we found an old two-story brick house in town, located just a short block away from the homes of her parents and sister Dorothy. There was no sidewalk on the street in front of the place, and no tub in the bathroom inside, nor was the garage finished or the driveway paved. But I could walk the two blocks to Main Street across the fields, we could take showers, and there was no money for a car anyway.

In fact there wasn't enough money for the house, which cost an astronomical $7,500. But I had three thousand—and, thanks to Marion's uncle Les Leibson, I was able to borrow a few thousand more at a nominal interest.

So in July 1953 we made the move. The house was carpeted and decorated within the strictures of our modest budget, and the exterior painted. Since we had a double lot, 120 feet by 120 feet, Marion began to cast longing looks at the huge vegetable garden and the areas suitable for planting flower beds.

But a look was all she got. The stress of moving brought on another crisis. A doctor in nearby New London put her in the hospital for observation, and after several weeks, brought in a verdict. The orthopedists and specialists in Milwaukee and Madison were wrong. She had tuberculosis of the bone.

There was only one way to deal with the situation. He ordered her to enter a state hospital some fifty miles away. And that's how we began our stay in Weyauwega. Sally and I held down the fort at home and Marion went to the sanatorium.

It wasn't an ideal beginning. Lacking transportation, I had to depend on the kind offices of her relatives to get over and visit every week or so. But there was a bright side to the picture. In the many years since Marion had been treated correctly for her ailment, new drugs had been developed as a cure for tuberculosis. She was being given the proper medication at long last, and it was working. Unfortunately, a side effect of the massive sulfa dosages prescribed resulted in a partial loss of hearing—but the fever disappeared, the drainage stopped, and the rest was a matter of patience.

She came home for a week during the holidays, and the following spring she was discharged—in time to begin gardening. I got weary of pulling weeds, planting, cultivating, and fighting mosquitoes, but in the end, as Marion took over supervision of the agricultural project, we had a continual source of fruits and vegetables, which came in very handy.

Because while Marion had a green thumb, mine was black and blue from hammering the typewriter in my office upstairs. A revised and expanded version of my unsuccessful novel was sold for paperback publication as *Spiderweb*. Somewhat encouraged, I began work on other novels at the behest of a new agent, former magazine editor Oscar J. Friend. The immediate results, *The Kidnapper* and *The Will to Kill*, also saw paperback publication, but I saw very little money. Despite turning out additional short stories to supplement my income, our residue of savings dwindled down to almost nothing.

It was then that Sid Stone came to the rescue. Sid, a cartoonist who had sold artwork to the Marx Agency, now had a highly successful agency of his own, and took over one of the accounts

I'd worked on. In addition, he was conducting "It's a Draw," a weekly cartoon quiz show over a Milwaukee television station.

He offered me a deal. Would I be willing to come down to Milwaukee every weekend to service the account, write the copy and appear as permanent guest panelist on the show?

Since I'd have to travel by bus—or a combination of bus and train, involving a four-to-five-hour trip each way—this would mean staying overnight. That cost me my weekends, plus transportation, meals and lodging. But he offered me a magnificent fifty-five dollars per week, and by imposing on the kindness of my many Milwaukee friends I was often able to cut down on expenditures for hotel rooms and meals. So in the end I averaged around thirty-five dollars in take-home pay. It spelled the difference between survival and going under.

The trips also spelled survival for what laughingly passed as my sanity.

Not that Weyauwega was a madhouse. On the contrary, it was a very pleasant rural community of 1,241 people, most of whom were friendly and well-meaning. Together with Marion's many relatives, they offered continuous contact and companionship. Unfortunately, their interests didn't coincide with mine, and their understanding of my professional problems was miniscule or non-existent.

Hunting, fishing, bowling and sports weren't my thing, nor was Saturday-night-at-the-tavern. Conversely, the life of a writer was alien to their special sphere, and I didn't intrude my work in conversation or social occasions. Although I listened politely and did my best to adapt to the local scene, inevitably I was considered a loner. While television reception in town seldom brought in the Milwaukee stations, I was occasionally glimpsed on the tube. And local wiseacres sagely concluded that my primary income was derived from being a TV celebrity, since they didn't see my books or stories. Nor could they hope to, in a community where the library was open twice a week; Tuesday nights from seven to nine, and Saturdays in the morning and early afternoon.

The good citizens of Weyauwega were not unlettered. Pete Walch, the editor of the weekly paper, had been the secretary of a congressman and we spent time together before he was supplanted, after a final illness, by Richard Prideaux. Aside from occasional write-ups in the local press, the latter, whose brother was on the staff of the prestigious *Life* magazine, tended to ignore my presence in town; he associated with the other literate and prosperous local dignitaries who lived on "the hill"—Weyauwega's answer to Grosse Pointe, where the community business leaders dwelt in air-conditioned luxury when not off on annual vacations to Hawaii or New York. Most of these folks had the advantage of a college education and a worldly sophistication acquired in the marts of trade; they had put aside childish things, and to them writing was an avocation pursued by lady poets whose work appeared in church magazines. Of course they knew there were *real* writers in New York and Hollywood, making *real* money, but certainly a local specimen could only be classified as an exotic eccentric.

Nevertheless, I cruised the Wolf River in the company of Don Shelp, the pharmacist. At times I made the rounds of the wayside pickle stations with Steve Tedesco, an Austrian expatriate almost as foreign to the community as myself, being both an immigrant and a Democrat. Occasionally I rode with Doc Maasch, the resident physician, on his house calls to outlying farms. And I was enlisted in a local advertising promotion by Ross Bauer, son of the proprietor of the leading funeral home and furniture store. Upon inheriting the business he decided to go in for a quality furniture operation which would bring customers from all over the state; I devised a presentation to major manufacturers which brought him franchises for their lines, plus newspaper advertising and an elaborate brochure for the remodeled store. The strategy worked, but I was paid a minute fee for my services, and while Ross became a close confidant he never really understood my way of life, nor did I share his. Marion's relatives were certainly cordial and hospitable, but they were largely farm-oriented and I didn't intrude my own interests upon family gatherings.

So the Milwaukee trips kept me going, even in subzero weather, with interminable delays, standing outside for hours in the freezing wind while waiting for the arrival of snowbound buses. And although as time went on we had many visitors—fans and writers from all over who happened to be passing through the area—it was the consistent contact with Milwaukee friends that linked me to the life I'd known.

During this time my correspondence with both fans and fellow professionals increased. From time to time I enjoyed contacts with various writers whom I esteemed and feel are now unjustly neglected. I have fond recollections of Philip Wylie, author of *Finnley Wren* and *A Generation of Vipers,* and Tiffany Thayer, once famous for his *Thirteen Men* and later the head of the Fortean Society. I also traded letters with William Lindsay Gresham, whose *Nightmare Alley* remains memorable.

My contributions to the proliferating science fiction fan magazines continued, later to be bound and gagged in two hardcover collections. And usually, twice a year, I managed to get away for a weekend to a science fiction convention. Since I never discussed specifics of my work or professional problems at home, these brief interludes supplied me with the companionship of my own kind—writers, editors, artists, publishers and readers.

In 1954 I served as toastmaster at the Worldcon in San Francisco, and there augmented my admiration for the protean Anthony Boucher—editor, author, critic, commentator, scholar, wit, linguist, gourmet, wine connoisseur; authority on detective fiction and real-life homicide, opera, pro sports, limericks, stud poker; and the only man other than me who was enchanted by Dave Chasen's performance in *Rain or Shine.* That long sentence scarcely begins to cover an enduring friendship. It was at that convention that I also met a fan named Samuel A. Peeples, a deputy police commissioner in nearby Colma who was a movie buff, book collector, authority on western Americana and himself the author of a score of paperback novels in that genre.

In those distant days when conventions were still labors of love, even the guests of honor were frequently forced to shoulder their own expenses, including the price of a ticket to the banquet held to celebrate their presence. The following year's Worldcon found me unable to afford the trip to Cleveland and I turned down the toastmaster's job. Tony Boucher had word of my refusal and, suspecting the cause, promptly suggested I write a story for *The Magazine of Fantasy and Science Fiction*, which he coedited with Mick McComas. The suggestion had to be prompt because the convention itself was only a week away. I sat down and wrote an eleven-thousand-word story in one day. Fortunately, "All on a Golden Afternoon" turned out well, and I had no qualms about cashing the check sent to me in time to attend the Cleveland affair. There I helped write and perform in a skit with fellow writers, which was somehow overlooked in the annual Drama Critics Awards.

In 1956 I again acted as toastmaster at the Worldcon in New York, with Arthur Clarke as guest of honor and Al Capp (then at the height of his *Li'l Abner* fame) as guest speaker. The traditional all-night poker games continued; after one of them I wandered the city streets at dawn with nonplayer Isaac Asimov, then later went on to breakfast with Arthur across from the Chelsea, which had once lodged the likes of Thomas Wolfe and Tennessee Williams. Though Arthur preferred his residence here, the actual convention was held at the Biltmore. After the fans had left, the hotel repaired their damages and changed its name to the Rebiltmore.

Somehow the '57 convention in London managed to muddle through without either my presence or Winston Churchill's, but in 1958 I was doing the usual in Los Angeles, which remains a memorable occasion for me in more ways than one. Following a round of festivities I spent several days at the home of Sam and

Erlene Peeples; he had moved down to Woodland Hills and become a television writer at a time when western series were beginning to dominate the medium.

In 1959 I again attempted to pull in my horns, but finally agreed to act as co-toastmaster, the other slice being Isaac Asimov. Together we appeared in Detroit to hand out the Hugo Awards, which for the past five years had been bestowed to the people and works voted best in the science fiction field by convention membership.*

Emulating the Oscar ceremony, Asimov introduced the categories while I opened the envelopes and announced the winners. To my stunned surprise, I found myself reading off the award for Best Short Story for "That Hellbound Train" by Robert Bloch. Until that very moment I actually had no idea this was even one of the nominees, nor would I have suspected as much, since the story was outright fantasy, not science fiction.

It was an occasion never to be forgotten—the first time I had ever gotten a prize since I'd stopped buying Cracker Jack.

---

*"Hugo," of course, is so nicknamed in honor of editor Hugo Gernsback.

TWENTY-SEVEN

Winning the Best Science Fiction Short Story award for a deal-with-the-devil fantasy wasn't the only strange thing that happened to work of mine during the latter years of the 1950s. There was, for example, "Water's Edge." This was a simple, straightforward little story which I thought would be ideal for the new *Alfred Hitchcock's Mystery Magazine*. The editor thought otherwise.

So did the editors at *Ellery Queen* and a half-dozen other potential markets. In the end the story saw the light of day—and a very dim light it was, at a penny a word—in *Mike Shayne's Mystery Magazine*. Imagine my surprise when, just a year later, the story was reprinted in a hardcover anthology entitled *Alfred Hitchcock Presents Stories They Wouldn't Let Me Do on TV*.

In the years that followed, the story continued to be widely reprinted here and abroad. Eventually it even ended up as a one-hour television episode.

Needless to say, the show on which it appeared was "Alfred Hitchcock Presents."

All through the free-lance period I kept experimenting with writing methods, all aimed at simplifying direct communication with the reader. My antenna went up whenever I saw or heard writers explain their work by describing it as a "metaphor." My feeling is that there's seldom a genuine need for metaphorical messages—if one wants to say something, why not say it straight out? All too often the term *metaphor* is used as an apologia for either obscurantism or sleaze, and quite frequently it euphemizes both.

Ideas for stories came from everywhere, but I never seriously attempted to develop them until I hit upon an ending. This frequently involved a plot twist or at least some sort of thematic summation. Then, once I knew where I was going, I sat down and wrote an outline which mapped out how to get there and described the happenings en route, together with the characters I enlisted as passengers in the vehicle chosen for the journey. If this sounds a bit confused, so was I. But over the years this procedure has seemed to work out, enabling me to write a first draft and correct it immediately. At least it served for short fiction.

I wasn't doing well with novels. A great deal of time and effort went into *Colossal,* a saga of silent-screen Hollywood during the twenties which ended with the advent of sound. It was planned as the first book of a trilogy; the second would continue the story through the early years of the talkies and WWII, while a third would deal with the coming of television. My characters were fictional, but some could be regarded as being modeled after D. W. Griffith, Erich von Stroheim, Lon Chaney, Buster Keaton, and other stars.

Success or failure in writing, as in many other fields of endeavor, is often dependent on timing, and mine was bad. The nostalgia boom wasn't "in," film historians were just beginning to probe the past, and biographies of stars and directors had yet to attain best-seller status. As a result I was stepping up to bat with three strikes already against me, and nobody wanted to play ball. In the end, it took a dozen years for the book to reach print in paperback. Even then the publishers disguised its contents by changing my title to *The Star Stalker,* with a deliberately misleading blurb and cover art to match. I was not informed in advance, let alone consulted, and can only offer a belated apology to all four of the readers who purchased it.*

During the 1950s I branched out into the new men's magazines—*Playboy,* which started with lowly reprints and small-pay new material, and its many imitators, including Bill Hamling's *Rogue.* I wrote a monthly column in the latter, just as I had in his earlier science fiction magazine, *Imagination.* Mystery and suspense stories were sold to appropriate markets.

Sadly, after a generation of precarious survival, *Weird Tales* went out of business. *The Magazine of Fantasy and Science Fiction* took up the slack. New science fiction magazines were springing up. Some of them promptly fell down again, but I managed to keep selling.

Any slight advance in income was offset by higher taxes plus the increased cost of living. And if luck turned bad I could easily find myself sharing the fate of *Weird Tales.*

Someone in Weyauwega found out I could speak and as a goodwill gesture I gave talks to the local Lions Club and service clubs in the surrounding area. All gratis, of course. Once in a great while I also did a talk or gave an interview in Milwaukee (where, incidentally, following a reasonably cautious approach to the situation, Harold Gauer and Alice Bedard were married after a courtship of twenty-five years). Marion's family seemed pleased by our presence in the community but we did little to expand the immedi-

---

*While I'm in a contrite mood, let me also apologize to both of the readers who bought a paperback containing my short story collection, *Terror in the Night* combined with an original novel titled *Shooting Star.* I have no particular qualms regarding the stories, but the novel is one of a dozen or more of my worst.

ate circle of acquaintances or alleviate the dullness of daily routine. I found rural existence to be more colic than bucolic.

Sally Ann was making friends, riding horses, running free as a teenager in the last refuge of freedom available to a rapidly urbanizing society.

Marion was not so fortunate. Much as she liked her relatives, she'd lived too long in the city and become too acclimated to the tastes and interests of our friends there. Unable to walk distances of more than a block or so without effort, she took to staying home much of the time, and—following Voltaire's advice—cultivated her garden. She wouldn't fly, hence didn't attend conventions with me, despite my urging.

On April 5, 1958, I turned forty-one. Over the hill now, for sure; ready to descend into middle age. Almost eighteen years married, with a daughter seemingly destined to spend her adolescence—and, perhaps, her lifetime—in a small-town environment with no opportunity to spread and test her wings against a wider horizon. Twenty-four years a professional writer, and what to show for it? A few published books, only two of which had appeared in hardcovers a dozen years before. Lots of short stories, most of them sold for one cent a word. A few in men's markets, some reprinted in anthologies; a bit of critical recognition, but this sporadic enough and hardly a food substitute in case the money ran out. A small bank balance, insufficient to pay off the mortgage or insure against disaster. Surely not enough to risk buying a car; I'd never owned an automobile. No prospects of shoring up what seemed increasingly to be a shaky marriage, no prospects of materially improving my work as a writer or my resultant status.

Forty-one. With varicose veins, leaky sinuses; living in virtual small-town exile. What would happen when the TV appearances stopped? What would happen when my markets dried up—or still worse, when my writing dried up? What would happen if my wife got sick again? What would happen if *nothing* happened and I just got older? Twenty-four years a writer, and still nowhere. Oh, yes, *somewhere*—I forgot. Forty-one. Over the hill.

All the places I'd wanted to see—travel, go abroad. All the people I was curious about, wanted to meet. And Hollywood out there, with the movies and television; I'd have enjoyed working in a field like that. But too little and too late. Forty-one. Over that big hump and nowhere left to go but down. Down and out.

If I'd had any common sense I think I might have considered shooting myself. Instead I just kept plodding along. And some months later, toward the end of the year, I wrote *Psycho*.

TWENTY-EIGHT

"**P**sycho all came from Robert Bloch's book," said Alfred Hitchcock, as quoted in an interview in *The Celluloid Muse* (1969).

But where did "Robert Bloch's book" come from?

Elsewhere (*The Quality of Murder,* edited by Anthony Boucher), I have recounted the story of the grim case which shocked Wisconsin in 1957 and led me, the following year, to write a novel in which a seemingly normal and ordinary rural resident led a dual life as a psychotic murderer, unsuspected by his neighbors. I based my story on the *situation* rather than on any person, living or dead, involved in the Gein affair: indeed, I knew very little of the details concerning that case and virtually nothing about Gein himself at the time. It was only some years later, when doing my essay on Gein for *The Quality of Murder,* that I discovered how closely the imaginary character I'd created resembled the real Ed Gein both in overt act and apparent motivation.

But at the time that I decided to write a novel based on the notion that the man next door may be a monster, unsuspected even in the gossip-ridden microcosm of small-town life, I set out to create my character from whole cloth.

My title derives, of course, from *psychotic* and also from *psychology* and *psychoanalysis*. It was from the latter sources that I sought a rationale for my protagonist—or, more precisely, an irrationale.

In order to become a successful serial murderer in a close-knit rural society, a man must adopt a reclusive existence: operating a motel on the outskirts of town seemed a solution. Sticking close to his business day and night would excuse him from participation in the social life of the community and at the same time physically isolate him from constant scrutiny. Also, the very nature of his occupation was such as to provide him with potential victims, and under the seemingly most ordinary and natural circumstances.

So I built a motel and put him in business. But it wasn't until I'd arrived at his fixation—accompanied by the transvestism that was to form his modus operandi, modus vivendi, and my "gimmick" all in one—that I hit upon his name.

Norman Bates.

The first name was a combination of two words, "nor man," a pun which contains the secret of the story: my killer is neither woman nor man.* Bates? I thought of his mother's sexual domination in childhood and youth: a domination young Master Norman could not escape except through masturbation. To say nothing of how Norman "baits" his trap and in another sense "baits" his pursuers.

Psychologically oriented punning prevails throughout the story. The Misses Crane for example: when peering, straining to see something which is hidden from view, one "cranes" one's neck. My hero operates a hardware store—he led a *hard* and *wearing* existence—but he is also *hard where* Norman is soft and

---

*There might even have been an echo ringing from my vaudeville attendance in childhood. Karyl Norman was a well-known female impersonator, rivaling the famed Julian Eltinge, and I may have seen him perform, though I can't recall doing so.

impotent. Mother, *Norma* Bates, of course derives back from "Norman" and from the secondary pun in her own: the murderer is neither Norman *Nor Ma,* but a combination of both.

There is also the reassuring phonetic association with "normal": students of trivia may recall that Edgar Rice Burroughs assumed a punning pseudonym for his first published novel— Normal Bean. The insensitive magazine editor, unaware of the connotation of "normal being," changed the byline to *Norman Bean.*

As for mother's mummified appearance—I had never forgotten seeing my own mother on her deathbed, yellowed, shockingly wizened and shrunken by the inroads of terminal cancer. It was partially in an effort to exorcise that shock that I must have unconsciously come up with the taxidermy gambit in the novel. "Mother" became "mummy."

I see I've used the term *unconsciously,* and it's quite correct: many of the examples I give here were not conscious contrivances at the time, and only since then have I been able to analyze some of the sources of various story elements. The use of multiple personalities as a plot device was, however, derived from sources familiar to me, viz, two short stories.

"Lucy Comes to Stay" (*Weird Tales,* January 1952) was one of the last pieces I ever did for my alma mater: a brief account, in the first person, in which a woman details the crimes of her best friend, Lucy. The friend, of course, is a figment of the imagination—"Lucy" is derived from "hallucination." Years later I adapted this story for the screen as a segment of the film *Asylum.*

"The Real Bad Friend" (*Mike Shayne's Mystery Magazine,* February, 1957) was a variation told from a masculine viewpoint and with a background of ordinary domestic life rather than an asylum setting. As such, it represented an attempt to bring the schizoid manifestation closer to the daily experience of the reader.

Now, in *Psycho,* I had to go a step further and develop a notion as old as *Dr. Jekyll and Mr. Hyde* into a seemingly fresh idea. I felt transvestism might help, but even more important would be a careful attention to the details of ordinary existence in ordinary surroundings, setting them up for the intrusion of the extraordinary.

From time to time I have been alternately amused and confused by various comments on *Psycho* as a film, written by Hitchcock admirers. These *auteur*-theorists express great appreciation for his innovations—for example, the effectiveness of murder in a shower stall, at a time when a person is most naked and vulnerable. They applaud the portrait of Norman Bates and the audacity of setting up a presumable heroine, only to kill her off outrageously so early in the story.

I, too, admire and applaud Hitchcock, but as several million readers of *Psycho* in its various additions can testify, these concepts came, as Hitchcock himself said, "from the book." One of the *auteur*-theorists mentioned my name once, and disparagingly, in his account of Hitchcock's creation; to the others I apparently don't even exist.

Hitchcock *did* make changes. The sex relationship I allude to in the novel becomes dramatized as the first scene in the film. A state trooper wearing ominous "shades" becomes a character in the girl's flight with the stolen money, which I treat in less detail in the narrative. Norman Bates is portrayed as being ten years younger than his namesake in the novel. Mary Crane becomes "Marion"—much to my own distress, since I happened to be married to a Marion.* There are perhaps a half-dozen other alterations but *Psycho* is still my story right down to the last line.

Of course I wasn't anticipating any such development at the time. When people asked about the book I was writing, I told them

---

*I later learned that when the film went on a location shoot in Phoenix, the phone book there listed a "Mary Crane," so the character's name was hastily changed to avoid any possibility of a lawsuit.

only that I felt it would be rather unusual, but due to the nature of its plot it would never make a movie.

Shortly after publication—and satisfyingly good reviews—I had a call from my agent, Harry Altshuler, in New York. He had been approached by someone from the huge talent agency MCA with an offer to buy *Psycho* for films. The offer was blind: the would-be buyer's name was not mentioned, only the price—five thousand dollars. This was no fortune, even in 1959, but it represented my first chance for a film sale in a twenty-five-year career, and I could certainly use the money. Taking a deep breath, I refused and told him to hold out for more. A few days later he called back; they'd increased their bid to $9,500. I accepted. My agent got ten percent, my publishers took fifteen, the tax people skimmed off their share of the loot, and I ended up with about $6,250. Hitchcock got *Psycho,* and the rest is history. Ancient history, really, yet people have never forgotten his brilliant film. And today, more than thirty years later, the novel is still in print.

From time to time people come to me and volunteer the information that after seeing the film they were unable to take a shower. I can only tell them that they're lucky I didn't kill off my victim on a toilet seat.

But in the summer of 1959 the film had yet to be made. The contract I signed identified the purchaser as "Shamley Productions." It took a while for my agent to discover that this was Alfred Hitchcock's company, and it was a newspaper publicity release that revealed Hitchcock would be making the film for Paramount. I was never contacted by Shamley or told directly of his intentions; not until years later did I learn some of the problems he faced.

To begin with, Paramount was not happy with his plans. Executives didn't like the story and were even opposed to its title. Unfortunately for them, Hitchcock's contract specified that he controlled the selection of material, and he wanted to make *Psycho.* He was also determined to use this title, so much so that he secured rights to the lettering design on the book jacket for use in advertising the film. After a series of financial obstacles were put in his path during negotiations with the studio, he lifted the roadblock by setting up a production deal involving an investment of his own. Whatever the arrangements, budgetary restrictions made it impossible for him to mount the usual technicolor opus featuring top box-office names. Hitchcock would settle for a black-and-white film without superstars in the leading roles. In a further attempt to head him off at the pass, he was told that due to previous commitments there would be no sound stages available for his use at Paramount during his shooting schedule. Undaunted, Mr. Hitchcock announced that while honoring contractual obligations to release the film through Paramount, he would actually make the film at Universal, where his television show was produced, and use its cinematographer as well. Which is precisely what he did.

I've since been told by one of his former associate producers that Hitchcock inquired as to whether or not I might be approached to write the screenplay, whereupon he was promptly informed by an MCA agent that I was not presently available. This, of course, was technically the truth; it's a long limo ride from Weyauwega to Universal City. Also I'm more or less convinced that the agent never wrote down either my name or Weyauwega's, and if he did, he misspelled both.

The writing assignment went to James P. Cavanaugh, whose efforts proved unsatisfactory. The next nominee was a radio writer, Joseph Stefano, who worked on the script for six weeks and, in Mr. Hitchcock's words, "contributed dialogue mostly, no ideas." It seems quite apparent that, as usual, the producer-director brought his own inspirations to the screenplay. The "Hitchcock touch" is very much in evidence throughout the film, and to good effect.

Many times since, I've been asked whether or not I would have liked the opportunity to do my own adaptation of the novel. Perhaps I could have added a few touches; I most definitely would have fought for a final explanatory scene only half the length of the one used in the picture. But the blunt truth is that it's just as well for me—and for the film—that I wasn't asked. Without any previous experience, I doubt I had the ability to have done a satisfactory screenplay, and at the time the thought never crossed my mind.

During the summer of 1959 whatever did cross my mind risked little danger of being run over. Mental traffic had slowed almost to a halt. My thoughts were running on empty.

Actually the slowdown was a long-awaited luxury. In a biographical essay, science fiction critic and historian Sam Moskowitz cites the story "The Funnel of God" (published in *Fantastic Science Fiction,* January 1960) as one into which I poured the "accumulated disillusionment" characteristic of my personal feelings at the time.

The truth of the matter was that the tale was written in a period of euphoria rather than depression; my fortunes already seemed on the rise and there was fresh hope for the future. What happened was that the magazine's editor pulled one of her customary stunts by sending a copy of the cover for a forthcoming issue illustrating the main feature, already titled "The Funnel of God." All the dear lady required from me was an appropriate story, preferably within the next twelve hours or so. I never did find out whose idea it was to come up with that ambiguous artwork and the title; for all I know, the miscreant still lives. But if there is any evidence of despair, it's because I had a horrendous job writing ten thousand words appropriate to the illustration and its designation.*

Somehow I managed, just as I'd earlier managed a short novel, titled *Sneak Preview,* for *Amazing Stories,* a sort of alternate-universe approach to *This Crowded Earth,* the short novel I'd written for the same magazine a year before. The previous effort had dealt with the problems of overpopulation and senior citizens in the near future, hardly matters of great interest or concern in 1958. My 1959 vision of things to come depicted a post-holocaust

---

*Boy, this guy sure takes himself seriously, doesn't he?

society ruled by the film industry. As such, it might be considered a companion piece to a story I'd done for the May 1959 issue of *Ellery Queen's Mystery Magazine.* This little yarn dealt with the immediate future, in which unscrupulous powers plot control of our society by grooming professional actors for election to political office.

Science fiction writers certainly do get some crazy ideas. Thank God nobody wastes time paying attention to the weird nonsense they come up with!

For the record, nobody has ever paid any particular attention to mine—not even amongst fans or fellow writers in the field— except, of course, for conferring that science fiction award on a fantasy story, "That Hellbound Train." In September of '59 I came home from the Detroit convention clutching the trophy to my breast—which, considering its rocketlike shape, was a hell of a lot safer than trying to sit on it.

Shortly after putting the thing on a shelf alongside a sixty-minute taped interview with a talking toilet seat,* I received a long-distance phone call.

My friend and colleague Samuel A. Peeples wanted to know if I'd like to come out to Hollywood and write a script for "Lock-Up."

---

*And a very well-educated one it was, too. This toilet seat could speak five different languages. In fact it could do almost anything, except flush.

TWENTY-NINE

"Lock Up," starring an actor named Macdonald Carey, was a half-hour television series about a crime-solving attorney who charged no fees. This, of course, made it a fantasy, but most people didn't seem to be aware of the fact. What appealed to me about the show was that its hero wasn't a gun-toter like the ones in the omnipresent westerns of that period, and his problems were frequently solved by brains rather than brawn.

But the major appeal lay in Sam Peeples's proposal itself. Another writer, Frank Gruber, had been responsible for bringing him into television and now he wanted to confer a similar favor on me. Knowing I wasn't interested in routine shoot-'em-up shows, he thought this one might be more to my taste. Since he'd done a number of episodes himself, he approached the story editor and recommended me for an assignment. Thirty years ago such things, while uncommon, were not yet impossible. And "Lock Up" was produced for syndication by Ziv, an outfit which was always happy to buy material for a song. All they were willing to warble for me was an offer to purchase one half-hour script for the lowest price allowed under the terms of their contractual agreement.

Whether or not they liked what I might write was, of course, impossible to foresee in advance. Should Ziv be dissatisfied with what I did, Sam would do a script of his own. Meantime he generously offered to lodge me while I tackled the assignment. This was my chance to discover if I could write for television for fun and profit. Maybe nothing would come of it, but at the very worst I'd end up with $1,135 and a three-week working vacation.

I was grateful for the opportunity and remain so to this day. Sitting at the typewriter in the spare room of the Peepleses' home in Woodland Hills, I studied an assortment of sample scripts from the show, then came up with a story line. Sam had kindly volunteered advice and assistance, which I declined with thanks. If I intended to learn to walk, I'd better do so without relying on a crutch.

Soon I was walking across the Ziv lot on Santa Monica Boulevard to deliver my first draft to the producer and his staff. One of the latter was Sam's neighbor, a young story editor from back East whose name was Frank Price. Since Frank happened to be a fantasy and science fiction fan I felt somewhat reassured, although the show didn't deal with such material. As it turned out I had no trouble making a few changes for the final draft, whereupon I was promptly commissioned with a second assignment.

Just as promptly, in accordance with the rules, I joined the Writers Guild of America. Meantime, across town, other writers were adapting two of my stories, "The Cure" and what they retitled "Is Betsy Blake Still Alive?" purchased for "Alfred Hitchcock Presents."

I was now beginning to feel as if I were a member of the Hollywood community, along with the great names remembered from my childhood—people like Skelton Knaggs, Lon Poff, Ub Iwerks, T. Hee, Sonny Bupp and Yakima Canutt.*

---

*You think I'm kidding? Yakima Canutt was perhaps the greatest stuntman in movie history; he doubled for John Wayne in *Stagecoach,* and I remembered him

In keeping with my exalted status I quit sponging off the Peeples family and moved into a lavish one-room furnished apartment in Studio City, directly across the street from what was once Republic Studio. "Lock-Up" kept on buying scripts and I needed an agent. Sam Peeples suggested I seek the advice of his representative, Gordon Molson. Since the Molson Agency handled only seasoned professionals, I was not qualified for their services, but Molson could undoubtedly recommend someone suitable.

It's a long hike from Studio City to Beverly Hills, so I took the bus, which probably got me there in at least fifteen minutes' less time than if I'd walked it. The time I saved was spent discussing my situation with Gordon Molson, and I walked out of his office as a client. He remained my agent and cherished friend until his sudden death twenty-two years later.

Shortly after we met, agency offices were moved to just half a block away from the Kuttner residence where I'd stayed during my first trip to California in 1937. Gordon and his associates—Bill Stanton, Ben Kamsler, Giulio Anfuso, and secretary Dorothy Schaff, who actually masterminded the whole setup—soon became a surrogate family. I frequently met one or the other for lunch, and each of them took turns driving me around to see producers and executive personnel. One of the first stops was Universal Studios, where I met the staff of "Alfred Hitchcock Presents."

For the record, this event took place in the late fall of 1959. Contrary to published accounts by no-accounts who didn't do their homework, I had no previous personal contacts whatsoever with either Mr. Hitchcock or his television show. They had nothing to do with my coming to Hollywood; nor did the success of the film version of *Psycho*. As a matter of fact, the picture was still

---

from as far back as the twenties. Imagine my shock when one night in the 1970s the phone rang and I picked it up to hear a voice announce, "This is Yakima Canutt." Turned out he was seeking information regarding one of his early roles for use in a forthcoming autobiography.

being shot when I arrived at the studio for the first time. And I later learned that Joan Harrison, the producer of "Alfred Hitchcock Presents," shared the grave reservations of many associates regarding this film venture. So much for the notion that *Psycho* launched me on a television and film career. At this stage of the game my identification with the novel was more handicap than help.

Miss Harrison had formerly worked with Hitchcock as secretary, screenwriter and production assistant. Her associate on the television show was actor/director Norman Lloyd, who had been one of Orson Welles's Mercury Players and appeared in the title role of Hitchcock's film *Saboteur*. A third member of the team was young Gordon Hessler, who acted as story editor and became a film director upon returning to England some years later. The trio and their secretary occupied one of the bungalows in what was then a wooded enclave south of the main gate, the domain of wild rabbits, domesticated squirrels, and tame employees of studio boss Lew Wasserman.

The reason for my meeting with the Hitchcock people was simple enough. They'd purchased those two short stories adapted for the television show by other writers and they'd learned that I wrote for television myself. So what could be more logical than to call me in to do a television script from a story by another writer? At least that's the way they were thinking at the time. Who was I to dispute them? Particularly not when they offered me Frank Mace's story "The Cuckoo Clock" for adaptation.

I said I'd think it over (which I did, for almost five seconds) and departed to prowl around the lot. I zeroed in on "the *Phantom* stage," the theater interior of the Paris Opera House, which was still standing and frequently used for other films. To my surprise, it was much smaller than I'd expected, but this was where it all started for me on film a third of a century ago.

I returned a few days later when, by remarkable coincidence, this became the stage where *Psycho* was being shot. In point of fact, this was the first time I'd ever been present at a shoot. My main concern, as I recall, revolved around just sneaking in without permission. Skulking behind some flats, I confronted the side of a building which had to be the Bates Motel just as Tony Perkins passed by on the walk. I did not see or hear Mr. Hitchcock, but some assistant, also invisible at the far end of the walk, yelled, "Cut!"

I promptly obeyed, cutting for the door, and thus ended my first and only personal association with the filming of *Psycho*.

Bill Stanton drove me home in his Corvette and I sat down to write the teleplay of "The Cuckoo Clock," not even waiting until I received and signed a contract. In a single step I'd moved directly from the bottom of the heap to one of television's most prestigious shows. Almost immediately following submission of the script I was offered a second assignment. I was sitting on top of the world.

A few days later the world was sitting on top of me.

Beginning on January first the Writers Guild would be going on strike. As a member, I would not be permitted to sell stories, write scripts, visit studio offices, confer with their occupants, or even say hello to a producer who might be standing next to me in the men's washroom.

I had no way of knowing just how long the strike would last. But I did know that there would be no further income until its outcome. Any possibility of bringing the family to California and settling down on a permanent basis would have to be deferred.

Instead I flew home over the holidays; uncertainty about the future made the occasion bittersweet. Having just experienced a capsulized example of the sudden reverses which can affect a writer's capital, I discussed that situation with Marion and Sally, as well as the risks they might run by such a drastic uprooting and change in life-style. We decided that the only sensible course was for me to return to Hollywood. When the strike ended and I knew what sort and source of income could be expected in the immediate future, we could make our final decision accordingly. They were both enthusiastic about the prospect of selling the house and snow shovel. And after all, we weren't in for more than a brief separation. How long could the strike possibly last?

The answer turned out to be damn near six months.

It was magic time. Overnight, that hotshot new Hollywood writer miraculously reverted to a penny-a-word hack, sitting in his one-room furnished apartment and pounding out stories and articles for dear life. During the months to come I wrote a score of pieces; some of them sold for better rates, but not enough to simultaneously support a mansion in Weyauwega and a luxurious life-style in California. I did, however, have prospects.

A new collection of short stories, *Pleasant Dreams,* would be forthcoming from Arkham House in the fall. While the advance payment was only $600, I would receive a gigantic $750 from Simon & Schuster on publication of my new novel, *The Dead Beat,* plus a fee for its magazine publication. And by midyear I'd have screen credit for the story of *Psycho,* though no additional cash. These considerations were enough to keep me chained to the typewriter when I wasn't walking over to the Studio City shopping area where I dropped off my laundry and picked up such gourmet delicacies as canned baked beans (with molasses, not tomato sauce), Chef Boyardee spaghetti, and Heinz vegetable soup. Fortified by this balanced diet, I dared to think ahead. Even though the strike dragged on interminably, sooner or later it would end before television network executives had to find honest employment. If the family was to join me afterwards, I had better learn how to drive a car.

Up until now I had been augmenting bus trips with assists from a growing and generous group of friends. In addition to the Peepleses, the staff of the Molson Agency, and various members of the Los Angeles Science Fantasy Society, I was in contact with a number of fellow writers. My high school friend Milton Gelman, married to actress Gloria Gould, had segued from New York to Hollywood in his television writing career. He was most helpful and hospitable. Richard Matheson was now active in both films and TV, along with a group of writers which included Charles Beaumont, William F. Nolan, George Clayton Johnson, Jerry Sohl and John Tomerlin. Fritz Leiber and wife Jonquil had also come west again, and like Gelman offered both occasional transportation and driving lessons. So did supportive fans like Djinn Faine and Elmer Perdue, who graced the local scene. People, I discovered, could be very kind.

I resumed contact with Forrest Ackerman, A. E. van Vogt and Evelyn Gold, who had come west to marry Paul Donner Spencer. I attended their wedding, along with Howard Browne, my former editor at Ziff-Davis, now a successful mystery novelist and television writer. There were also monthly meetings with the Mystery Writers of America, an organization I'd joined in the Midwest. All in all, while I missed the family, the one-room apartment wasn't the equivalent of solitary confinement.

As a matter of fact, I soon discovered neighbors, or, more accurately, they discovered me. One of the Molson Agency's clients was William R. Cox, a reporter-turned-writer who had graduated from a long career in both pulps and slick-paper magazines to doing screenplays and then television scripts. He and his wife Lee were gregarious and enjoyed entertaining a wide assortment of friends in the profession. During the first six months of 1960 they were heavily involved in the strike proceedings, but that didn't seem to slow their hyperactive social life. I soon became a part of it, once we were introduced and they discovered I lived only a block away. Many of Bill's buddies were former free-lance writers from back East whose careers paralleled his own and who enjoyed a mutual interest in outdoor sports and indoor refreshments. That wasn't the case with me, but Bill had his quieter moments which we shared, along with a mutual admiration for various old-timers in show biz. Sometimes, when we might have a drink together late in the afternoon, nostalgia set in.

On such an occasion I told Bill that one of the first movies

I remembered was a two-reel comedy starring a wonderfully inept and even more wonderfully inventive little man who built a boat. I never forgot the film or its star, and through my lifetime I followed his fortunes and misfortunes on screen and off. Thanks to Bill, almost forty years later I had the privilege of meeting that man at a baseball game in Griffith Park between a team of actors and a team of writers on strike.

The umpire of this epic contest was actor Dick Foran, who showed up wearing the regulation cap, chest protector and a black patch over one eye. The writers were, I admit, a somewhat sorry collection of geriatric jocks, their only qualification for participation in sports being a case of athlete's foot. Some idea of their level of competence may be established by the fact that they selected me to play second base.

The actors were for the most part younger and more agile; their ranks included such stalwarts as Dan Blocker, the hulking star of the television show "Bonanza." But the star of the team, and the star of the occasion, was a sixty-five-year-old catcher—none other than the boat-building buffoon of my childhood memories, Buster Keaton.

Bill Cox had met Keaton some years earlier when Lee had served as script girl on Buster's local television series. Together with Buster's wife Eleanor they formed an enduring friendship. I learned this later; at the time all my attention was focused on this diminutive, bald-headed, elderly man whose ready laughter and almost constant grin robbed him of any resemblance to the legendary Great Stone Face. But suddenly the game began and the miracle took place. The moment he started to move, the little man became Buster Keaton. He hurled pitches, slammed out hits, ran bases, slid and somersaulted into them with the same unmistakable combination of precision and derision of danger which had characterized him during the great days of his stardom.

Not that those days were entirely over. Buster was, after the hiatus of long and lean years, regaining recognition as one of the classic clowns. He was doing cameo roles in films, guest star appearances and commercials on television, and live theatrical performances. His silent comedies were being rediscovered here and abroad.

In the great days when those comedies were being made, Buster chose his associates very carefully; one of the major qualifications for employment was the ability to play baseball. Barring unforeseen delays, work was halted every day at three-thirty in time for a game to begin. Even now he remained a baseball freak.

Since I was probably the worst excuse for a ballplayer Buster had ever encountered, he must have noted the fact and taken pity on me. After the game I found myself with the Keatons in their new brown Cadillac, en route to the ranch for dinner.

The ranch was actually a five-acre spread in Woodland Hills, a suburb presided over by Buster as honorary mayor. In addition to the house proper it boasted a swimming pool, a full-sized barn and a chicken coop that was a model of the old-fashioned little red schoolhouse. Needless to say, the grounds were spacious enough to accommodate baseball games. They were patrolled by Elmer III, a huge Saint Bernard with the ferocious disposition of a field mouse. Standing on hind legs, Elmer was considerably taller than Buster; in that position his front paws rested easily on my shoulders. Everybody coming to the Keaton home as a guest would be warned to wear casual clothing because Elmer was likely to shed on them during his displays of affection.

The Keatons loved animals and animals loved them back. They loved people too, with the same results. At parties, when amongst friends, Buster was usually the extrovert; he'd bring his ukulele and entertain, plunking away as his hoarse, gravelly voice rendered songs popularized in turn-of-the-century vaudeville. During his childhood as a member of the Three Keatons he had known and worked with virtually every star performer. It was fascinating to hear him mimic them, and even more fascinating to hear his ready laughter as he reminisced.

At home he was often quieter and inclined to introspection. Eleanor, who always addressed her husband affectionately as "Babe" although she was some twenty-odd years his junior, mother-henned his activities in public but kept a low profile herself. It was in her own domain that this warm-hearted and gracious lady blossomed forth.

Buster Keaton was the first authentic genius I ever met. Much has been written about his tragic and turbulent career and the even more tragic and turbulent personal misfortunes which befell him before Eleanor Norris entered his life. In the many analyses of the dichotomous simplicity and complexity of the man and his work, I don't recall anyone remarking upon what I noted as a salient characteristic. His attitudes, interests, standards and values, shaped in childhood, were those of a typical midwesterner.

Despite the rough-and-tumble of vaudeville which robbed nine months of his childhood every year, it was the other three he remembered most fondly—the months spent at the family's summer place in rural Michigan. Here he'd led the ordinary life of a small boy, along with his younger brother and sister, and experienced an existence far removed from the ordeals of show biz. Even as an adult he took particular pride in his membership in one of the hometown fraternal organizations. His tastes and enthusiasms—in food, sports, entertainment—were recognizable to anyone who, like myself, had been exposed to similar early influences.

It would be a mistake to identify Buster with his screen image, for he was neither unsophisticated nor unworldly; during the glory years he had mingled on equal terms with the renowned and the elite. Unconsumed by the voracious ego which so frequently devours members of his profession, Buster was nevertheless aware of his identity. Perhaps his proudest boast was that even during the darkest days of his career he could still walk into a good restaurant anywhere in the world and be given the best table. Now doesn't that sound like a typical midwesterner?

But few midwesterners have a toy electric train running between the kitchen and the swimming pool to bring drinks from the refrigerator. That's because very few of them ever made silent comedies like *The Electric House,* where the train served dinner. And no one except Buster Keaton ever made films like *The General, The Navigator, Sherlock Jr.* and the rest of his classic titles. Needless to say, we talked quite a bit about the pictures and the people of that period. But he lived in the real world and many of his and Eleanor's guests were young actors and actresses.

I met a number of them there, and more at the Cox residence, then still more at the home of Suzanne and Dick Foran. Former football star, film actor once typed as a "singing cowboy," presently active on both the big and little screen, Dick had an intelligence and wit his image belied, to say nothing of a pack of weimaraners which might easily have held their own with Elmer III. Probably only Suzy, who later became a psychotherapist, could have explained why Dick and I hit it off so well. Perhaps, as with Buster, he enjoyed reminiscing and I enjoyed listening. Having worked with everyone from Shirley Temple to Mae West (and W. C. Fields, in *My Little Chickadee*) he had an endless supply of anecdotes. It was at his house that Buster had a reunion with Sally Eilers, his 1930 leading lady. From a slightly later period came the ebullient "Judgie"—Arline Judge, leading lady and comedienne whose five marriages included both of the millionaire Topping brothers. Since one of them owned a baseball team, Judgie was granted lifetime use of a box at the ballpark as part of that particular divorce settlement. Occupying it with her in the company of the Keatons and Forans was always an interesting experience; it was more fun watching their antics than following the game. Judgie was far from the femme fatale, and her own recollections involved experiences as a teenage chorus girl in the gangster-owned speakeasies of New York, hobnobbing with the likes of Ruby Keeler, Texas Guinan, Mayor Jimmy Walker and killer "Legs" Diamond.*

Spring sprung, but the strike remained struck, or is it stricken? Even so I fulfilled one of the promises I made to myself earlier and bought my first car, a used Mercury, then quickly sat down and started another novel in hopes of paying for it. I also wanted extra cash to cover future moving expenses and the leasing of a home, since Marion and I had decided after long deliberation that we'd make the move once the strike was over.

In June it finally ended and I found a small furnished house on Valley Vista in Sherman Oaks. When Sally's school semester ended I flew back to Weyauwega, where Marion had already arranged for packing our possessions and putting the place up for sale.

We said good-bye to her family and friends, as well as to the Milwaukee contingent, then arrived in Chicago, where sister Winifred and brother-in-law Frank hosted a farewell dinner party attended by virtually all my remaining relatives, including niece Barbara and nephew Peter. We saw more than two dozen, many for the last time, before boarding the Union Pacific for Los Angeles. There Milton Gelman drove us to our home for the year ahead. Upon arrival I heaved a sigh of relief; the family had come out at last.

So had *Psycho*.

---

*What's the matter—don't you ever get tired of reading footnotes?

THIRTY

1had already seen *Psycho* before its theatrical release. Much to my surprise I received a call inviting me to come to Universal one afternoon and attend a private screening.

The screening, in one of the small rooms devoted to such procedures, proved to be very private indeed. Only a half-dozen unidentified studio and production personnel were present that afternoon, but among their number were three whom I promptly recognized. The composer of the film's score was Bernard Herrmann, a pudgy, bespectacled and irascible little man with one of the biggest talents in the history of motion picture music. Seated directly behind me was Janet Leigh, accompanied by a male escort named Alfred Hitchcock.

There were no introductions, no preliminaries. The moment we settled in our seats the lights dimmed and the screen brightened. I steeled myself for the inevitable, remembering how little remained of John Buchan's *The Thirty-Nine Steps* and Somerset Maugham's *Ashenden: The Secret Agent* after Hitchcock transferred them to film.

What I saw up there on the screen was indisputably his

production, but it was also recognizably my book. Some of the episodes I merely alluded to in the beginning were elongated for visual and dramatic effect: a tryst between the heroine and her lover, a detailed version of her flight ending at the Bates Motel and, of course, the detailed version of her own ending there. Although expanded, all were essential elements in the novel. Later on, Mr. Hitchcock disposed of my insurance investigator on the stairs instead of at the front door of the Bates house, but the story itself continued to follow the book right down to its final line.

I conceded the cinematic logic of making Norman Bates the beneficiary of a Pritikin diet and presenting him as a younger man, and sat still for the excessively verbose explanatory lecture near the end. Relieved by the film's fidelity to my story, I was dazzled by the virtuosity with which Hitchcock had presented it—not just the now-acclaimed shower sequence but the cinematography and editing which created the illusion of Norman's mother.

When the lights went on and I rose to depart, I recognized Mr. Hitchcock's voice as he murmured to his companion, "Well, my dear, what did you think of it?"

Miss Leigh's response was emphatic. "Hitch, when I watched that knife going into me on the screen I could *feel* it!"

Hitch chuckled. "But my dear girl, that knife never touched you on screen—not even once."

It was true, of course. The art of cutting lay in the editing, not the knife itself. Aside from the murder of my insurance investigator, there is no graphic violence in the film; the rest is merely suggestion. Even today it jolts an audience's imagination, and at the time of the first showing it was truly a daring, innovative shocker.

As I left the screening room the others followed. It was strange to emerge from such gothic gloom, and the late-afternoon sunshine offered only a pale reassurance. Evidently Hitchcock required more than that, for he now moved up beside me. Quickly verifying my identity, he uttered the fateful question. "What do you think of the film?"

A long pause. A deep breath. And then, the truth. "Mr. Hitchcock, I think this is either going to be your greatest success or your biggest bomb."

Fortunately for Hitchcock (and for me) the first half of my prediction proved to be the case once the picture went into release. But if audiences hearkened to the verdict of most film critics back in 1960, they would have had quite a bomb scare. *Psycho* got better reviews as a book than it did as a film at the time. And thanks to the film, sales soared for the first six paperback editions.

Throughout the remainder of that year I busied myself with television and printed fiction. Completing work left unfinished during the strike I went on to new assignments. Meantime, as anticipated, my novel *The Dead Beat* appeared, pleasing Simon & Schuster with its reception, but with no spectacular sales. The short story collection, *Pleasant Dreams,* didn't make August Derleth an overnight millionaire at Arkham House either.

Marion and Sally grew accustomed to the newly leased house and the new surroundings; Sally also found new friends with greater ease than her mother. But our life-style was not radically changed. I still worked at home, with the typewriter now occupying a small desk in an alcove of the hallway. My principal recreation was book-hunting with Sam Peeples.

And despite the work schedule and our modest social life there was spare time for such pursuits. Hollywood was not exactly banging on my front door, let alone breaking it down.

This was in part due to a premeditated decision. Not being a complete idiot* I knew what should be done in order to get ahead in films and television. With *Psycho*'s hugely successful re-lease, my cue was to invest every dime I could spare in retaining

---

*I'd had my tonsils removed, remember?

the services of a top public relations firm to tie my name to the film. The next step would be borrowing more dimes to acquire the proper home address in Beverly Hills, the proper car to park at that address, and the proper wardrobe for lunching, dining or partying with people, proper or improper, attracted by my phony celebrity.

The catch was that if this plan succeeded I would have to spend my time being successful. What little I'd seen of Hollywood's high-speed social life wasn't all that attractive, and in all candor I was just too old for the fast lane. Certainly Marion wanted no part of it, and a teenage Sally would be driving at her own risk.

Even if I'd opted for such a course my professional instincts were at odds with the attitudes of many contemporary Hollywood filmmakers. I did not arbitrarily believe, as they seemed to, that louder is funnier, bigger is better, or new is always superior to old.

I did not find it credible that anyone wearing tight-crotch designer jeans could jump into any parked car at any time and promptly roar off because the door was conveniently unlocked and keys had been left in the ignition. Nor, a few years later, was I convinced that the same character, now wearing a designer mustache, could encounter similar circumstances whenever he saw a helicopter, which he would immediately lift off like an expert pilot. I didn't even believe that all detective heroes were divorced, had unerring skill with any weapon they happened to grab, and always slept in the nude. The truth was that I had few of the qualifications necessary for being a Hollywood writer.

That fact was borne home to me upon receiving a surprise visit from a writer friend whom I'd known in the Midwest. Having once enjoyed his hospitality at his place of work when he'd been employed as the night watchman in a coffin factory, I didn't hesitate to invite him and his new bride over for dinner. Marion had no objection to this last-minute arrangement, but neither of us anticipated that our hospitality would also be extended to my friend's brother-in-law, the brother-in-law's wife and several small children. After the initial shock, Marion put a valiant effort into assembling the dinner. I contented myself by serving as bartender before the meal.

By the time it reached its conclusion my services were unnecessary. While his relatives plagued away at the food like locusts, my writer friend addressed his attention to the drinks.

After dinner he addressed his attentions to me, asking innumerable questions about business and finances more appropriate to an IRS audit than to a party with friends in a private home. When at last his supply of questions and my supply of liquor was exhausted, he staggered to his feet with an ominous belch.

"Better grab what you can get right now," he warned. "You won't last long out here."

Fortunately, Gordon Molson Associates, as they were officially known, didn't agree. Molson himself, soft-spoken and hard-headed, was a staunch ally. Bill Stanton opened doors for me in the television area without creasing his Brooks Brothers suit; former teacher Giulio Anfuso brought a scholarly approach to films. Ben Kamsler was perhaps the only member of the team who might fit the image of the typical Hollywood agent, and it was he who brought me to Warner Brothers for my first feature.*

"The Couch" was the title of a brief story treatment by Blake Edwards. Owen Crump, noted for his television documentaries, was Blake Edwards's uncle. If I could concoct a script from the treatment, Uncle Owen would direct it. He impressed me as being both kindly and knowledgeable, and I was comfortable with his nephew's story line. Warner Bros. hiring honcho Steve Trilling ran no risk of bankrupting the studio when he employed me, so everybody was happy with the deal.

In short order I was installed in what was then still the

---

*"My" is a proprietary term notable for the impropriety of its usage in the industry. Everyone who has any connection with the production of a film tends to refer to it as "my" picture.

Writers' Building, a two-story frame structure northwest of Jack Warner's tennis court. I found an office and a secretary awaiting me on the first floor, and none other than my old friend C. L. Moore on the second floor. Henry Kuttner had died of a sudden heart attack in 1958, and Catherine abandoned science fiction for a successful career as a television writer. She was presently doing episodes for "Maverick," the western comedy show. Every afternoon we knocked off work and let our secretaries transcribe the day's dictation while we drank coffee in her office.

As the years went by, Catherine and husband Hank had both become increasingly introverted. They'd invited me out to vacation in their South Laguna home in 1947, and while our visit was convivial, only once did we venture into the wilds of Los Angeles. Even then we saw no one there except Norma Talmadge, flickering on screen at a picturesque picture house called The Silent Movie. Hank and Cat continued their collaborative career, and in the last years of his life Hank inaugurated a series of novels about a psychiatrist-detective, which abruptly halted with his tragic death. For a time Cat had become almost a recluse, although she was presently dating the man who would eventually become her second husband. In these circumstances she turned to me as a confidant.

When not playing the role of Dear Abby, I wrote a screenplay. Dealing as it did with a psychiatrist and his patient, I was hard put to avoid static scenes and lengthy dialogue. In order to counterbalance the confrontations between the shrink and the shrinkee, I decided to present a number of intervening sequences from the patient's point of view. Since the patient was, happily, a homicidal maniac, his point of view could become quite interesting, particularly when he hallucinated.

The front office didn't object to his delusions, but had none themselves when it came to considering the budget limitations for one of Brynie Foy's B pictures. Jack Warner having taken off for Europe, director Owen Crump had no one he could appeal to, and the psychotic fantasies of dummies in store windows coming to life and Los Angeles in apocalypse were removed.

My dismay and disappointment were partially alleviated by the excitement of peripheral involvement in the shoot which followed. One day on location at the County Stadium was followed by a night session downtown, during which I appeared—with very poor lighting—as a pedestrian who encounters the antihero on a deserted street in the opening shot.

The lead was Grant Williams, who'd taken the title role in friend Dick Matheson's *The Incredible Shrinking Man,* so we had grounds for immediate rapport. Shirley Knight played the heroine, with Broadway actor Onslow Stevens as the psychiatrist. Stevens, like many talented performers, apparently had psychiatric problems of his own. On several occasions I was called to the set because my presence seemed to have a calming effect on him.

The real star of our little film was the celebrated "Limey" Plews. He'd probably worked on more pictures than anyone else in Hollywood's history, with the possible exception of Charles Lane, Irv Bacon, or Bess Flowers. Unlike these players, his face wasn't familiar to audiences, but he'd gained off-screen fame for his irreverent comments and conduct while working on the set.

It was "Limey" who arranged for me to have a director's chair with my name on it. Apparently my naive acceptance of this intended mockery disarmed him, for I subsequently received nothing but genuinely hospitable treatment. The same held true for everyone else I met during the production, and the sneak preview in the company of the studio brass resulted in no changes or re-editing. But the bottom line also remained unchanged; *The Couch* was a B picture, released as such without fuss or fanfare, and once its play dates ended, it was seen only by couch potatoes watching the small screen.

What little lingered on was embodied in my novelization of the screenplay, which had been solicited by a paperback publisher;

twenty-five years later, after several foreign translations, it was exhumed to form part of a hardcover trinity of my older novels.

At the time I was somewhat more interested in a second paperback novel venture, *Firebug,* which was also to become part of another hardcover trio of novels after a number of paperback reprints and translations during the intervening quarter of a century. It didn't reach any readers until 1962, when Regency finally risked publication. Regency was an obscure outfit which at the time employed an obscure editor named Harlan Ellison on its staff. I don't know if he was the original reader of the manuscript or the instigator of its acceptance, but I do know he called to say the book had come up around twelve hundred words short of their standard length. Interpreting my ten minutes of nonstop profanity as an indication that I was currently involved with a television deadline, he volunteered to add the necessary wordage at the beginning of the novel. I most gratefully accepted this gracious offer, and thus Harlan collaborated with me in much the same manner I had once collaborated with Edgar Allan Poe.*

All by myself I'd assembled another collection of short stories which Simon & Schuster published under the title *Blood Runs Cold.* Somebody suggested it might benefit from a transfusion by Alfred Hitchcock. As I was now supplying stories and scripts for his television show and he had done rather well out of his deal with me on *Psycho,* it was assumed he might be willing to do an introduction to my collection.

The assumption was correct. His company, Shamley Productions, promptly advised my publishers that Mr. Hitchcock would be most happy to have his ghostwriter, Jimmy Allardice, furnish a one-thousand-word introduction to which Hitch would sign his name for one thousand dollars.

---

*The chief distinction between the two situations being that Poe is dead and I am still alive—although the difference is somewhat less apparent today.

Inasmuch as my advance payment for the entire collection only amounted to $750, my literary agent regretfully declined. Some while later another and more prolific contributor to the Hitchcock show brought out a collection of his own, prefaced with an introduction by the Master of Suspense. It was not visible on the bestseller lists and seemed to vanish rather quickly, so perhaps my agent saved me some money. Certainly I didn't make a fortune from *Blood Runs Cold,* although it later came out in paperback and was reprinted in half a dozen foreign editions.*

My book got good reviews but *The Couch* was either ignored or dismissed as the B picture it was. Nonetheless I was already embarking on another screenplay for Samuel Goldwyn, Jr. Titled *The Merry-Go-Round,* it was a freewheeling vehicle based loosely on Ray Bradbury's short story, "Black Ferris." Changing the Ferris wheel to a carousel was only the first step, and I kept right on toddling in my office over at the Goldwyn lot.

Young Mr. Goldwyn exhibited none of the abrasive personality traits which perturbed people who had labored for his father. He was likable and levelheaded, and I found it a pleasure to work with him. Unfortunately I did not find a satisfactory solution to the problems posed by my first-draft script. But Goldwyn didn't lose faith, and it was mutually agreed that I would return to *The Merry-Go-Round* for another ride later on.

There was no shortage of activity. Because of my film work, most of the stories I sold to television had to be adapted by other writers during this period. I do recall squeezing in (or out) an episode for "Whispering Smith," an undistinguished western series starring the distinguished war hero Audie Murphy. My motives were ultra-ulterior; I wrote "Poet and Peasant" to showcase one of my longtime favorite actors, Alan Mowbray, as a character very similar to Oscar but not quite so Wilde.

---

*I particularly like the Japanese translation, although it has several typos.

As a Southern California member of the Board of Governors, I joined the Mystery Writers of America regional vice-president in a trip to New York headquarters, seeking more autonomy for our fast-growing local chapter. It was gratifying to meet so many colleagues for the first time and renew my acquaintance with Clayton Rawson, who had been my Simon & Schuster editor on *Psycho,* or whatever its name was. Rawson was the author of some notable mysteries which featured a magician-detective, the Great Merlini; he himself was a prestidigitator whom I'd met several years before at a magicians' convention in Chicago.

Aside from this quick trip there was no break in the work routine, or in the flow of material featured on television or the newsstands. As permitted under my Arkham House contracts, August Derleth sold the two collections of short stories for paper-back reprint. The paperback outfit outsmarted him, because the two books were drawn and quartered for subsequent publication in *four* separate volumes under new titles.

Now it was Derleth's turn to outsmart himself. One day Gordon Molson called to tell me a special screening had been set up for me at his request, over at Twentieth Century-Fox. I arrived at the appointed time and settled down in my seat to view the pilot for a proposed one-hour series called "Nightmare." Oddly enough, the pilot turned out to be a dramatization of my short story "I Kiss Your Shadow." It made its magazine debut in 1956, and reached book publication in my Arkham House collection, *Pleasant Dreams.* Twentieth Century-Fox had bought the story directly from Derleth, and was under the impression that he owned theatrical rights to everything that Arkham House ever published.

That was definitely not the case, and Gordon Molson exhibited my original contracts as proof. The studio offered an embarrassed apology and a thousand dollars for the use or misuse of my story. What they offered to Derleth I wasn't told, and he never offered an explanation. Suffice it to say that "Nightmare" didn't become a series.

THIRTY-ONE

$\mathcal{T}$he next adventure also involved Twentieth Century-Fox, which was prepared to distribute a film by longtime independent producer Robert L. Lippert. He'd been negotiating with a French expatriate, Roger Kay, who had a background in television and film but no full directorial credit on a feature. Now he intended to obtain it with a remake of the German silent classic *The Cabinet of Dr. Caligari*.

Later on, comparing notes, I learned he had first approached Bradbury with the project but Ray, far more studio-street-smart than myself, backed away.

I leaned forward, and fell flat on my face.

Roger Kay was an artful persuader. Sharing my interest in old nightmares on old nitrate film, he proposed that I drop the *Dr.* from the original title but do a story with enough similarity to be recognizable as an homage.

Agent Giulio Anfuso was intrigued and so was I. Though the proposed budget was not astronomical, or even half astronomical, it represented roughly three times the amount alloted to *The Couch*, and I could indulge in on-screen illusions.

Indulging in off-screen illusions was my downfall. Once I'd signed, I shared off-lot office space specially rented for that purpose on Wilshire Boulevard by director Kay. As I dictated to a stenographer he spent much of his time devising what he frankly defined as an ironclad contract with Lippert. He confided that he had earned his own law degree in France. His film experience, he revealed, included working with both Chaplin and Orson Welles, both of whom were notoriously unwilling to share credit on their productions. This would be a long-awaited opportunity for him to come into his own.

I could easily do an entire book on my experiences with Roger Kay, but this is an autobiography, not a horror story. Enough to say that during the time I spent on the screenplay he not only hammered out his unbreakable contract but nailed down a producer credit as well. Then he was ready for me.

The story I'd evolved was not a clone of the original though it bore a recognizable resemblance. My central character was female, but unmenaced by a somnambulist. Whatever sleepwalking there might be in the film she'd have to do on her own. The supposed villain of the piece was, as in the original, an asylum director.

My director, in this office which sometimes took on certain characteristics of an asylum, approved. What I wanted was to tell the story in a fashion which would appear utterly realistic and convincing to an audience. There would be no telltale expressionist set designs, no grotesque costumery or makeup, no clues of aberration in the miming or dialogue. Only the film's climax would reveal that everything seemingly experienced by the heroine was hallucination.

As luck would have it I was the one experiencing hallucination. The script kept expanding to include Kay's suggestions and I pointed out the necessity of trimming dialogue and cutting scenes, but he would have none of this. His approach, Kay explained, was a variation of William Wyler's. Wyler was notorious for ordering endless takes of scenes when shooting a picture, thus giving himself the widest possible choice of what might be included in the film. Kay's idea was to provide such choices earlier on, in the script itself. He wanted scenes lengthened, the same dialogue rephrased and repeated. Once the script was completed he could visualize the film as a whole, selecting specific content and editing out the rest. The final result would be a screenplay of normal length, containing exactly what he needed, and representing the very best of my output. In my deluded state this sounded as if it might work.

I certainly was working. In the end, obeying instructions, I turned over a script almost as thick as my stupid head. Roger Kay beamed with delight and promised to cut and edit for immediate submission to Mr. Lippert.

During the interval I focused my thoughts on the unsolved problems of the screenplay for young Sam Goldwyn. Then thought went out of focus again when Roger Kay called. Everything, he said, was under control. Lippert liked the script in its edited version, but insisted on some changes in the story line. This meant I'd have to do some quick revisions in order to meet the deadline for the start of our shooting schedule, working from my own first draft and cutting as I went along. This went against the original plan but Kay said he trusted my judgment. I told him it would be impossible to do the kind of job we both wanted in so short a time.

Not to worry, he said; there was a way out. With Lippert's consent, he would put a second writer on the payroll. While I fashioned a working treatment for revised scenes, this writer would contribute appropriate dialogue, subject to my final approval. According to the terms of his contract he would or could do nothing more, and it was expressly specified that he claim no screen credit for his contribution.

Meanwhile the clock was ticking away and Roger Kay had now set up shop in offices at Twentieth Century-Fox. He wanted me to join him there immediately and get to work. In view of his haste there'd been no time to make the proper arrangements in advance and he apologized for the drab confinement of my temporary quarters, as well as the lack of a permanent parking slot. But these were minor inconveniences; my concern was the script.

Once I arrived, Kay lost no time in introducing me to the young man who was doing the anonymous dialogue polish. Out of charity I shall not introduce him to you. Let me say only that this clean-cut young writer had, to my knowledge, a single screen credit and ambitions for a film-writing career. In those pre-yuppie days he would have been described as someone who wanted to join the jet set. He asked courteous questions about the script and was grateful for my suggestions; I was satisfied our work project would proceed without conflict.

But not without surprises. Again because of haste, the studio management had neglected to assign me a stenographer. About the time I emerged from self-exiled seclusion with the revised pages, I notified agent Giulio Anfuso that I'd not received a check for several weeks and asked him to make diplomatic inquiries to Robert Lippert's office. He promptly did so, and reported back that they had terminated my services after I had completed the first draft of the script.

I was surprised to hear this, they were surprised to learn I was still working, and Giulio Anfuso was surprised to confront a situation he had never encountered before.

It wasn't until he sorted things out that we began to understand what had happened and why. Apparently Roger Kay submitted the overlong first draft he'd insisted on my writing, with no cuts whatsoever. And Mr. Lippert, understandably disappointed with this unprofessional mishmash, told Kay to inform me there was no longer any need for my dubious services. But Kay said nothing, of course. He needed me to edit the script down to its proper size and hoped I'd do so before discovering that I was eligible for unemployment benefits.

Naturally I left in a huff*. My agent contacted Lippert to tell him the circumstances, and it was only then that our suspicions were fully confirmed.

There was nothing suspicious, however, regarding the terms of Kay's ironclad contract. As if in anticipation, it prevented Lippert from firing him under these or similar circumstances. The best Mr. Lippert could do was forward a check, make a gentlemanly personal apology to me over the phone, and ask if I would be willing to return on salary and polish the script according to my own wishes.

I informed him, quite sincerely, that he had both my respect and best wishes, but I could not feel comfortable doing any further work on a project involving Roger Kay.

Instead I returned to the Goldwyn studio and the refreshing company of Samuel, Jr. *The Merry-Go-Round* revolved again, and this time one of the new riders was Buster Keaton.

It had occurred to me that the script might benefit from the addition of another character—an elderly ex-magician neighbor of the small-boy hero. When the youngster discovers and returns a strayed rabbit, the magician puts on an impromptu magic show for his benefit, and in so doing conveys to him the difference between illusion and reality.

Writing the sequence with Buster in mind was a great pleasure, and a great contrast to the sort of thing I'd just gone through on my previous assignment. Showing it to Keaton and receiving his enthusiastic approval was even more gratifying. The next step was to broach the matter to Mr. Goldwyn. He too was pleased; Keaton had done a cameo appearance for him in another film. He wondered if I might impose on Buster to come in and discuss the role.

So it came about that a few days later the brown Cadillac

---

*Huffs are no longer manufactured, and most of what has replaced them comes from Japan.

drove onto the lot through the Formosa Street entrance and the Great Stone Face confronted Mr. Goldwyn in his office. I was present, and count that afternoon among my fondest memories.

Buster had come not to discuss the role but to perform. It was my privilege to be part of an exclusive audience of two, watching Buster Keaton's pantomime as a bungling comic magician who mislaid props and demolished his own act. It was silent comedy at its best, Keaton at his best.

Unfortunately his performance never reached the screen; nor did *Merry-Go-Round* itself. Maybe Goldwyn, Sr., advised against it. Perhaps the timing was wrong for a film with a small boy in the leading role. Possibly it was just a lousy script.

My twenty-twenty hindsight suggests a combination of all three factors. Whatever the reason, the younger Goldwyn didn't reproach me. Instead he came up with a suggestion for another venture—nothing less than a remake of the old Lon Chaney vehicle, *The Unholy Three,* with Alec Guinness playing the ventriloquist. I thought it was a brilliant notion, and Guinness, in 1962, would be ideally cast. Accordingly we repaired to MGM for a special screening of their 1930 sound version. Both of us realized that major changes would be necessary in order to update the story line, but our enthusiasm wasn't dampened until MGM threw cold water on it by refusing to sell the rights.

The studio's decision came after a long delay. In Hollywood, a pregnant silence often results in an aborted project.

Some while earlier (July 1961, to be exact) the family had moved to more spacious quarters. The house we leased on Vantage Street in Studio City was considerably larger, with furnishings that included a piano. Its grounds contained a badminton court and what was either a large sunken bathtub or a small swimming pool. I later acquired a new red convertible to park in the driveway.

At times I drove Marion to meetings of the Mystery Writers of America and dinners with Kay Martin or Boyd Corell, two members she found congenial. We also saw Sam and Erlene Peeples, Frank Price and his then-wife, Phyllis, the Gelmans and a few others. Very few, actually, because Marion didn't feel comfortable with many of my colleagues or their families. On occasion we got together with the Forans or the Coxes; she enjoyed the Keatons but Buster was now spending a good deal of his time filming outside the country.

Averse to dinners or entertaining at home, Marion frequently shunned occasions where my presence was obligatory. Sally graduated from Valley High to enroll at Valley College. She'd become a regular patron of a stable near Griffith Park and rode regularly. After Marion's sister came for a visit she invited Sally to her place in Oregon. There a friend of hers fulfilled my daughter's dreams by offering her a horse. Sally would probably have been happy to ride it back to California but I demurred. My recollection of how we got the horse down from Oregon remains unclear; perhaps we had it sent by pony express.

Soon my sister moved from Chicago to Tustin, in neighboring Orange County. Husband Frank had been transferred to this territory; the change suited both the children and Winifred, who had been afflicted with multiple sclerosis for almost a decade. At least we now had an opportunity to meet on a regular basis. Back in Chicago, branches of our family tree were becoming increasingly bare.

With my fiction output curtailed, I didn't scan the daily mail for letters or checks from New York. But one missive now arrived to command my attention. It was a notice from the Writers Guild informing me that sole writing credit for the forthcoming film *The Cabinet of Caligari* was being claimed by Roger Kay.

I imparted this delightful news to the Molson Agency and, not having been invited to a preview screening of the film, requested a look at the shooting script. According to Guild rules I could appeal the credit, but first it seemed appropriate to see just how much of my own work had been appropriated.

As it turned out, the story and scene-by-scene sequence

seemed structurally intact, the characters, relationships and motivations unchanged. What had been drastically tampered with was the dialogue. The affected and frequently ineffective substitutions replaced realism with theatricality, thus destroying my attempts to make the events of the film seem plausible at its outset. Somehow the style wasn't what I'd expect from the uncredited writer hired for a ten-day stint. Instead, the flowery and often overripe speeches were more like echoes of conversation from Roger Kay.

All in all, the script seemed a portent of disaster. My first impulse was to evacuate the area by abandoning any claim to screen credit. But when I mentioned the problem to the junior Goldwyn he advised me otherwise.

"Whether you want the credit or not, you've got to get it," he said. "If you don't you'll be setting a dangerous example for other writers to follow. Once word gets around that scriptwriters can be stripped of their rightful credits without a fight, other producers and directors will do what this man is trying to do to you."

His opinion made sense, but I was still reluctant to make waves. As my birth certificate attests, I'm a born coward. The last thing I wanted was a Writers Guild arbitration hearing where I must somehow anticipate and manage to refute Kay's claims. My friend Goldwyn persisted. It was his conviction that even though Mr. Kay and the truth were not always on speaking terms, I owed it to myself and my colleagues to seek justice.

While still pondering a decision I received an unexpected phone call. The anonymous young writer whom Kay had commissioned to "polish" my dialogue had just been shocked and outraged to learn about the tentative writing credit, and now volunteered some polished dialogue of his own. If I intended to ask for a hearing, he would be only too happy to appear and testify on my behalf.

After expressing my gratitude, I promised to get back to him later. Then I informed Gordon Molson of this conversation and

Mr. Goldwyn's opinions. Molson agreed that I must stick by my guns, but felt the young man, however well-intentioned, might be a loose cannon. He didn't even want agent Giulio Anfuso to appear. And while Molson offered to set up a hearing and accompany me there for moral support, he believed that my best option was to send the arbitration committee a statement of the facts in advance and then face them alone. "Don't bring in interested parties as witnesses," he told me. "Keep it as simple as possible. Just go in there and tell them the truth."

I followed Molson's plan up to a point. I did send in a statement, he did set up a hearing and went with me to Guild headquarters on the appointed evening. But the rest of his instructions—about just going in there—were put on hold.

So were we, because upon arrival it turned out that Roger Kay had shown up early and was closeted with the arbitrators in a private session. Molson and I sat in the outer office and waited. Time flew by on leaden wings. Almost an hour passed. What the hell was he doing in there, as if we didn't know?

Finally the door flew open and Kay emerged, clad in his customary all-green outfit, sweeping past us without a glance or a word. One glimpse of the smile on his face was all I needed, but as the outer door closed behind him someone beckoned me into the inner office.

"You're on," Gordon Molson murmured.

He was so right. I was on—on the spot, to be exact. The members of the arbitration committee turned towards me as I entered, rivaling Buster Keaton with their stony stares. Even today I've no idea just how long Roger Kay had taken to voice his claims. My portion of the hearing lasted about fifteen minutes.

After all, as I told them, if they had read my letter explaining what had happened, there wasn't much more to say. And if they had read both my script and Roger Kay's, they would note that his claim of authorship was based almost entirely on changes in dialogue. As I understood the rules, rewriting dialogue did not in itself constitute grounds for screen credit. Was I correct in this?

Maybe so, but judging from the reaction to my statement I was still facing a committee of Keatons. Whatever Kay had told them must have been very convincing. A man who could match wits with an experienced producer like Lippert and a major studio like Twentieth was bound to come prepared with a story that would satisfy these arbitrators.

To persuade them my claims were true would require the talent of a Machiavelli, and I didn't even know how to spell his name.

As usual, lacking anything profound to dredge up, my naïveté surfaced. Grasping at straws, I suggested that if they wanted corroboration of my account they might check with the young gentleman whom Kay hired to help out on dialogue. I was certain he'd cooperate because just recently he had phoned me and volunteered to appear at this very meeting to verify what I'd stated.

Keatonesque stares vanished amidst a dropping of jaws. There was a moment of what I can only describe as stunned silence. Then the committee chairman cleared his throat.

"I think there's something I'd better show you," he said.

What he produced and offered for my inspection was a letter addressed to this committee, voluntarily informing them in the interest of justice that the "warp and woof" of the *Caligari* script was indisputably the work of Roger Kay. The letter was signed by the anonymous dialoguer.

Apparently the committee had come to fresh conclusions about what had happened. In their eyes it seemed evident that Kay tried to set me up with the dialogue-polisher turned apple-polisher, probably promising that if he surprised me by offering false testimony at the hearing Kay would later reward him with a writing credit on the next film he produced or directed. But when the plot failed because I didn't ask the young gentleman to appear, Kay drafted a letter for his signature instead, anticipating it would serve the same purpose. Which it might have, if I hadn't blurted out my dumb remark which unwittingly revealed the connivance of the other claimant and his dupe.

"Dupe" is indeed the proper word for it. Obviously, since the eager young man had already signed away any claim to writing credit under the terms of his contract, once Roger Kay succeeded in getting my name removed through arbitration he would be left with sole credit himself. He had used the young gentleman just as he had tried to use me, hoping to end up as sole producer/director/writer, which had been his intention all along. Machiavelli, eat your heart out!

In the end it was Roger Kay who went on that sort of diet. The Writers Guild decision gave sole screen credit to me. Not too long thereafter Kay departed for Europe. I don't know if he is alive or dead at this writing, but apparently he never got another such opportunity. A few years back, someone in France told me an elderly man calling himself Kay still popped up from time to time and, despite the Writers Guild legal determination, which is a matter of record, he still claimed the writing credit on *Caligari*.

As far as I know, his ambitious young collaborator (if not on the script, at least in the scheme to deprive me of my credit) never made it as a member of the jet set. Apparently he got lost in the jet stream.

So did the film. Despite the work of fine actors, Dan O'Herlihy as Dr. Caligari and Glynis Johns playing the hapless heroine, the picture played to poor business. It took twenty years before I ventured to see the film for the first time, on television. When I did, I wished I'd waited a little longer—another twenty years, at least.

THIRTY-TWO

$\mathcal{T}$he Mystery Writers of America had some unusual guests at their monthly meetings in the early sixties. It was at one such gathering that I had a drink with local underworld kingpin Mickey Cohen, who was eager to find someone to script his biography for film. The leading role, he confided, would be ideal for actor George Raft. I gently hinted that Raft's career had gone into steep decline. If I'd mentioned anything about Cohen's career I probably would have gone into a deep decline myself.

As far as can be determined *The Mickey Cohen Story* has never been made, not even as a musical.

Another guest was Anthony Boucher, who was in town for several days. I recall hauling him down to Bradbury's house, where we spent the evening in the basement, poring over Ray's collection of old Sunday newspaper comic sections.

In a more varicose vein, I had surgery on both my legs at Cedars of Lebanon Hospital. What they called a bilateral ligation took four hours under local anesthetic, during which time smoking, drinking and folk dancing were strictly prohibited. As preparation for the procedure I had driven out to a local cemetery, Forest

Lawn. It's a nice place to visit but I wouldn't want to live there.*
The purpose of my expedition was to acquire a variety of the
souvenirs sold there to tourists; these I distributed to hospital
visitors following my surgery.

It must have been during convalescence that I concocted a
paperback novel, *Kill For Kali,* which the publishers retitled *Terror.* Antiheroes, still comparatively rare at the time I wrote *The
Scarf,* were now quite common; as a switch, this time around my
main character was a moral and law-abiding young man. Perhaps
I should have listened to reason and done the biography of Mickey
Cohen instead.

Since there'd been so little time available for the production
of new material I welcomed opportunities to resurrect the old. A
rather unusual volume was issued in both hardcover and paperback
editions by the specialty publisher Advent Press. Under an esoteric
title, *The Eighth Stage of Fandom,* they offered a collection of
articles, essays and fiction I'd contributed to science fiction fan-
magazines over the years. As far as I know this sort of venture had
never been attempted before, and I was relieved for their sake when
it succeeded.

So did *Atoms and Evil,* a compilation of stories I selected
from my work in professional science fiction magazines. Its editor,
Knox Burger, was genuinely appreciative of writers and later espoused their cause by becoming an agent.

After the long film stints I spent a few days soaking in the
mineral baths of Desert Hot Springs. It must have been during the
first of those autobaptismal occasions that I came up with a short
story which won a prize upon appearing in *Alfred Hitchcock's
Mystery Magazine.* Having contributed to quite a few of Hitch's
half-hour shows I continued the practice now that the program had

---

*When I'm ready to die I plan to rent a U-Haul hearse and convey myself to the
nearest drive-in mortuary.

expanded to hour length. After adapting Patricia Highsmith's *Annabel* for the longer format I did the same for my prize-winning yarn which they purchased for that purpose. This wasn't an easy task because the published story, "A Home Away From Home," was another of my many variants on old buddy Eddie Poe's lunatics-take-over-the-asylum theme, and my version was only a few pages long.

Somehow I managed. I also managed to have a short visit with Aunt Gertrude, Aunt Lil and Cousin Bea in Chicago while attending the science fiction convention there. Many writer friends were present, including Charles Beaumont, who had flown in from the Coast to do a piece for *Playboy*. As usual, Chuck did a brilliant vocal imitation of the late Bela Lugosi. In our private conversation he confided he was fed up with today's Hollywood and resolved to forsake both films and television. Upon finishing his chore here, Beaumont intended to go to Rome, where he would complete work on a novel.

Until then he was in residence at the Playboy mansion, and a few nights later Hugh Hefner invited a group of writers from the convention to join him for late-night festivities. Most of us were contributors to the magazine, but since many convention attendees were accompanied by wives or working equivalents the occasion was not orgiastic. Although we may have slid down the fire pole to the pool level below, we didn't dive in to join the nubile females there nor make any attempt to fish them out. It was, nonetheless, a pleasant evening with a pleasant host.

As for friend Beaumont, after a short time he came back to Hollywood. I was already at work there.

One of the major television studios called upon me to write the pilot for a new game show—an area of entertainment which I rank somewhat above geeking but slightly below turtle-racing on a muddy track.

The format, while hardly novel, was interesting. The first half consisted of a mystery film, a whodunit cut off just before the identification of the culprit. In the second half a live panel—a moderator and guest "experts"—would attempt to solve the crime and guess which suspect was the guilty party. The miniature mysteries were not meant to be taken too seriously, and the panelists would be selected for their wit as well as their status as crime buffs. My job was to write the mysteries, inject the necessary clues and at the same time mislead the audience sufficiently so that the solution wouldn't be easy to guess. Then the panel would take over for an impromptu session.

The producer in charge of the project proved to be a courteous and charming gentleman, which is why I won't embarrass him by using his name in this incident. He quickly realized this assignment was trickier than it seemed on the surface. In order to serve their purpose, the mysteries had to be bizarre enough to provoke conversation from the panel, yet sensible enough so that their solution seemed logical. A half-dozen characters must be presented in quick succession, each of them firmly established as possible suspects, and their actions and motivations must be made clear without interfering with the rapid thrust of the plot itself.

We discussed these matters at some length and found ourselves in mutual agreement. I turned out several different complete scripts, together with synopses of a half-dozen others.

The next step was to select one of the scripts for the pilot film, and it was here that my efforts were reviewed by another member of the production staff. Learning that he was the son of a famous European star whose work I'd long admired, I complimented him upon his choice of father.

That was my mistake. Apparently, as is the case with the offspring of some famous and egocentric parents, he was jealous and resentful of his father and hated anyone who praised him. I can think of no other valid reason for what followed, for I had no further personal contact with this man.

But, along with the producer, he read my scripts. And while the producer was pleased and enthusiastic about the material, this son-of-a-father defaced it with complaints and objections which illuminated nothing except his personal animosity. One in particular I shall never forget—in the margin opposite a comic sequence he scrawled, "Where is the *Fun*???"

This broke me up, but it didn't break up my relationship with the producer, who promptly filmed the script. The next step was to audition panelists. It was decided to test the candidates "cold," before a live audience.

So one evening, following the televising of a Steve Allen show at a local theater, the attendees were invited to remain and view our little pilot project. Then, with Carl Reiner as moderator, a group of show biz panelists including Betty Garrett and others of equal caliber sat down for the guessing-game session which followed. Thanks to Reiner's expertise and the enthusiastic cooperation of the guest panel, the show came off very well.

The next move was to restage the audition for a group of advertising executives representing potential sponsors. But a funny thing happened on the way to the theater.

Groucho Marx had terminated a long and successful television engagement as the emcee of "You Bet Your Life." Many celebrities, despite accumulation of fame and fortune, seem to resemble the protagonist of H. Rider Haggard's *She*, who achieved eternal life by exposing her body to the flames of a sacred fire. Groucho was apparently of a similar disposition and longed to immolate himself in the limelight.

Someone—could it have been the unrisen son who was searching so despairingly for the "fun" in the script?—decided without me that Groucho would make an ideal permanent panelist on our show.

Accordingly, when the big night arrived and the network and advertising men joined the audience, the film was run and a new cast of "guest experts" took the stage, headed by Art Linkletter, Jr., as emcee. He was a bright young man and I had no reason to question his presence, but I was a bit disturbed to find that in place of seasoned professional panelists were several bimbos whose exact profession seemed open to question. Groucho himself was nowhere in evidence during their introduction.

Then, on cue, the band struck up the familiar strains of "Hooray for Captain Spaulding" to the accompaniment of a stentorian pronunciamento along the inspired lines of "Here comes our star—in person—*now*!" Groucho strutted forth and took his place with the other panelists.

Suddenly our little whodunit project had turned into "The Groucho Marx Show." While Linkletter strove valiantly to question various panelists about clues, Groucho kept up a barrage of interruptions and non sequiturs. He leered at the young ladies, commenting upon their cleavage and crudely impugning their moral status. His ad-libs were not funny, merely vulgar, his impertinence an ego trip, and a bad one. My longtime admiration for this man's comic achievement suffered a severe setback, and so did the show. By the time it ended—in a complete shambles—I knew that there would be no series on the air. And there wasn't.

Maybe Groucho had an off night. But there's no doubt that the show was off due to the effects of a common Hollywood syndrome—the generally prevalent belief that if A is good and B is good, you can add the two of them together and come up with a sensational C. Almost invariably the end result turns out to be an F.

I had another encounter with celebrity shortly thereafter. Warner Bros. television lineup had been sent to the showers after a disastrous playing season, and a new coach was hired, at a reported salary of two million dollars—which, in the early sixties, was still regarded as a rather handsome stipend.

But the recipient, Jack Webb, was a prestigious figure, whose radio and TV success with "Dragnet" had established him as a genuine wunderkind. "Dragnet," one of the pioneer "police procedure" shows, was chiefly distinguished for its use of laconic and supposedly naturalistic dialogue: a sort of highly stylized pseudo-

Hemingway language which all the characters spoke with tense monosyllabicity. But the novelty appealed, and no one had reason to dispute Webb's acumen. He moved into the studios with a large suite and staff at his disposal, plus seemingly complete autonomy in guiding their television production plans. He would create new shows, new series, new excitement, and restore Warner Bros. to preeminence in the field.

Time passed, and when new projects were presented, the networks passed too. In the end, the only series set for the coming season was something called "Jack Webb Presents GE True." The explanation for this title proved to be simple, in every sense of the word. Jack Webb's name was incorporated for the prestige audiences presumably attached to it. GE—the General Electric Corporation—was sponsoring the program and felt *their* name carried prestige too. *True* was mentioned because the show itself was based on stories from that magazine.

The format of the show was a hybrid, a fictionalized version of a "true story" presented as a documentary. Mr. Webb, standing center stage under a spotlight in a limbo setting, introduced each weekly episode. Since the scripts did not involve police procedures, his presence was hardly appropriate—but again the Hollywood syndrome prevailed, and he was slotted to add "name-value" and "strength" to the show.

Came the time when I was called in and offered a script assignment by the pleasant and highly professional story editor. Mr. Webb stopped by to be introduced, and then the editor took over, handing me a magazine account of a WWII effort to salvage a cargo of sunken silver in the face of Japanese opposition. I was immediately informed that one of the catch phrases from "Dragnet," "Only the facts, ma'am," was not necessarily applicable to the content of my script. It had to be "dramatized." A story line was discussed and approved.

I went home and wrote. What I came back with did not meet with general favor. The story editor was somewhat at a loss to point out precisely where I'd erred; the plot and characterizations followed the agreed pattern, and all he could tell me was that "somehow it seems to misfire." He suggested that I take my time and do some thinking about the script and its undefined deficiencies.

At this juncture the first few programs were already appearing, and I viewed them for telltale clues. The answer came almost immediately, but when I returned to the story editor, I posed it in question form.

"Is it possible that Jack Webb wants all these shows to be written in Dragnet dialogue?" I asked. The story editor did not blush, nor did his gaze meet mine. He merely nodded.

"That's okay for Webb's narration," I said. "But what about the Navy characters? Would the enlisted men talk exactly like the officers? And must the Japanese sound like Jack Webb too?"

This time he only shrugged. I followed suit, then went home and rewrote the script. The grammar-school dialogue read poorly, and I knew it would sound even worse.

When I brought my revised version to the studio I was directed to Webb's office to deliver the script. The reception area was imposing, and several personable secretaries labored within its confines. But its chief attraction was a series of huge glass-fronted display cabinets which featured an impressive array of literally scores of framed citations, medals, gold and silver trophies and awards presented to Webb for "Dragnet."

As I stood goggling at this overwhelming evidence of success, the door to the inner office opened and Webb himself emerged. He may or may not have recalled my name and used it in his greeting; this I can't recollect. What I do remember is the perverse impulse which came over me.

Nodding at the staggering display of prizes and trophies, I said, "Gee, Mr. Webb—you must have done a lot of bowling!"

These were my last words. The show was never produced, and the series itself vanished from the television screen shortly thereafter. At the conclusion of his contractual season, Mr. Webb departed from the studio and went on to fresh and deserved triumphs elsewhere. No doubt he added many new statuettes and awards to his collection.

As for me, I have never received an Emmy for my dialogue.

THIRTY-THREE

Boris Karloff had made his first big success at Universal, playing the monster in *Frankenstein* and the horror films which followed. Now, thirty years later, he was returning to the scene of his crimes as the host of a new one-hour anthology series called "Thriller."

While the show was still in the planning stage I was invited to adapt somebody else's story. Quite honestly I remember neither the name nor the plot; all I can recall is that there were no thrills in it, nor any way of injecting them without substituting an entire new story line.

As usual, my naïveté surfaced. I complained to the producer, not knowing at that time he was the man Hitchcock had hired, then fired, as *Psycho*'s screenplay writer. Obviously anyone remotely associated with that particular project was bound to evoke unhappy memories for James P. Cavanaugh. He hadn't been the one to hire me for this project and wished no one else had either, but was now stuck with my services. Obviously he was also stuck with a show he didn't understand; if you asked him what it was about, he'd tell you it was about an hour.

Since Cavanaugh offered little by way of suggestions or cooperation, I took my complaint to a higher court. In those primeval days the studios still employed story editors. Universal's was a knowledgeable lady with classy legs, an ancient secretary, and a still more ancient pet poodle, all housed in a beat-up building which must have been standing when Uncle Carl Laemmle bought the ranch back in 1915.

The lady had lent a friendly ear to me in the past, and it was only natural that I should bend that ear now. The ineptitude of the "Thriller" producer seemed bad enough, but how could a show hope to succeed by putting material on the screen which by rights ought to be put in a shredder? Whoever was responsible for selecting this story should have been a candidate for retroactive abortion.

To these and other sentiments the lady heartily agreed, and it wasn't until several months later that I discovered she was the person who had picked that particular story for the program. By that time it didn't matter; she was no longer the studio story editor and Mr. Cavanaugh was no longer the "Thriller" producer. Relieved of command, he had fired a parting volley of anathema via the pages of *TV Guide,* and made it appear the retreat was of his own choosing.

Voluntary or involuntary, his departure was a fortunate one, both for the show and for me. The inappropriate story was tossed out, but I wasn't tossed along with it. Instead I found myself adapting one of my own published tales, "The Devil's Ticket," which by coincidence would star Macdonald Carey, for whom I'd written all those episodes of "Lock-Up" upon arriving in Hollywood.

The new producer was William Frye, and he was a joy to work with. The same can be said for associate producer Douglas Benton and story editor Jo Swerling. Together with a lady of title named Rita who served as secretary and general factotum, the production unit took over what had once been a schoolhouse for the juvenile delinquents appearing in Universal's films.

We seemed to hit it off well together, and during the following two seasons I wrote seven shows for them and had four additional stories of mine adapted by other writers when I wasn't available to script them myself. This, together with the teleplays I did for Hitchcock and the theatrical film projects, kept me from running down to MGM. As a result I never committed myself to "Twilight Zone," which was securely in the hands of Rod Serling and the Matheson Mafia—Beaumont, Nolan, Johnson and other friends.

Universal was closer to where I lived and "Thriller" offered a close approximation of ideal working conditions. For one thing, there was a wider choice of material than other shows allowed: Hitchcock would use nothing supernatural or science-fictional, while "Twilight Zone" used nothing else. On "Thriller" I had the opportunity to vary my work, just as I did for publication purposes. In a number of instances my scripts were shot from first draft. Whatever rewriting seemed necessary was the result of mutual discussion and decision. Although I didn't sit in on the editing, I did enjoy a privilege which hadn't been offered to me by any other show I worked on: an invitation to attend the first cast rehearsal sessions. These were eye-openers to me.

Wandering around studio lots I'd already been fortunate enough to enjoy meetings and conversations with old-time performers like J. M. Kerrigan, Neil Hamilton, Otto Kruger and Sam Jaffe—the latter having abandoned playing the bugle for playing a producer in one of my Hitchcock scripts.* At social events such as the one Milton Gelman's friends staged to celebrate the seventieth birthday of veteran actor Francis MacDonald, I ran into people like Jack Oakie, Julia Faye, Chester Conklin and Monte Blue. As a longtime film buff I naturally freaked out on meeting face to face

---

*For some unknown reason he had elected to do the part with a thick accent, which surprised me. I never realized that Gunga Din was Jewish.

those whom I had seen only face-to-screen in childhood. But what took place at those first readings of my "Thriller" scripts was even more exciting.

It was their sheer professionalism that intrigued me. Young actors like William Shatner or such veteran performers as Henry Daniell, John Emery, Edgar Buchanan and Oscar Homolka could sit down at the big table, pick up a script and deliver a cold reading with an impromptu interpretation which was a tribute to their insight. And when the distinguished descendant of a famous theatrical family, George Macready, would consult me as to whether or not I was satisfied with his rendering of a Latin incantation, it was a heady moment indeed.

So were the lunches I shared with some of the show's directors. The truly multitalented Ida Lupino told me ghost stories based on personal experience and surprised me by rattling the family skeleton of one of my childhood favorites, her late uncle Lupino Lane.

John Brahm, who had formerly directed abroad, told me of D. W. Griffith's trip to England to remake his silent *Broken Blossoms* as a talking picture, with Brahm as assistant director. Upon screening the original, Griffith shook his head. "I wouldn't change a single shot," he said. The elderly man, who was never invited to direct a film again, walked away from his classic and Brahm took over the film, which starred his then-fiancée Dolly Haas. Out of respect for Griffith, he duplicated the famous closet scene performed by Lillian Gish in the original version.

Robert Florey proved to be another raconteur I appreciated. The French director had arrived in Hollywood simultaneously with the Roaring Twenties and was now a walking encyclopedia of that era. He soon became a sitting-down one during our luncheons together. Florey had written half a dozen books about American filmmakers but none were available in translation; it seemed a pity because he'd been a firsthand assessor of Hollywood's golden years and the baser metals compounding them.

Soon after arrival he became a friend of Douglas Fairbanks, who introduced him to other major stars; for a time he was a guest of Rudolph Valentino's and an intimate of Charlie Chaplin's circle. Both Fairbanks and Chaplin were, he felt, well armored by their egos, but Valentino was a tragic figure. The Great Lover of the silent screen was not, as some alleged, homosexual or bisexual; he suffered from impotence, due to a gonorrheal infection acquired during his early years in New York. On a somewhat less unhappy note, the handsome matinee idol was extremely myopic. Vilma Banky, his leading lady in *The Eagle* and *The Son of the Sheik,* was also quite nearsighted. Without their glasses, both faced serious problems when the cameras rolled; Florey recalled they frequently had trouble finding one another for a seemingly spontaneous embrace during love scenes. At times their awkward antics were almost as amusing as those of the Marx Brothers, whom Florey directed in *The Coconuts.**

Most of Florey's memories were mellow, but some of his experiences left scars. Chaplin had lured him into working on *Monsieur Verdoux* with the promise of a codirector's credit. "For a picture with Charlie I would even have been satisfied to be listed as an assistant director," Florey told me. "But I ended up with nothing."

For much of his career, this man's skills were lavished—and often wasted—on B pictures. This was largely due, he believed, to another broken promise made to him right here at Universal in 1931. He had been offered the directing assignment on *Franken-stein* and prepared a script which included the finale he devised after seeing a windmill used as an advertising emblem by a local bakery. Since the studio wanted Bela Lugosi as the star, Florey shot

---

*Shot on the East Coast because the brothers were appearing nightly onstage in *Animal Crackers,* this was Florey's second directorial effort, with assistance on the musical numbers.

two reels of test material to define the characterization and makeup of the monster. Due to circumstances he still found inexplicable, the film was taken away from him at the last moment, along with any share in its writing credit. Lugosi stalked away and the new director, James Whale, created a new monster called Boris Karloff. To calm their outcries, the studio shoved a pacifier down Florey's and Lugosi's throats: a hastily mounted production of *Murders in the Rue Morgue.* Florey did his best, some of which was relegated to the cutting-room floor before the film's release. The ultimate result of all these mishappenstances was that now, thirty years later, Robert Florey was directing occasional segments of a television show starring Boris Karloff as its host.

Karloff had loomed large for me on screen ever since his initial monsterpiece, but during the early days of "Thriller" he could have more suitably been identified with the title role in *The Invisible Man.* Although he did appear in a few individual episodes, he had nothing else to do except for his hosting stints. These, cleverly concocted by Doug Benton, were filmed for several shows during a single shooting session, so Mr. Karloff was not at the studio on a daily basis.

I met him one Sunday at the home Bill Frye shared with Jim Wharton in Coldwater Canyon. Amidst a number of interesting guests he and Ida Lupino stood out most prominently. He and I sat looking out over the pool as it shimmered in the late-afternoon sunshine, and it was there that we shared the first of many reminiscences about his early career in films. The moment the subject was broached Karloff visibly stiffened, bracing himself for the inevitable. I recognized that reaction, for in a period of just two short years I'd already learned that when anyone mentioned the word "career" to me it meant he was going to ask about *Psycho.* And Karloff, over a thirty-year period, must have endured endless repetitions of questions and remarks concerning *Frankenstein.*

Thus it came as something of a shock to him when I said, "Mr. Karloff, there's one of your films I've always wanted to ask about. How did you feel about those scenes with Mabel Normand in *The Nickel-Hopper?*"

"Good Lord!" Karloff grinned. "Nobody's mentioned that picture to me in donkey's years! Where on earth did you hear about it?"

"Maywood, Illinois. I saw it there, back in 1925 or thereabouts. The Silent Movie theater on Fairfax ran a print just last year. It seemed strange to see you doing a bit as a truck-driver type."

"Not to me." Karloff chuckled. "In those days, when I wasn't working in a film I *was* a truck driver. Also a gardener and at times even a manual laborer."

"But you were in a lot of pictures," I said. "I remember you from *Two Arabian Knights* and *Tarzan and the Golden Lion.* It seems to me there was a shot of you as an Arab in *Old Ironsides.*"

Karloff shook his head. "I wasn't in that one," he told me.*

He also told me of his off-screen life in the silent era, making early-morning rounds of the casting windows where studios hired the extras and bit players necessary for that particular day. Those who didn't luck out usually ended up footsore from the quest and sought rest in the shade of the pepper trees on Melrose Avenue.

It was when film jobs became too few and far between that Karloff returned to his manual or menial chores. But even then he reserved every Tuesday evening for a visit to the fights. All Hollywood attended the weekly boxing matches, and Karloff never missed them.

"Never saw them, either," he said. Again the chuckle. "I couldn't afford such luxuries. But I made a point of showing up outside the entrance before the fights began, so I could see and be

---

*Karloff did play in the film. He is visible on screen for all of two seconds. It would have amused him to know that when the picture was released several years ago on VHS, his name was listed as one of its stars.

seen by every casting director or film producer in the crowd. Helped jog their memory, you know."

It required roughly ten years of jogging before Karloff's career finally took off. There had been hard times and hard labor, false starts and bitter disappointments, but I didn't learn of them until much later.

During the next several years we met a number of times. My first vivid recollection of Mrs. Karloff is connected with a luncheon attended by Charles Beaumont and Richard Matheson. The Karloffs were then staying at the Chateau Marmont, an unedifying edifice which basked above Sunset Boulevard as Hollywood's answer to the Hotel Chelsea in New York. I picked them up and drove them to the restaurant for a lengthy and laughter-filled lunch. It was then that I first observed Evelyn Karloff's fortitude in the face of her husband's fans, her patience and tolerance. She graciously put up with puns, in-jokes, even Beaumont's *Dracula* imitation, if only because Karloff seemed to enjoy the occasion. I was coming to recognize that so-called horror-film actors were very much like so-called horror writers; they took their work seriously, but not themselves. By the time Karloff got around to a droll description of the Chateau Marmont's plumbing, I realized he felt at ease in the present company. After all, he'd edited two volumes of fantastic tales and was as conversant with our work as we were of his.

At this period Dick Matheson had written a screenplay for American International Pictures which gave Karloff a starring role, and I was shortly invited to spend the day at tiny California Studio, where *The Raven* was being shot. There I had my first meeting with Vincent Price and exchanged brief words with Peter Lorre and a juvenile lead named Jack Nicholson. Later, on another Karloff vehicle, I spent a few hours with Basil Rathbone. The occasion marked a reunion for him, Karloff and Vincent Price; all three had worked together on *Tower of London*. This version of *Richard III* was played more for shakes than Shakespeare, and required Rathbone and Karloff to drown young Mr. Price in a wine barrel. Unbeknownst to their victim, they had dumped garbage, cigarette ashes and whatever else was available into the liquid already in the barrel, and it was thus that Vincent Price was baptized into horror films.

Several times since then I had the good fortune to share the podium with him and learned to admire the wit and erudition he displayed throughout the course of his lengthy and successful career.

Peter Lorre and Basil Rathbone, both with attributes similar to those of Price, fared sadly. So many do, in Hollywood—and everywhere else, for that matter.

As I came to know Boris Karloff better, he voiced a truism which I've since heard repeated by virually every successful individual who ever ventured to speak frankly. "Remember, dear boy," he told me, "ten percent of everything you do requires talent. The other ninety percent is luck."

THIRTY-FOUR

Readers who have stayed awake thus far will note I have avoided any description of current events after WWII. But this doesn't mean I was unaware of what was occurring in the outside world.

The one constant in life is change.

When I was a young man it was commonplace to see the necks of older women grotesquely disfigured by huge saclike protuberances called goiters. During the years that followed, goiters disappeared, along with garters and gaiters. Someday even guitars will disappear, though I'm sure many readers find it impossible to believe this.

I do want them to believe, however, that I wasn't unmindful of important happenings that took place beyond the path I wore between my typewriter and the wastebasket. It's just that there isn't enough time or enough space for matters better dealt with in histories rather than autobiographies.

As previously observed, *Psycho* made me neither rich nor famous, but it gradually invested me with a small amount of notoriety. Somewhere around this period a friend named Dean

Grennell moved to California from his residence in Fond du Lac, Wisconsin.* Formerly a salesman with a route which included Weyauwega, he took it upon himself to ask some of his customers if they had known me there. Since they didn't realize he and I were friends they spoke quite freely.

One of the shopkeepers identified me as an eccentric who paraded around in strange attire partially obscured by a long beard. Another report had it that I was a wheelchair-bound paralytic who never left the house. Still another source combined the best of both worlds by informing him that I spent six months of each year working at home and emerged to spend the other six months in the asylum.

But I couldn't place the blame for all such accounts on small-town gossip. In metropolitan Milwaukee the clerks in the book department of a downtown store said a man used to frequent the rental library section and proclaim himself to be the author of *Psycho*. He was by no means the only one to do so over the years.†

As the sextuplicate decade grew out of its diapers I had no time to claim authorship of anything; I was too busy writing. Sally spent much of her free time outside, Marion spent much of her free time inside, and I operated both in and out, but always on the run. Once in a while there were poker games with the Spencers and Louis and Bebe Barron, whose electronic tonalities had scored the film *Forbidden Planet*. But my longtime addiction to penny-ante antics was ebbing, particularly in view of Marion's disinterest. I went to current films with Marion, saw old movies with Sam Peeples. As for television, she watched it and I wrote it.

Our social encounters with Suzy and Dick Foran eventually

---

*And friend he was indeed: he built me the desk on which I wrote *Psycho*.
†Why anyone would want to be known as the author of *Psycho* is beyond me. For some time I've attempted to persuade the editors of *Who's Who* to amend my listing as follows: "Robert Bloch is the author of *The Iliad*, *The Odyssey*, and *Romeo and Juliet*." So far I've had no success, but I keep trying.

Taking deadpan lessons from the master: Buster Keaton, 1961.

William Castle, Leif Erickson, Joan Crawford, and unidentified bystander. *Photo © 1964, Universal Pictures Inc.*

With Christopher Lee, 1966. I've got a hazy recollection that this shot was taken at Bradbury's home, in which case, *photo courtesy of Ray.*

"We are the last of the dinosaurs," said Fritz Lang to Boris Karloff when they met at our home in '68. It was a prehistoric occasion.

Forrest Ackerman presents an award at the 1972 premiere of *Asylum* at Hollywood's Pantages Theater. The cloak is from Bela Lugosi's *bar mitzvah*.

The year is 1968, and I've bought a new bowtie. Elly has washed her earrings.

Sally, 1989. My daughter climbed on a horse when she was ten and never got off.

A stray kitten wandered into a 1986 convention at Huntsville, Alabama, and Andre Norton promptly christened it "Robert." The result is this very unusual picture: Most Guests of Honor refuse to be photographed with thinning hair.

resulted in Dick's proposal that he and I buy a small boat together. Our outboard motor polluted the waters of the Colorado River on the rare weekends that could be devoted to fishing trips. At least they were rare on my part; Dick was presently undergoing a career slump. Somewhere along the line our fishing boat turned into Foran's small camper, as a result of a trade he'd negotiated with friends.

I had yet to learn how to deal with such transactions. A financial failure at the time of my arrival in Hollywood, I couldn't tell you whether the hundred-dollar bill bore a picture of President Grant or Elvis Presley. My education soon improved as various friends solicited loans; in due time, when repayment was due, I ended up with fewer friends and less money. That's all I ever learned about economics.

It was during this period that Warner Bros. asked me to write a pilot script. Actually none of the Bros. except Jack was still alive and the request came from his son-in-law. Apparently somebody had the notion that a series about a parole officer would be a viable variation of the usual cops-and-robbers shows. This in itself didn't particularly interest me until I learned that much of the action would be centered in San Quentin. To that end a four-day research trip to the penitentiary had already been planned.

Years before, the Marx Agency had donated its services to a prison welfare volunteer organization, and once my employer and I met the lady in charge for a day at the state prison. The occasion proved more memorable than any of us had anticipated. As we joined the warden for lunch, the inmate acting as our waiter approached the table, his smile a combination of surprise and delight. "Hello, Bob!" he said.

I too was surprised, though not necessarily delighted, to recognize an old schoolmate from Lincoln High. He was here to serve both lunch and a term for murder.

As far as I knew, none of my friends were incarcerated at San Quentin, though for a few this was just a matter of luck. But the idea of prowling around one of the most famous penal institutions in the nation was intriguing; at least I'd have the opportunity of seeing just how the inmates differed from the average employees at the local studios, if at all.

At my urging it was agreed we be allowed to tour the penitentiary's premises without prearrangement. Accompanied by a guard (there were no such things as "security officers" in those days), we would come and go as we pleased. The prison authorities promised they wouldn't phone ahead to warn of our coming; as a result we would see no cosmetic changes in the regular routine. Nothing would be off limits to us except the hospital and the cell interiors of the maximum security area.

Our own quarters in a downtown San Francisco hotel were pleasantly plush, but we spent little time there. Warner's son-in-law was accompanied by a buddy from the executive echelon of the studio, and when not at the prison they took off together for parts unknown. I was left in the coruscating company of a gentleman named Harry, whose conversation sparkled like a bottle of $1.98 champagne.

Not that I was disappointed. Harry turned out to be one of the last of a dying breed—a genuine Hollywood "gofer." Like Robert Florey, he'd come to filmland as a young man; unlike Florey, he didn't become a director. Or, for that matter, much of anything else. Somehow he stumbled into the movie business as a messenger and gradually his duties expanded to those of an errand boy. Over the past thirty-odd years nothing had changed, except that his initial fifteen-dollar weekly salary had risen to a hundred and fifty dollars, because he was now running errands for more important people. He moved from studio to studio and from one employer to another, but was never out of work. Due to his long tenure everyone knew him and he knew everybody in town.

It was this that made him so fascinating to me, his lengthy career as the little man who wasn't there. He was the guy who had always been around, the one nobody even noticed being in the room while the deals were cut, the schemes were plotted, the crucial decisions barked into the phone. He had more of an inside view than an intestinal parasite.

Be assured that while noodling in Chinese restaurants and during the evenings that followed, I asked a lot of questions and got a lot of answers. Unfortunately some have slipped my memory, because the prison sentence took its toll.

Every morning, not so bright but all too early, our reunited foursome lunged past the gates of San Quentin in a limousine. The rest of the long day was spent largely on foot, except for lunchtimes very similar to the one I had enjoyed in Wisconsin, though these felons were all strangers to me.

In retrospect they're even more strange to me today. It seems incredible that we could have so casually broken bread with men whose modern counterparts would have broken our heads. At the time we thought nothing of it, nor felt fear for ourselves when mingling with a thousand or more long-term convicts as they milled around in the recreation area. A single guard conducted us through the prison shops and everywhere else, from library to laundry. Only when passing the solitary-confinement cells did we ever encounter the slightest evidence of hostility, and that was merely verbal as well as highly understandable under the circumstances. By and large the men we talked to were friendly and helpful, once they learned our mission.

My favorite stopping place proved to be the office of the prison psychiatrist. Naturally I had many questions to ask him (almost as many questions as I had to ask Harry) and his input was welcome. But what really intrigued me was his hobby.

One of mine, back in Weyauwega but since abandoned due to lack of time, had been oil painting. The psychiatrist was not himself a painter, but he did collect pictures—all sorts of pictures—created by the prisoners suffering from mental illness. He had hundreds of them, stacked high on shelves and piled deep in drawers, everything from simple pencil or crayon doodlings to

elaborate creations in watercolor, tempera or oil. It was his intention to someday compile a book of such work with an appropriate
text, but there was another reason for the collection. He encouraged patients to indulge in artistic expression for use in diagnosis
and treatment. With the aid of such efforts he could analyze their
fantasies and disorders.

So could I. After inspecting several hundred specimens of
artwork I found myself classifying them without using clinical
terms. While the degree of artistry varied, there were some disturbing common denominators. By far the majority of the settings were
graveyard scenes. The background was always nocturnal and inevitably the moon was full. Why did so many mentally disturbed
criminals fantasize about graves yawning open in midnight moonlight? These constants evoked uneasiness, but the variations in
content raised questions even more unsettling.

Why did one artist portray the moon as a staring all-seeing
eye, while another sketched it as a grinning skull? What prompted
the differing locations of the knives embedded in corpses both
within coffins or sprawled at the grave site? Why a single knife in
this drawing and a half-dozen knives in the next? What about the
frequently disproportionate sizes, either too large or too small?
What determined the profusion or the total absence of bloodstains?
And above all, why did so many of the scenes depict a helpless
victim being savagely attacked by a black panther?

It was in these examples that one noted possible clues regarding the degree of the artist's disorder. Whether simply or sophis-
ticatedly rendered, lines tended to be more jagged, brush strokes
formed by slash or splash. Almost without exception the victim was
scarcely more than a stick figure; all the effort went into delineating
the attacker. I don't know what Carl Jung would have made of
these recurring symbols, but they fascinated me.

Unfortunately the main purpose behind this prison visit proved
much less fascinating when I started scripting back in Burbank. In

time the network concurred, and the project went to its final rest on that Great Shelf Up in the Sky.

Probably it also was joined by the material for the book on psychotic artwork.

When I get there I'll have to look it up.

THIRTY-FIVE

Although I had been working in Hollywood now for several years, my firsthand knowledge of film production was limited. True, I'd visited sets during shooting, seen dailies and rough-cut screenings of *The Couch*. But in most instances, once a script was turned in to the butchers I went on to the next assignment, and I had no control over what came out of the meat grinder. All I could do was hope that not too much sawdust had been added to the sausage, and if the end product turned out to be baloney, this was presumably not my affair.

Such was the situation in the late winter of 1962 when I accepted a film deal with William Castle at Columbia. Bill Castle (né Willie Schloss) was a gray-haired heavyset man of nervous temperament, much given to growling and floor-pacing; my first impression was of a polar bear who smoked cigars. But he was a longtime veteran in the industry, with a record dating back to the thirties. During the past half-dozen years, he'd been turning out low-budget "exploitation features" in the mystery and horror-film genre. Bill made personal appearances with his films and personal contacts with exhibitors, and had achieved a reputation as a sort of minor-league Alfred Hitchcock.

What he now proposed was inspired by a news item involving a murderess who killed while in disguise. The particular gimmick he had in mind was a "fat-suit," a rubber garment that could be blown up and worn by the villainess so that she could commit her crimes without risk of recognition. It seemed a grotesque premise, but I found Bill compatible on first meeting, and was pleasantly impressed by the direct, no-nonsense attitude of his associate producer, Dona Holloway. I came up with a story treatment which expanded the central character beyond the dimensions afforded by the fat-suit. What hooked me was the notion of an ax murderess—a sort of latter-day Lizzie Borden—who had been incarcerated in an asylum after her crime, then released as sane many years later, only to be accused of new and similar slayings. Of course the real culprit donned the fat-suit to throw unjust suspicion on the now-reformed lady. But humanizing a former victim of mental illness seemed interesting and I worked up a script to direct audience sympathy to a somewhat unusual heroine.

Bill liked what I had done, and so did the powers that be, or were, at Columbia. Basking in their approval, he set about casting—hampered, as usual, by the nickel-and-dime budget customarily applied to his productions.

Working on the script in an adjoining office led to some unexpected bonuses. One of them consisted of daily luncheons in Columbia's executive dining room, a hallowed sanctuary once presided over by the redoubtable Harry Cohn. His ghost was still very much in evidence at the long table, where various holdovers from his regime—including the brothers Briskin and nephew Bobby Cohn—held sway. From their lips, and those of longtime Cohn employee Jony Tapps, I heard many inside stories and bits of privileged information regarding the famous (and infamous) tycoon. I also had the pleasure of rubbing elbows with writers, directors and actors either visiting or employed on the lot—Guy Endore, Richard Brooks, Johnny Green, Frank Capra, Gene Raymond, Lee Tracy, Lew Ayres, Edie Adams and others.

In addition, a constant parade of visitors passed through our offices, people like Rock Hudson and Cary Grant who had known Bill for years and still sought him out for auld lang syne.

Dona too had her following and protégés. Thus it was that one afternoon I was present at the hastily organized, almost impromptu wedding of comedian Dan Rowan and Adriana, who were married in the office by a civil judge while Dan was en route to an appointment with his barber. During the brief cake-and-champagne aftermath to the ceremony, I suggested to Adriana that the marriage was not necessarily legal, since the judge who performed it had been sent over by central casting.

It was proposed that I sit in on casting interviews for the picture, which I'd titled *Strait-Jacket*. I immediately made two nominations: one was unsuccessful, and the other proved a mistake after a few days of filming, forcing a replacement. But other decisions rested in Bill's hands, although I was consistently consulted. In short order, character roles were assigned to Leif Erickson and Rochelle Hudson—two people whose work had long been familiar to me. Leif was a bluff, hearty man with a booming voice and laugh. Rochelle—"Shelly" to her friends—was returning to films after a long absence, but she'd obviously forgotten nothing of her competent technique.

A much more knotty problem involved the casting of a loutish and brutal villain. The third or fourth candidate had the proper physique and seemed to handle his lines well, but he lacked the coarseness and menace of the character. Sensing our reservations, he asked if he could come in the next day for a second reading.

The following afternoon he showed up dressed in dirty dungarees; his face and hands were filthy, his hair a tangle, his gait shambling, his voice a grating mumble. And his nose was broken, lending a sinister cast to his grinning countenance. No doubt about it—he *was* the character I'd written in my script. It still pleases me to know that I had the privilege of working with George Kennedy.

Our big question now was whom to select for the lead. It was a "fat part" in every sense of the term, but difficult to cast with our emaciated budget. Finally Bill settled on Joan Blondell. She was just pleasingly plump, but Bill intended to pad her costumes if necessary. As an added inducement, he promised to see about padding her part.

But before that happened, a message came down from New York, where Leo Jaffe presided over the Columbia empire. He'd read the script and was favorably impressed, so much so that he'd sent a copy to another actress who owed him a commitment. She saw the potential of the part, and Jaffe was willing to work out a deal with her, even to the point of paying off Joan Blondell in full.

The rest was up to us—me, in particular. Could the role be rewritten? More specifically, could Bill and I fly to New York during the next forty-eight hours, see the lady, and sell her on a revised version of the story?

The question was academic. Bill had already assured Jaffe we were on our way. Here was the opportunity he'd been waiting for—a chance to do a film with a bigger budget and a bigger name. I asked him to drop the name on me.

"Joan Crawford," he said.

I went home and started packing.

On the plane, Bill began to worry. Crawford was a legendary lady. How would she react to working on a tight, fast shooting schedule? Was she temperamental, did she insist on maintaining a glamorous image at the expense of her role? How would she feel about playing a dowdy ex-mental patient and murderess? The only possible solution to these problems lay in presenting her with a story she couldn't refuse.

A story we didn't have.

But as we zoomed over the Rockies I started to dump excess baggage. The first thing to go was Bill's beloved gimmick.

"The fat-suit is out," I told him.

"But that's our whole picture!"

"Not anymore. Crawford is our picture now."

In his autobiography, Bill succumbed to a natural temptation; he tells of arriving in New York, meeting with the lady, and being crushed by her demands for a completely new script—whereupon we returned to our hotel and sweated out a different version. As a director, his instincts are correct. It's a much more dramatic situation when told this way.

Actually, that's not quite how it really happened. Our two evenings in New York were spent attending the theater. The new story line we came up with was worked out in advance, on the plane. I broached my ideas and Bill approved, then added touches as our enthusiasm mounted.

But enthusiasm wasn't enough to carry us through. By the time we arrived, met with Leo Jaffe the following day, and went with him to Crawford's apartment, both of us were beginning to suffer from the same pangs Bill's actors experienced when they came in to read for a part. But now the situation was reversed. We were the ones who had to audition.

Our tension was heightened as we went through an elaborate security check before being admitted to Crawford's imposing Park Avenue residence. She occupied a two-story penthouse apartment on the corner, with a magnificent view of the park, and its decor was designed to emphasize the superstar image.

She herself greeted us at the door, wearing an apron. "We're having lunch," she said.

Was *this* the glamorous Joan Crawford? This little five-foot-three housewife with steel-gray hair was a far cry from the screen siren I first recalled seeing in an obscure film called *Paris,* back in 1926, and even further removed from the later Crawford of the great days at MGM and the Oscar-winning triumph which launched her on a career at Warner's.

Like a housewife, she cautioned us to please remove our

shoes; she'd just put in new white carpeting. Like a housewife, she played hostess during lunch; like a housewife, she showed us through the apartment; like a housewife, she busied her nervous hands with knitting as we talked afterwards.

But the woman who sat behind the executive desk of her organized office-at-home and listened to me tell the revised story was a housewife no longer. She listened intently, questioned minutely, and evaluated decisively.

"I'll do it," she said.

So it was back to Hollywood and the typewriter. The revised script went to Crawford in New York, along with Dona Holloway, who served admirably as diplomatic liaison in setting up arrangements for the star's stay on the local scene.

To our delight, she reported that Crawford approved the script as written. But her contract also required approval of cast, cinematographer and costumes; she would have her own hairdresser, her choice of makeup artists. There were specifications regarding her dressing room, and even one regarding air-conditioning—the temperature on the set must be lowered to sixty degrees at all times during actual shooting.

Bill's misgivings about star temperament returned full-force as he listened and gulped.

"One thing more," Dona said. "Crawford would like to spend her first two days in Hollywood with Bob, going over the script."

Now it was my turn to gulp. The request was unusual, and it had an ominous ring.

"It's not in your contract," Bill told me. "You don't have to do it."

"Oh yes I do."

And I did. The following week Crawford arrived and I climbed the stairs to the quarters assigned her—Rita Hayworth's former suite. The star wasn't in residence. Instead I found the housewife. She was down on her hands and knees, scrubbing the bathroom floor.

"Always do it myself," she said. "I like cleanliness. I'll be with you in a moment."

Crawford came out of the bathroom, wearing a smock. She went over to the table, put on her glasses and picked up the script.

"Now, dear heart," she said. "Shall we begin?"

"Begin what?"

"Didn't they tell you?" The big blue-gray eyes peered at me over the top of the eyeglasses. "I'm going to read my lines—tell me if I'm giving the interpretation you wanted."

I don't know what I said, if indeed I managed to say anything. But I know what I was thinking. Here is a woman who has been a top star for thirty-five years. And she wants *me* to tell her how to read her part?

"After all, you wrote it," she said. "You're the one who has to be pleased."

This was a temperamental movie queen?

She read—and I was pleased. The glamour image was for the public, but behind that image was the real star, totally dedicated, genuinely eager to learn anything that would aid her performance.

At the end of our two-day session she asked a favor. Would I be willing to stay on the picture, through the shooting and the postproduction? My answer was an emphatic yes. Now it was my chance to learn, from a vantage point directly behind the camera.

During lulls in the shooting I got acquainted with other cast members: Diane Baker, John Anthony Hayes, Howard St. John, Edith Atwater, Michael Cox. Then the picture went on location at Riverside, where a farmhouse had been rented outside the town. The company stayed at the rambling old Mission Inn, and it was here that I had the opportunity to learn something about the backgrounds of my new associates—Leif's stint as a vocalist with Ted Fio Rito; Shelley Hudson's impressions of W. C. Fields and Peter Lorre; George's army experiences. But much of the time was spent visiting with Joan and getting a firsthand account of what it had been like to work with Lon Chaney, the Barrymores, Gable and all the greats. For a lifelong movie fan like me this was the ultimate trip.

And the working routine—from early-morning arrival on the set to watch Bill block out the shots and staging with cameraman Arthur Arling to the early-evening screening of the dailies with Bill, Dona and publicist Linn Unkefer—was fascinating. Bill's direction was deft and his involvement total. My only personal dissatisfaction stemmed from his insistence on shock-for-shock's-sake; where the script called for George Kennedy to lose his head in a shadow sequence on the wall, Bill shot the decapitation on-camera with a dummy, much to George's distress and mine. Subtle it wasn't, but by today's standards such a scene would be considered tame; in 1963 it raised a yell from the audience and a shriek from the critics. I resigned myself to the realization that we were turning out a horror film, although a lengthy sequence, shot exactly as written, did achieve the sort of mounting suspense I'd hoped to bring to the entire picture.

We came back to town to finish our shooting at Columbia. One more day remained, followed by a day of postproduction work. Joan had asked Bill to film four television spots for some charitable cause to which she was committed; this involved four complete costume changes for which she would wear her own jewelry—diamonds, emeralds, rubies and pearls. These goodies would be conveyed to the set by a Brink's armored car and guarded by security personnel. In addition, I'd been commissioned to write a five-minute promotional film, *How to Commit a Movie Murder*—starring Joan, Bill and me.

But first we had to get through the final day of shooting, and it was a long one. There were a few pickup shots involving Joan, culminating in the grueling opening scene of the film in which she would be introduced writhing in a straitjacket.

Everyone was tired, and Joan most of all; she was on-camera

all day. Late in the afternoon we reached the next-to-the-last sequence. Joan, moving through the darkness outside the farmhouse, stumbles upon an ax projecting from a woodpile and picks it up.

That's how the scene was shot, and Bill was satisfied. But Joan, ever the perfectionist, called him over. "Could we do another take? I think my timing was a little off."

Bill consented; out came the clapper, and once more the familiar litany rose: "Roll 'em! Speed! Action!"

Joan came around the side of the farmhouse in the shadows. But this time she really stumbled—not upon the ax but upon the woodpile. Our star went down in a tangle of jagged, splintered kindling.

Blood. Confusion. A doctor summoned. A consultation. "She's pretty badly cut up. Better get her home at once," said her physician.

Joan shook her head. "Can you bandage me after you stop the bleeding?"

"Yes, but—"

"Then get with it. We've got to finish the picture."

The bandages were applied. Joan got up. She repeated the shot—perfectly.

Two hours later she was down on the studio floor, thrashing about in a straitjacket.

And the next day she appeared on the set bright and early. Her legs were a mass of cuts and purple bruises from ankles to thighs—but they were hidden under the gorgeous gowns she wore during the shooting of the four television spots. Her jewelry sparkled, and so did she.

"How're you doing?" I asked.

"Okay. Now let's get on to your promo film."

"You think you're up to it?"

"Wouldn't miss it for the world."

We did the film, in several takes. Bill and I fluffed a few lines, but Joan was letter-perfect. She moved without the slightest hint that she was in pain.

And when we finished, about five o'clock, it was time for the traditional cast-and-crew party. Catered by Chasen's, no less.

Joan had retired to her dressing room, and we expected she'd leave after a brief, token appearance to bid farewell to her fellow workers. Appear she did, but not briefly. She had another job to do—as hostess—and she wouldn't shirk. And when the music began to play and an elderly gaffer whom she'd known since the days at Metro asked her to dance, Joan danced with him. Then she drew Bill, Dona, publicist Linn Unkefer and me aside as the men from Chasen's began serving food.

"Don't eat anything," she said. "Just stick around until the others have gone."

Puzzled, we obeyed. And when the last members of the cast and crew departed, Joan went to her dressing room and brought out the casseroles she'd hidden there. "Baked beans and sausage," she said proudly.

"Where'd this come from?" Bill asked.

"I cooked it myself, last night."

And so it was that we sat down to a private meal of baked beans and champagne with Joan Crawford. A hell of a cook. A hell of a sport. And one hell of a star.

THIRTY-SIX

A warm night in October 1963. Insomnia was my bed partner and I couldn't sleep. Quietly, so as not to disturb my daughter in the adjoining bedroom, I rose and tiptoed into the darkness of the kitchen, searching for a cigarette. The apartment was hot, stuffy, and the walls were closing in on me.

I opened the front door and stood there, looking out across the gray motionless surface of the pool, then up to the gray, motionless sky above it. I was gray and motionless too.

The thought didn't pleasure me.

That morning I'd had my day in court, an appearance made after months of anguished anticipation, ending in anticlimax. A few minutes of quiet questioning by the judge, a moment of testimony by Paul D. Spencer, who'd volunteered as a witness on my behalf, had resulted in the granting of my interlocutory divorce decree.

Twenty-three years of marriage—half my present lifetime—vanished, gone up in smoke like my cigarette. *Warning: The Surgeon General Has Determined That Marriage Is Dangerous to Your Health.* Like smoking, it has its pleasures and its perils. But quitting is never easy, not after all those years. It's only when your health—

physical, mental, emotional—is threatened that resolution can be summoned to kick the habit. A matter of self-preservation.

Or was this just a selfish rationalization on my part?

Selfish, yes; rationalization, no. In recent years my state of health had been threatened and impaired by marital discord—discord as much of my making no doubt, as Marion's.

No sense arguing the rights and wrongs of the situation or attempting to assign blame. The plain truth was that she could not or would not adjust to the demands of this new way of life here in Hollywood—the problems, the patterns, the people. She was unhappy and showed it; her unhappiness created an emotional climate in which I couldn't survive. Inevitably I'd lost enthusiasm for work, and had fallen into an attitude of "What's the use? Why go to all this effort if she's unhappy, I'm unhappy, our daughter's unhappy?"

It was what I'd feared—and warned Marion about—when the opportunity to come out here had first arisen. I'd anticipated the uprooting wouldn't be easy, the adjustment might be disruptive. Given the physical limitations to her activity, the necessity of adapting to a new environment, new professional and social demands, the risks seemed obvious; I'd discussed them earnestly and at great length. But she wanted to make the change and did her best to go along with it.

Unfortunately, it hadn't worked out. Not for her, not for Sally, and not for me. Much as I'd tried to avoid drastic changes in our life-style, much as I'd deliberately avoided the Hollywood party and public-appearance routines, there were still certain minimal obligations which had to be met, certain friends whose invitations must be honored and reciprocated. Marion couldn't accept or enjoy them, nor could she accept or enjoy the domestic routine which she had to face alone when I was working at the studios. Sally felt the tension, the sense of stress and schism, and suffered accordingly. And I was smoking more and enjoying it less, working harder and wondering why.

In Hollywood, writers' wives I knew were singularly prone to finding themselves prone on the psychiatrist's couch, even when they boasted a self-confident self-image which Marion wasn't blessed with. Writers' children often fouled up too. And as for writers themselves, I'd seen too many ulcerated specimens preserved in alcohol—not really preserved, but merely kept bobbing afloat temporarily before sinking forever.

The point seemed simple: if I went under, we all went under. If I couldn't work, none of us would survive.

Returning to the Midwest was no solution; twenty-odd years of near-poverty brought an appreciation of today's creature comforts which Marion and Sally shared. But if we were to continue to enjoy those comforts, I'd have to continue to function.

A hard decision to make, and a harder one to implement. I'd waited until our two-year lease was up, then gone to work hunting a house to buy, selecting one which I thought might fill the needs of the situation. I found one a block or so away, so that Marion wouldn't find herself alone in a new neighborhood without friends; it was within walking distance of shopping, because she didn't drive. The place required little effort for upkeep, and Sally would still be attending the same school. Only after its purchase did I break the news that I wouldn't be moving in.

It was a painful announcement to make, and the period of transition was painful too, for all of us. The business with the attorney, working out a settlement and income to provide for the future, the mechanics of moving, the trauma of dissolving a family relationship—all took its toll.

After a few weeks in a motel, I moved into an apartment about a mile and a half from the new house, so that I'd still be available to run errands, assist Marion in shopping for furnishings, and help make the change less harrowing. While friends knew of the situation, there was no public announcement, and I stayed on the job at the studio without anyone there being aware of what had happened.

Since the apartment was modestly but adequately furnished, my own requirements were few; I had a living room, kitchen and two bedrooms, one of which I converted into a work space. At least that was my intention, but three weeks after I took over, Sally appeared. She had decided to move in with me, though she meant to maintain regular contact with her mother and use her car to provide transportation whenever needed. Meantime she planned to continue school and keep house for me.

I didn't question her reasons, but I questioned her future. For the moment, however, the arrangement seemed to work out; somehow we'd managed to get through the months of waiting until the divorce hearing and the granting of my decree.

So now it was over, and at long last I was free.

I stood there in my doorway, stubbing the cigarette beneath my heel. Messy gesture; should have used an ashtray. Sally would have seen to it that I did, but she was asleep. I wondered if she would rest as easily if she were aware of potential problems in the future. Certainly she'd had problems in the past, problems which contributed to my decision to seek at least a partial solution in divorce. Still, she was young, and with a little luck she'd find her way to a deserved measure of happiness. And so, I hoped, would Marion.

But what about me?

I'd continue to work, of course, as long as I could survive in the Hollywood jungle. At the moment there was nothing to fear. Nothing to fear—and nothing except work in which to find satisfaction or fulfillment. The property settlement and alimony arrangement which both judge and attorney deemed more than equitable would impose a perpetual obligation, but I still had enough for ordinary needs. I didn't have to continue living in a side-street furnished apartment in the valley; I could move anywhere I chose. And then—

I began to think about other writers I knew, divorced men in similar situations. Several went the health-kick route, spending their free time working out at the gymnasium, playing handball, golf or tennis, hunting or fishing or backpacking in the mountains. Others gambled their lives away at the card tables of so-called "country clubs," and a goodly share dedicated themselves to sexual activity with any available partner, amateur or professional. Some even remarried.

I pondered the alternatives without enthusiasm.

Since learning to drive, drinking had appealed to me less and less as a pastime, let alone a full-time avocation; solitary drinking, never. Drugs were for suicides. I'd never cared for sports in any form. As for aerobic sex, I lacked the aggressive qualities which seemed concomitant with continual success, and let's face it—at forty-six I lacked the insatiable drive of youth. One thing I was certain of: when it came to marrying again, no way. I'd just emerged from almost a quarter of a century of confinement in that particular institution, and had no desire to serve another sentence.

I have no complaints about my daughter's culinary skills. Since her marriage she has become a gourmet cook, and even when she moved into the apartment with me back in '63, she prepared excellent meals, despite her school schedule. But it was a difficult period for us both, a period of adjustment when each of us, in our own way, sought to gaze into the future and, try as we might, could see only the dim outlines of a huge question mark.

Sally's escape was in horseback riding. Mine was the occasional company of friends. And when an invitation came for a sit-down dinner followed by a social evening, I welcomed it eagerly.

One such invitation arrived shortly after the holiday season. Jo and Gerry Morrison asked the Gelmans and me to dinner on Saturday, January 18, at their Beverly Hills home. There would be one other guest, a recently widowed lady whom I'd never met, but that hardly concerned me: the principal attraction was gastronomic.

The Gelmans picked me up en route from their home near

my apartment and drove me up past Pickfair to the Morrison residence off Summit Ridge Drive.

When we got there, the other guest had already arrived. Her name was Eleanor Alexander, and she had lost her writer-producer husband, John Alexander, just three months before. This was her first social evening since the night of his sudden and fatal heart attack.

Mrs. Alexander and I started to talk. Shortly thereafter, she excused herself and went into the bedroom.

I followed her and proposed marriage. We had known each other for exactly twenty-two minutes. The rest of the evening is a blur even to this day. I know that she politely declined. I know that we ignored our host and hostess and the Gelmans most shamefully. I know that the Gelmans eventually drove her home to Santa Monica and that I sat beside her in the back seat of the car, suggesting we meet for brunch the following morning.

We did indeed have brunch, at the Santa Ynez Inn on Sunday: we met again for dinner on Monday evening and again on Tuesday.

From then on we saw one another every day with the exception of a three-day period I spent in Mexico with Bill Frye, scouting possible locations for a film project in San Felipe.

In retrospect, the whole situation seems incredible. I am not normally impetuous, nor was I actively seeking a long-term relationship. The notion of marrying again had no more appeal than the risky athletic feat of jumping out of a frying pan into the fire. As for Elly, she mourned the loss of her husband and had deliberately withdrawn from full-scale social contacts. It was only with the utmost persuasion that the Morrisons had induced her to come to dinner. When informed that a stranger would be present, she almost panicked. Upon learning this stranger was the author of *Psycho* she was still further upset. She'd not read the book or seen the film, because the subject matter repelled her, and she had no desire to meet the kind of person who could conjure up such morbidity.

But that's the way it happened.

In a few weeks we broke the news to Sally. By July we'd purchased a home, and while I remained at my apartment, Sally moved in with Elly as she furnished and decorated the house.

Somewhere along the line we compared notes and learned of a coincidence. Elly had lost her husband on the same day I received my interlocutory decree of divorce. On the night that I stood in the doorway of my apartment, wondering about the future, Elly returned from the hospital to which her husband had been taken following his sudden, fatal attack after dinner—and she too had faced an enigmatic, empty tomorrow.

Born in Canada, of Ukrainian parentage, she had come to Chicago in her late teens to live with an older brother. She became a fashion model, taught courses at the Powers Modeling School, then began a career as a cosmetician at Marshall Field's. In the late forties and early fifties, I made many trips to Chicago on weekends to visit my father during his stay there. Almost invariably upon arrival, before proceeding to the South Side apartment, I'd spend a half hour at Marshall Field's book department, which was reached by a route that took me past the cosmetic counters. It's very likely that we saw one another at that time: but what's another salesperson in the eyes of a passerby and why should he be singled out by a cosmetics expert interested only in potential customers?

Elly was then enjoying a full social life as a stunningly attractive and unattached young lady with a bright professional future in her chosen field, and I was married, harried, and preoccupied with the perennial problems of sheer survival. Had anyone told us that we were destined to meet a dozen years and two thousand miles from then and there, following a marriage for her and a divorce for me, I doubt that either of us would have entertained the possibility.

But here we were together, in 1964—together, and inseparable. My final divorce decree was granted on October 11; five days later, on the sixteenth, we married and departed for a Tahiti honeymoon.

Actually, it wasn't all that simple.

Marion had sold the house I bought for her and purchased a home in Desert Hot Springs. Seemingly, she'd adjusted to a new life. Much to everyone's surprise, she bought a car, learned to drive, and made an immediate place for herself in the community. She was far more active than at any time during our marriage, and I realized that I had done her a disservice over the years by serving as a crutch, establishing a dependency which she really didn't need after her physical condition improved. Now she blossomed in the sunshine of her freedom, and in this I found consolation for my conscience. My remarriage might come as a shock to her but would not induce any lasting trauma. And she had the continuing solace of alimony.

The problems arose from unexpected sources.

During my stay in Hollywood before the family joined me, and even thereafter, when Marion chose to abstain from many social involvements, I'd made a number of friendships and renewed others. I'd enjoyed much hospitality, and reciprocated it whenever possible. So had Elly. Her brief period of widowhood automatically transformed her into a loner, available for the casual visiting and companionship of friends who didn't want to see "poor Elly" suffer solitude.

I had never thought of myself as "poor Bob"—but I'm sure that divorce conferred that label upon me in the minds of many. During the period of my interlocutory decree, I thought it advisable, for Marion's sake as well as my own, to keep a low profile. Elly gradually came to meet some of my friends, and I met hers, but apparently even the announcement of our intentions met with skepticism in some quarters. Many people were stunned when they heard of our plans; such precipitous resolution seemed to them to be completely out of character for us both. And, since they felt that they really *knew* us, they tended to disbelieve we'd actually go through with the wedding. We were wrong for each other, it couldn't last, and besides that, it wasn't going to happen.

Early on, Elly and I discussed the logistics involved in tying the nuptial knot. I'd been introduced to her friends, Annie and Ferde Grofe. Ferde's compositions had long been favorites of mine and I was delighted to meet him. Confined to a wheelchair following a stroke, Ferde was nevertheless a charming host and an endless source of anecdotes about the great days with Gershwin and Whiteman. He was pleasantly astonished at my interest and my knowledge of his more obscure work. When he discovered that our birthdays came only about ten days apart, he suggested a mutual celebration at their home, giving me carte blanche to invite my own friends. The occasion was memorable: at Elly's urging I did invite a number of people, and of course Ferde's guests included musical notables from both the jazz and classical fields. Shortly thereafter we escorted Annie and Ferde to dinner and revealed our marital plans. The news took them completely by surprise and for a moment it seemed that Ferde might suffer another stroke. But he quickly recovered, and almost immediately he and Annie proposed that we be married at their home. They had a large garden, with an arbor, and they'd instruct the gardener to begin floral plantings now. It would be a gala affair, for several hundred people—

We considered the matter and then declined, with thanks. The birthday party had been gratefully accepted, but it seemed a little too much of a good thing. And a formal wedding, involving several hundred guests, was something neither of us could face. Nor did we feel we could impose on the generosity of the Grofes to such an extent.

Elly had many friends, and I had mine—plus a multitude of acquaintances and business contacts in the industry. Both of us had more friends and relatives in the Midwest, and Elly had scores of others in Canada. If we went public with a wedding, all would have to be included. And no matter how long we labored over our list of invitations, there were bound to be people we'd omit or overlook. The inevitable result would be hurt feelings, and what began with good intentions would end in disaster.

So when our dear friend Dona Holloway—Bill Castle's associate producer—suggested a quiet ceremony in her home, we gratefully accepted this solution to the problem. Dona arranged for a judge to perform the legal incantations. Joan Crawford sent us our wedding cake. The judge included Elizabeth Barrett Browning's lines—"How do I love thee? Let me count the ways"—in the ceremony. Since this, by coincidence, happened to be Elly's favorite poem, the occasion proved a moving one. Following the ceremonial champagne toasts, we left for the airport and our flight to Tahiti.

THIRTY-SEVEN

1n recent years there seems to have been an increasing output of nonlinear novels. Nonlinear autobiographies might be just as easy to write, but I have a hunch they're a helluva lot harder to live.

Since I never got around to making the attempt, there have been times when I had the feeling I was existing on many levels simultaneously. That certainly holds true for the median years of the sixties. I was, in rapid succession, a divorce plaintiff, a suitor and a newlywed; meanwhile I continued to be an author of short stories, a TV scripter and a screenwriter. At times the combination of these activities tended to interfere with my leisure.

They didn't, however, interfere with my social life. I was meeting Elly's friends and she was meeting mine. Some months earlier Tom and Terri Pinckard had inaugurated a contemporary counterpart of the traditional literary salon. Once a month a group of local writers plus personal friends met at the Pinckard home. Invited speakers, in many cases visiting from elsewhere (or even further), would hold forth, followed by a question-and-discussion period, followed by a mad rush for the refreshments.* I took Elly to one such gathering but didn't mention our impending nuptials.

In a small town like Los Angeles it's almost impossible to keep a secret. Inevitably the day came—a Sunday afternoon, to be exact—when Elly and I were invited to an affair at the home of George Kennedy and his family. Much to our surprise the Pinckards also showed up as guests; the only thing that saved us from discovery was the fact that I hadn't revealed our plans to George. Everything went smoothly until former actress Marjorie Reynolds and her husband arrived. Spotting us, the first words out of her mouth were, "How do you like your new house?"

Since she and her husband had sold us our new home in the Hollywood Hills, the question was normal enough under the circumstances. Not so, however, was the reaction of our friends, who promptly scrambled around on the floor looking for the jaws they had dropped.

From that point on word spread rapidly as tom-toms started to beat in the jungle. Among the first to learn the news was Joan Crawford.

As is generally observed during a film shoot, the working conditions often lead to an instant intimacy which is dissolved with equal swiftness once the picture has reached its wrap. But the release of *Strait-Jacket* didn't terminate my pleasant association with some of the cast members, including Miss Crawford.

She toured with it during its first play dates on the East Coast, phoning in regular reports of good business plus caustic comments on two unfavorable reviews—one from a personal

---

*The Pinckard Salon deserves a book in itself. Over the years it entertained guest speakers ranging from astronauts to cryogenics pioneers. They entertained such writer-members as Fritz Leiber, Philip Jose Farmer, Jerry Pournelle, Larry Niven, Norman Spinrad, A. E. van Vogt, Forrest Ackerman, Kris Neville, Florence and Sam Russell, Walt Daugherty, plus a dozen others who will be upset because their names were left out. Which is all the more reason there should be a book.

enemy of hers, the other from a foe of Bill Castle's. I tended to take such matters less seriously, but Joan's instincts were correct; it is excerpts from these two particular reviews which have been either quoted or paraphrased in most mentions of the film to this day, thus denigrating her disciplined performance. Reviewers also ignored the superior values of a low-budget offering which boasted the contributions of famed production designer Boris Leven and makeup expert Ben Nye, plus one of the Westmores. It took almost two weeks of combined effort on the part of Bill and myself before Columbia brass met my demands to decapitate the lady who bears the torch of freedom in their screen emblem. I thought it might give a subtle hint to audiences and reviewers that the film wasn't to be taken all that seriously. Whether audiences got the message is problematical, but not one single critic ever seems to have noticed that somebody chopped the head off the Statue of Liberty. But enough of art.*

When Joan returned to Hollywood she signed for a costarring role in *Hush, Hush, Sweet Charlotte,* came down with pneumonia, relinquished her part and ended up in the hospital. It was there that she learned of my plans to commit matrimony (finally got it in, didn't I?) and promptly phoned to demand a summit meeting with my bride-to-be.

Elly and I drove to Cedars of Lebanon. She didn't quite know what to expect, but what she got was an RN escort to a two-room private suite where Miss Crawford awaited us propped up in bed, surrounded by apparatus which promptly disappeared as soon as the RN left. It pleased me that Joan seemed well on the road to recovery, a trip she was undertaking in good spirits.

We had not been her only visitors today—Butch Romero had

---

*Will somebody please tell me just how all this got in here? We were talking about Joan Crawford learning that Elly and I were to be married. At least I was talking about it, and trust you were paying attention.

just left, she told us—but not to worry, all was prepared. In the middle of the room was a smorgasbord setup and the essential components of a wet bar. Pushing aside the portable oxygen tank, Joan lighted one of the inevitable Herbert Tareytons and smiled at Elly. "Can I get you something to drink?" she inquired.

Elly glanced at me as I semaphored with my left eyebrow; then she nodded to her hostess. "Perhaps a small vodka and tonic," she ventured.

Joan was already out of bed and en route to the serving area. She filled a tall glass with hundred-proof Smirnoff and—when I demurred—added a soupçon of tonic. Elly sipped gingerly.

We had intended a short stay, but half an hour later both of the ladies were down on the floor and Joan was demonstrating a series of weight-reduction exercises to my fiancée. So much for the health-care program.

Elly's first encounter with Joan was not her last; the two proved congenial and it was Joan's custom to touch base whenever she visited the Coast. As those visits became less frequent in the years that followed we continued to maintain contact through correspondence and by phone. Like scores of others who enjoyed similar friendships we remember her fondly.

Another holdover from *Strait-Jacket* was Leif Erickson. He and I spent time together while on location in and around Riverside. What I didn't know was that he and his wife Ann had been friends of Elly and her late husband. And Leif, of course, wasn't aware I even knew Elly.

Shortly after becoming unofficially engaged, she and I were the objects of morbid curiosity on the part of her friends. Mary Kay and Johnnie Stearns invited us to their home for dinner and a covert inspection of my fingernails. When Elly learned Leif and Ann were also to be present she suggested that they be told she was coming with her intended husband, without mention of my name. "Let it be a surprise," she said.

Arriving at the Stearns' home on the appointed evening, Elly walked in while I parked and locked the car. The Ericksons were already in the living room and when Leif saw Elly he immediately grabbed her in a bear-hug embrace. As he did so, he looked up just as I came into view in the hallway beyond.

"Why, you son of a bitch!" he boomed. And grinned.

It was a very pleasant dinner.

Leif wasn't the only friend Elly had in show business. I soon had the pleasure of meeting Frances and Cecil Howard. Cecil was a titled gentleman and his wife was the former Frances Drake. I had seen her repeatedly thirty years earlier, at which time she was married to people like Boris Karloff and Colin Clive on screen. It was still easy to see why Peter Lorre had so ardently pursued her in *Mad Love,* and I couldn't quite believe that this same luminous lady was now offering to read my palm. Frances subsequently indulged in palmistry on at least a half-dozen occasions and unfailingly noted that I have an exceptionally lengthy life line. Thus far her observation seems correct, and I intend to devote my remaining years to proving it so.

While she was reading my palm and the hospitable Cecil was preparing to press a drink into it, I might easily have glanced through the window and noted the house across the way. It was some months later that Elly and I paid a visit there, and only after she'd queried me first.

"Would you like to meet Fritz Lang?" she asked.

Foolish question.

The only question, for me, was what I could possibly have to say to the director of *Metropolis, Siegfried, M* and many other films made here and abroad which had given him his international reputation. As Elly and I drove past Pickfair en route to the Lang home on a Sunday afternoon I pondered the problem.

It was Lang himself who solved it the moment we were introduced. "Tell me," he said, "whatever became of your radio show, 'Stay Tuned for Terror'?"

Needless to say he had made a friend for life.

Fritz and his longtime companion and wife-to-be, Lily Latte, were indeed just that. So was Peter Martini.

I saw a good deal of Peter in the years to come, although we never had very much to say to one another. In fact Peter seldom spoke, but Fritz admired his patience as a listener. They often dined together and had shared each other's company in travels throughout the world. At times Fritz even permitted his friend to wear some of the numerous medals he had received for directorial achievement. It is an incontrovertible fact that Peter was one of the most spoiled and pampered stuffed monkeys in the world.

On first glance he might easily be mistaken for a teddy bear in a sailor suit, but Peter was indeed a simian simulacrum. And in addition to being an ideal listener and travel companion he was also the perfect guest. Many times late in the afternoon Fritz would observe the cocktail hour, and after catering to my needs he invariably asked Peter what he wanted to drink. Peter's response, which I confess was not always audible to me, was unchanging. He opted only for martinis, as befitted his name, and his choice pleased Fritz. What pleased Fritz even more was that Peter never touched his drink, so in the end Fritz had to drink it for him.

I once had occasion to ask Fritz why he was taking a certain course of action.

"Peter makes the decisions," he told me.

It was Peter who made the final decision, many years later, to join Fritz in the grave. Elly and I took custody of his wife and child; they dwelt in our living room for several years. Peter's spouse was a mail-order bride sent to him by actress Joan Bennett and her husband. Some time later Fritz announced that she was pregnant and in due time (whatever the gestation period may be for stuffed chimpanzees) the infant appeared. There is no doubt whatsoever that Fritz Lang looms large in cinema history as one of the great directors, but he wasn't above a bit of monkey business.

Failing vision had virtually forced Fritz to withdraw from directing, and the health problems which come with age were not always easy for him to accept. There were times when Elly accused him to his face of being an "old barracuda." One day she went to the hospital for what used to be called an operation. Among the get-well cards she received after surgery, the first was a message bearing a hand-colored cartoon drawing of a fish. It was signed "Barry Cuda."

All this, of course, came following the marriage; during the months prior to the wedding there wasn't that much free time to get well acquainted with so many new friends.

There was work to do. I did my final hour-long Hitchcock shows, one for "Run for Your Life," and a story for "I Spy," the series which brought Bill Cosby into prominence. I also readied a few short stories for magazine debut along with a collection, *Tales in a Jugular Vein*. But most of my time was devoted to a film titled *The Night Walker*.

William Castle had moved his base of operations from Columbia to Universal, and it was here that he summoned me for a new assignment. An Australian housewife had sent him an unsolicited screenplay. Story line, characters, dialogue and setting were all impossible to consider, but Bill was interested in what remained. The basic concept was the dilemma faced by a person who could no longer clearly differentiate between dream and reality.

It was a concept Bill was willing to buy, along with the script, for a thousand dollars. He then threw the script away, called me in, and asked what I could do with the premise itself. What I did eventually evolved as a story and script of my own, though the resultant noctambulation sometimes lurched in a manner I had not prescribed. Nor was I responsible for the pedestrian approach to *fx*.

One of the reasons the film often seemed to get out of step was a budget problem. Its cause was simple—Bill opted to spend his money on cast rather than production. After his experience with Crawford he decided that heading his cast with a star name was good insurance. Accordingly he set up a luncheon for us with

Rosalind Russell. I enjoyed the encounter, but to me Miss Russell was the direct antithesis of my heroine. Bill noted as much and there the matter rested. Returning home I rested too, content that he'd seek an actress more appropriate for the role of damsel in distress.

But a short time later I was the one in distress upon learning that the damsel he'd selected was Barbara Stanwyck. If anything, I rated Miss Stanwyck's ability greater than Roz Russell's, but she too seemed an unlikely choice. The key attribute of my heroine was her vulnerability. Somehow I just couldn't picture Barbara Stanwyck's screen image in that light. The part called for a lady in her thirties; Stanwyck, who had defiantly eschewed the artifices of Beverly Hills beauty salons, had let her hair go prematurely white.

Even so, Bill considered her his film's insurance policy—and just to be on the safe side, he now insured his insurance by signing Robert Taylor as costar. Taylor and Stanwyck had been husband and wife during the height of their stardom. Divorced for well over a dozen years, he had remarried while she remained single, and during that time their paths had not crossed professionally or personally. Beyond a doubt Bill saw publicity and promotional possibilities in their screen reunion. In any event, I wasn't consulted, merely confronted with a fait accompli.

Once the film reached completion Bill himself had to confront the irreversible. Taylor was a competent, seasoned veteran, good-natured, unassuming and totally professional. "Missy," as she was known to everyone in the business, proved to be Crawford's equal in terms of ability and knowledgeability, with a dry, self-deprecating wit. There wasn't a moment of embarrassment or friction between the two stars, and they played their scenes together deftly. But time exacts its toll, and that, combined with cuts in both the budget and the shooting schedule, caused *The Night Walker* to stumble badly.

Once more I spent some time on the shoot, visiting with supporting players Lloyd Bochner and Hayden Rourke. Bill again cast Rochelle Hudson in a minor role. Shelley offered anecdotes about working with Mae West and W. C. Fields (though not, like Dick Foran, in the same picture). Taylor and I visited in the monster trailer he hauled onto the lot in preparation for a postproduction camping trip. I can't recall who was responsible for hauling in a different sort of monster, but distinctly remember that Stanwyck and I spent the better part of a morning outside the soundstage with a leopard on a leash.

Unfortunately it wasn't being used in our picture. And once the film was over Missy retired to her habitual seclusion. Elly and I visited her home for an evening following the death of her brother, but Stanwyck had none of Crawford's gregarious traits. It was ironic that in private life she actually possessed the vulnerable qualities which her screen image as my heroine didn't project. None of which interfered with her professional presence, and I have much fonder memories of the star than I do of the picture.

At Castle's behest I again wrote a special trailer for the film, this one featuring Pat Collins, aka "The Hip Hypnotist," but gimmickry could not atone for gimcrackery.

Bill must have realized I wasn't too happy with the results of our endeavors, for he made no effort to interest me in his next project; it was my old pulp-writer friend from the Ziff-Davis days, William P. McGivern, whom he turned to for another film with Crawford. But Castle took steps to maintain our friendly personal relationship and Elly and I spent our first New Year's Eve together at his home.

Or almost together. I got hung up in a long (and to me fascinating) account of big-time vaudeville from old-timer Ken Murray, and nearly missed the midnight celebration.

As usual, Ellen Castle played hostess to a star-studded cast for dinner, and that night it was Bob Taylor who carved the roast. If I'm not mistaken, other friends were among the many present: the multitalented artist Lou Litchenfield, who was soon to marry Dona Holloway, and publicist Linn Unkefer with his bride, Betty.*

Sometime before dawn on January first we returned home. There, in a newly furnished house, with a newly furnished wife, I awaited what 1965 might bring.

---

*But I could be mistaken, particularly after the second drink.

THIRTY-EIGHT

One thing the new year would bring was a horde of refugees and boat people from the East and the Middle West. Like myself, some would come by invitation; others arrived armed only with anticipation.

As previously noted, William P. McGivern was already on the scene, together with his wife, writer Maureen Daly. So was our mutual friend and former editor Howard Browne, who'd long since established a successful foothold as a television writer.

Now, seeking a toehold, came Fredric Brown, my onetime Milwaukee compatriot. Despite the fact that his second wife accompanied him to meetings with producers, or perhaps because of it, Fred didn't find a place for himself in Hollywood and ill health forced him to retreat to a desert home.

Horace Gold, former editor of *Galaxy* and *Beyond,* was another who didn't luck out, but he stayed on. Jack Denton, my longtime friend since the days when he emceed "It's A Draw" in Milwaukee, came as a stand-up comic. Bette and Philip José Farmer called Los Angeles home for a number of years, during which he continued his fiction career while daylighting as a technical writer.

Harlan Ellison appeared and almost instantaneously assumed the role of tempest in the local teapot. He managed to bubble in film, boil in television, continue to steam ahead in print, and is still simmering today.

And what about me?*

I was approached by actor Sebastian Cabot to work out a premise for a series which could star him as a psychic investigator. My own sixth sense told me that this possibility would never materialize, and it didn't. Over the next few years several pilots for similar series were launched at places where ours had been shown around, but you'd be surprised how far the long arm of coincidence can be stretched in Hollywood.

Another actor, John Ireland, commissioned me to do him a film script involving the assassination of Leon Trotsky. Apparently he never found financing, because the next time Elly and I encountered him was at the press party for *I Saw What You Did*, in which he appeared with Joan Crawford. Joan amused Elly by plunking herself down at our table and immediately asking how we'd enjoyed our Tahiti honeymoon, then constantly running off to be interviewed by successive reporters before Elly could ever respond to the question.

Meantime, in darkest England, a recently formed production company called Amicus† had filmed one of my short stories, "The Skull of the Marquis de Sade," under a shorter title, *The Skull*. Now producers Max Rosenberg and Milton Subotsky, both expatriate Yankees, wanted to go further and have me write and script a new project, which would wind up as *The Psychopath*.

Not content with this (and to tell the truth, neither was I, particularly) they invited me to come over during the filming.

It befell that the World Science Fiction Convention would

---

*I thought you'd never ask.

†Latin for "low-budget."

befall in London over Labor Day weekend. Coincidentally my agent, Gordon Molson, planned to be in England at the same time. Elly and I decided to map out a Grand Tour, the kind of lengthy expedition which requires no less than two suitcases and a complete change of socks.

We arrived at London's Grosvenor Hotel on August 26, then scooted over to the Mount Royal at the opposite end of Park Lane. That would be convention headquarters, and there we found a group of early attendees including guest of honor Brian Aldiss, his future wife Margaret, author John Brunner and, of all people, Arthur C. Clarke. Quite a few writers had come over from the colonies; Elly met them and their spouses for the first time. Forrest J and Wendayne J Ackerman she already knew.

The next few days passed in a round of newspaper interviews, publishers' cocktail parties and convention sessions. One of the drop-ins was Christopher Lee, already saddled with identification as the star of British horror films. Ackerman steered him to us and we steered him back to our hotel for tea.

The following day Gordon Molson arrived to attend the banquet, where I was one of the speakers. Elly, who had never been subjected to a convention before, was startled when I began insulting the guests. Gradually she relaxed, particularly after learning British law forbade capital punishment.

It seemed everybody had congregated in London that weekend; even Barbara Norville, my current editor at Simon & Schuster, showed up. Writer Judy Merril flew in from Canada and Irish fan Walter A. Willis came over from Belfast with wife Madeleine. At their urging we agreed to visit them after we left London. A day or so later I joined some of my fellow colonials to drink lunch with Kingsley Amis. By that time, what with a party at the Planetarium which we attended with Arthur and an East Indian curry dinner with a Yugoslavian editor I was ready for a penicillin shot.

As for Elly, by now she was ready for just about anything. But the following morning, when I made my way alone to the Mount

Royal for an interview, she decided to enjoy a rest and breakfast in bed. The drapes were still drawn against a dark and rainy day as she snuggled under the covers in the shadows.

The phone rang. She picked it up and a somewhat sepulchral voice inquired if Mr. Robert Bloch was there. Elly explained where I'd gone and asked who was calling.

"This is Boris Karloff," the voice replied.

Like hell it is, Elly told herself, remembering that I'd warned her about science fiction fans and their fondness for hoaxes and practical jokes.

"Is this Mrs. Bloch?" the voice queried.

"Yes." Elly's answer was hesitant. But the voice echoing from the receiver here in this darkened room sounded frighteningly familiar and all too convincing.

"Evie and I were wondering if you'd be free to come visit us tonight."

It must be Karloff. Why didn't Bob tell me he knew him? Elly braced herself, turned on the lamp, and accepted the invitation.

Before venturing off to Sheffield Terrace we fortified ourselves with cocktails at Christopher Lee's elegant and book-filled flat, located at an address formerly shared by Karloff. There Christopher, who had worked with him, reassured Elly that Mr. Karloff was really a charming man and not the least bit like the on-screen Frankenstein monster that had frightened her as a little girl.

Joined by the Ackermans we met Christopher's Danish wife Gitte, a former high-fashion model with whom Elly formed an instant rapport. Without any words being spoken I already knew in my heart of hearts that they would end up going shopping together.

Then the Ackermans left and Elly and I took off for Camden Hill. Here the Karloff residence proved equally pleasant, and Elly relaxed, though I noticed she never turned her back on Boris. He and Evie gave us a tour and we were both impressed by what she had done to their kitchen. The walls were uniquely papered by a montage of covers from the *New Yorker*. The mental image of such a decorating scheme doesn't do justice to the reality; somehow the variations in style and color blended instead of clashing. So did we and the Karloffs, joined later in the evening by another couple.

The next morning I taped for television, then repaired with Elly to the Dorchester Hotel, where Paramount had a cocktail party for me. By this time the penicillin was working so I didn't drink. The members of the press who attended were working too, but this didn't stop them from drinking. Elly and I met Milton Subotsky, director Freddy Francis, Paramount officials and other riffraff. There were countless (to say nothing of pointless) interviews. In the end even Elly slogged through one for *Woman's Own.*

The following day we moved to the Europa Hotel, ominously close to Oxford Street and other shopping areas beyond. Then we began tourist activities, interspersed with more socializing at various private clubs. One standout Sunday Ronald Kirkbride and his wife took us to the country, and the next morning a limo took us to Shepperton Studios, where we lunched after watching Freddy Francis helm a scene for *The Psychopath.*

The scene that morning was one I had indicated as taking place at the bottom of a staircase leading to the upper floor of a house. But everything they actually shot now took place at the top of a staircase which descended to the cellar. What I wrote up they put down. And when I took director Francis aside and questioned him about the change he pointed out that building a set with a stairway was expensive. Shooting from a high angle into the re-dressed recess beneath a soundstage trapdoor saved money.

In other words, I was right back on *The Couch* with *The Night Walker.* A low-budget film always operates on the same principle, that is to say, no principle whatsoever except saving a buck, even if it means losing the potential of the picture.

Despite this I later consented to meet with Gordon Molson, Milton Subotsky and partner Max Rosenberg about doing a second and seemingly more promising script, this to be an adaption if H. F. Heard's *A Taste for Honey*. After a prolonged consideration of such criminal activities our subsequent visit to Madame Tussaud's was something of a disappointment.

The same does not apply to our visit to the Shepherd's Bush station of Scotland Yard, where Chief Inspector of Detectives De Rosa invited me to discuss the serial murders of prostitutes by a killer whom the press dubbed "Jack the Stripper."* Two hundred operatives were on the case, but the homicides remained unsolved. Inspector De Rosa sighed as he indicated the widely scattered murder sites on a huge wall map. "Wheels," he said. "That's the problem. Today killers move around at will and can pop up anywhere. Think of what might have happened if your friend Jack the Ripper had wheels at his disposal."

On and off, Elly and I had wheels during our final week in London. Some of them were affixed to convenient cabs and others to the vehicles of newfound friends, but they rolled all over London. We visited everyone, from publishers to readers, including such fans as Ella Parker and clever cartoonist Arthur (Atom) Thomson. We dined and visited with Christopher and Gitte, and the worst of my fears were realized—Gitte and Elly went shopping.

Eventually it was time to pack for Ireland. All during the flight I sat shivering in anticipation of what would happen when Elly encountered Irish linens. But upon arrival in Belfast our host, Walt Willis, arranged that our first encounter was with typical Irish food; he took us to a Chinese restaurant.

Walt, Madeleine and their offspring lived in Donaghadee,† on the edge of the Irish Sea. The weather was cold and wet during our stay, but we thrived in the warmth of their hospitality, and that

---

*So christened because of his habit of strangling his victims with their stockings or pantyhose and dumping their nude bodies at various locales on the outskirts of London.

†Probably the Gaelic spelling of "chow mein".

of fellow writers Bob Shaw, James White, John Berry. They made our stay a memorable one, but their spouses eagerly guided Elly to the linen shops.

While ships and cargo planes were still packing Elly's purchases we flew to Chicago. We visited with my aunt Gertrude and cousin Myrtle on the North Side, Aunt Lil and cousin Bea on the South Side, and some of Elly's friends in the area in between. She met my old friends in Milwaukee during the days that followed. The past paraded before her at dinner parties and gatherings at private homes; half the people previously mentioned in these pages showed up.

It was quite a social whirl, and just about the only one we didn't meet was the dude who invaded our hotel room as we slept and glommed on to Elly's purse. She awoke, thinking I had gotten up in the dark, but turned to see me sound asleep beside her. A prod, accompanied by a passing reference to robbery, brought me to my feet. Upon realizing the situation my first reaction was to do the sensible thing and hide under the bed, but hotel beds aren't built that way except in French farces, so I had no choice. Spotting the shadowy figure, I stupidly ran after him as he bolted for the unbolted bathroom window, slid out, and dashed across the flat level of the rooftop beyond. In his flight he dropped the empty purse on the windowsill. Oddly enough the purse had been empty when he picked it up; Elly had stowed its contents in another bag before retiring and neglected to put this one away.

After a cordial three A.M. visit with the police and the house detective we moved to another room which didn't afford a view of a flat roof every time we went to the bathroom.

Now that she'd met everyone from Gus Marx and family to my favorite bartender and even my osteopath, it was only fitting that Elly also confront the Milwaukee Fictioneers. We were driven to the Wisconsin Regional Writers' Conference at Elkhart Lake, and when I finally took pity on the audience and stopped talking she was introduced to some of my longtime *compadres*.

After I got a treatment from Dr. Pearl Thompson, my former osteopath,* we packed and took off, arriving home before the linens did.

This gave me a chance to rest up and sober up. The past month had been a heady and intoxicating experience, but the party was over; Cinderella had had her ball and turned into a pumpkin, or whichever way the story goes. It was time to remind myself that being newsworthy abroad didn't prevent one from being news-unworthy at home. In Los Angeles most writers were a dime a dozen (one of the few rates which has not been affected by inflation) and commanded no more attention than that accorded local authors in Milwaukee years ago. I wasn't any exception; to the best of my knowledge, here in town I had only three fans. One of them was dead, but the other two hadn't noticed.

It was time to begin work on the second project proposed by Messrs. Rosenberg and Subotsky, the Rosencrantz and Guildenstern of Amicus Films.

After learning how fondly Christopher Lee regarded Karloff and confirming Boris's reciprocal respect, I altered the excellent Heard novel only where necessary to establish Christopher and Boris in the leading roles. Boris could accordingly ignore infirmity by playing much of his part as a supposed invalid and end up as the villainous monster we always admired. Christopher would delight both color enthusiasts and fish lovers as the reddest of herrings.

Needless to say, it didn't turn out that way. In real life Cinderella gets nothing from her glass slippers except a visit to the podiatrist, and Prince Charming doesn't turn out to be a foot fetishist.

Once the completed screenplay arrived in England, the problem of matching stellar schedules—and salaries—put the roles into other hands and the script itself into the hands of its director. As

---

*You thought I was kidding?

is often the case he decided to improve it, with the aid of a writer named Anthony Marriott, but apparently without the knowledge of Rosenberg and Subotsky, who left prior to production. Both of them had liked my original version, but by the time they returned the screenplay had been improved past recognition and the shoot was already beginning.

Sometime during 1966 the film was released under a new title, *The Deadly Bees*. As such it soon buzzed off into critical oblivion, unwept, unhonored, and unstung.

THIRTY-NINE

Elly was a fine cook and a gracious hostess, even when her only guest was her own husband; we dined by candlelight and I don't believe there was such a thing as a paper napkin in the house. Over the next decade her hospitality extended to visiting friends or relatives; we entertained fifty or more at a party for August Derleth.

We had particular reason to remember an evening when just three other couples were present. Elmira, our trusted ally on such occasions, served us coffee and after-dinner drinks in the living room, then retired to the kitchen.

Hearing a slight sound from that direction, Elly sent me there. I found Elmira lying on the floor; Bill McGivern brushed me aside to administer CPR, but she had died instantly of an embolism. It was a tragedy we deeply mourn to this day.

Buster Keaton was the next to go, a victim of cancer. And in the east my aunt Gertrude went into a nursing home, a sad end to a long lifetime of work and an all-too-short period of retirement. It was a bad beginning to an inauspicious year.

For a brief while I had sporadic contact with an actor whose film career as leading man began in the silent era. Richard Arlen had come a long way since *Wings,* but he was no longer flying high. A schoolmate of Gelman's and mine was supposedly at work writing Arlen's biography; it was perhaps just as well that the actor died before discovering no manuscript existed. Arlen's recollections of stardom were tinged with bitterness, for though he survived the coming of sound and remained on screen until the sixties, his career never brought adequate recognition or recompense. He learned, the hard way, that putting your name up there in lights doesn't mean a thing after the bulbs burn out.

Of course for every rule there are exceptions. Arlen had received billing as an actor in 1925, the same year that another young man made his modest directorial debut. Now, after the passage of more than forty years, Arlen was forgotten, but his contemporary, the director, was flamboyantly famous.

Word came down from on high, in the form of a contract, that Alfred Hitchcock wanted to collaborate with me on a film project. More specifically, the game plan called for meeting with him and discussing various possibilities until we reached mutual agreement on an idea. I was then to write a story treatment; once this too was discussed and any changes were agreed upon, I would then prepare the screenplay.

Although Mr. Hitchcock never allowed himself any share of the writing credits it was common knowledge that he usually contributed substantially to the scripts of his films, so I had no qualms about this aspect. In truth I was so pleased and flattered by his personal invitation that I gave little thought to the sordid details of our working agreement.

At the appointed time I presented myself for a gourmet luncheon accompanied by wines of appropriate bouquet and vintage. While (with my knowledge and permission) a tape recorder functioned faultlessly between our feet underneath the table, Mr. Hitchcock and I discussed murder in general and speculated as to the come-what-mayhem of a possible film premise. The only conclusion arrived at was that we must shortly meet again and resume our deliberations.

Once I returned home I called Gordon and asked him to ease me out of this commitment. Much as I enjoyed the gourmet meal and the prospect of even gorier ones in the future, it finally was beginning to dawn on me that there is no such thing as a free lunch. According to the fine print of the contract, I would not be paid until Hitchcock and I were in mutual agreement on an acceptable story treatment. Since there was no time limit stipulated, these luncheon sessions could go on for six months, or until Hitch had used up all the salami in the fridge. Meanwhile I'd lack any income, since the Writers Guild forbade working on more than one contract assignment at a time. Mr. Hitchcock was in a position to proceed at his leisure, but this was a luxury I just couldn't afford. One can only conjecture what we might have eventually come up with had things been otherwise. Opportunity knocked, but I couldn't come to the door.*

A question I'm frequently asked is, "What was Alfred Hitchcock really like?" I can't answer that, but I know what he *wasn't* like. Alfred Hitchcock was not the kind of person anyone would call "Al."

So much has been written about him by cineasts, his genius not only minutely dissected but also sliced and diced, that little remains to be shred. First identified by his fleeting trademark appearances in each of his films, his name further established in the titles of numerous anthologies and a monthly magazine, Hitch became a great media personality on the television screen. As such, he also became one of the great media victims, imprisoned within

---

*Later, at Molson's behest, I did come up with a suggestion of a story based on the so-called "Cleveland Torso" serial murders. Hitchcock, apparently miffed at my rebuff, chose instead to make *Marnie, Torn Curtain* and *Topaz*. He'd have been better off in Cleveland.

his own on-screen image. It is my firm conviction that Alfred Hitchcock spent most of his final years impersonating himself.

The year rolled along. Since my fiction agent had begun editing *Show* magazine, I responded to his request with a series of articles on various facets of films and wrote few stories as a result.

I also responded to a request from a new television series, "Star Trek." Producer Gene Roddenberry, star William Shatner and story editor Dorothy Fontana were already known to me; Dorothy had started in the business as secretary to Sam Peeples some years before. As a matter of fact, Sam had written a second pilot script for "Star Trek," though he never contributed any episodes to the series.

In its initial season I came up with two, and then did a third. "What Are Little Girls Made Of?" and "Catspaw" were light-weight, tongue-in-space efforts. "Wolf in the Fold" was the result of Dorothy Fontana's suggestion that I launch my old friend Jack the Ripper into orbit. She provided considerable assistance in the final draft.*

At the time neither I nor my fellow-Treknicians had any inkling that the show would become an enduring favorite. As a matter of record it didn't survive to the end of its third season, during which the episodes deteriorated to a point where I lost interest in coming up with any further contributions.

It was really the efforts of fan Bjo Trimble which sparked the revival of "Star Trek" after a premature cancellation decision and its subsequent popularity in reruns. Today one can posit the series' appeal more easily against the context of the times. In an era of

---

*Writing these lines, I suddenly realize that in the hundreds of thousands of words I've read about "Star Trek" since it became a cult phenomenon, I seldom saw a scriptwriter give credit to Dorothy or another member of the staff, though I know that in some instances the writers taking the bows lent little more than their names to the shooting script.

social conflict at home and the Vietnam War abroad, young viewers escaped into outer space. Captain Kirk's crew was the surrogate for a united family, and one could rest assured that Lieutenant Calley would never be beamed aboard the *Enterprise*.

Our actual moon landing in '69 lent a touch of added credibility to the theme of extraterrene exploration, and the years that followed only heightened the need for role models and value judgments in an increasingly spaced-out generation. If anything, that need has intensified over the twenty years which followed.

Meanwhile, back in 1966, plans were under way to change its enumeration to 1967. Eleanor Keaton and Buster's sister Louise were our guests when we quietly ushered in the new year.

It was a time of changes. Daughter Sally resided in her own apartment and had become executive secretary for an electronics firm, where she'd met—and, in April, married her Jim, an engineer and consultant in the company.

My own relationship remained bigamous; espoused to Elly, I was still wedded to my work. But now the nature of that work was undergoing a change.

Motion pictures were no longer the product of the old-time studio system, and had become subject to outsiders' corporate control. Television's dependence on individual advertisers bankrolling their programs had given way to a more profitable system of selling spots to multiple sponsors; as a result the networks made creative decisions. In print the once-popular magazines were going out of print at a steady pace as paperback book publication boomed. A relaxation of censorship bans had created a market for soft-cover hard-core. Hardcover hard-core held its own, along with the so-called men's magazines and their feminine counterparts. Genre fiction was gradually being affected, though at a slower pace. If anything there was more demand than ever for anthology reprint rights to my short-story output, and I could always write and sell a conventional piece like "Underground."* But the tendency to go with the flow was unmistakable. When Harlan Ellison established the theme of his original-story anthology, *Dangerous Visions,* the Jack the Ripper yarn I wrote for it wasn't exactly the sort of thing I'd done for *Weird Tales.*

By a strange quirk some of those old *Weird Tales* stories were undergoing resurrection by Rosenberg and Subotsky, Amicus Films' answer to Burke and Hare. I was also involved in this grave robbery, adapting four of my published stories to an anthology film for which Milton Subotsky had synopsized a wraparound opening and close.

It seemed at the time that using work already proven popular in print might help make the resultant script more foolproof, or at least director-proof. My surmise proved only half correct. Two of the stories remained substantially unchanged and were, I thought, fairly effective. The opening and closing items had been "improved" by the kind of cosmetic touches you might expect after turning a plastic surgeon loose on the *Mona Lisa.*

Not to be outdone, someone well acquainted with the arcane and recondite reached back to the turn of the century and ripped off Octave Mirbeau's title, *Torture Garden.* I still blush to think of the misappropriation and the misnomer; there is no garden anywhere in the film and the only torture is that inflicted upon the audience as a result of the changes.

Joan Crawford was gradually winding down her extended goodwill tours for Pepsi Cola (a role assumed during her late husband's control of the firm) and California visits ceased, although we remained in touch. The Karloffs came to town occasionally, usually staying with old friends like Ralph Edwards.

---

*Though the editors, if only to remind me who was really in charge here, immediately altered the title to "The Living Dead." Somebody ought to come up with disposable titles; like diapers, they are changed so frequently.

Among the newer faces staring at us across the living room from time to time were Mr. and Mrs. Max Lamb, biographer Charles Higham and Mr. and Mrs. Rouben Mamoulian. I was, of course, highly impressed by the wit and intelligence of the man who had directed *R.U.R.,** works by Eugene O'Neill, *Porgy and Bess* and *Oklahoma!* in the theater, plus his award-winning films. It was quite an experience for us to be seated beside him during a screening of the 1932 *Dr. Jekyll and Mr. Hyde* while he explained what the censors had done to the black cat and attempted to do with Fredric March and Miriam Hopkins. Today regarded mainly as an innovator during the first decade of sound films, Mamoulian awaits the recognition he deserves, along with King Vidor and other true *auteur*-directors. He was also a charming and delightful private person.

Throughout this period my convention attendance continued. While functioning as toastmaster at the World Science Fiction Convention in St. Louis and guest of honor in Dallas I was accompanied by Elly. However, I attended several gatherings unchaperoned and on successive years made the acquaintance of two young ladies—budding writer Chelsea Quinn Yarbro and flowering editor Judy Lynn Benjamin. Both eventually became our dear friends. Ms. Yarbro went on to become a leading talent in the field and Judy Lynn (who changed her last name to del Rey when she married Lester a few years later) had an outstanding editorial career.

While I always did have an eye for the ladies, I found the vision in the right one increasingly impaired as the year drew to a close. As a result I went in for cataract surgery and came out with a contact lens. For the first time in forty years I was able to get around without wearing glasses.

By the time summer started I managed to get around as far

---

*Look it up, dummy!

as London once again, and promptly lost my right lens when standing in a queue for tickets to *The Four Musketeers*. While I'm looking for the damned thing I might as well explain the reason for my return to England.

Now that the Hitchcock show jogged along only in reruns, Joan Harrison was about to produce *Journey to the Unknown,* a joint venture of Hammer Films and Twentieth Century-Fox. In a moment of folly and madness she asked me to join the team in London and do a couple of scripts for the new anthology series.

At my request I was put up at the Dorchester, not in the Oliver Messel suite but on the same floor. Ms. Harrison's headquarters were on Grosvenor Square, catercorner from the American Embassy; she and her husband, celebrated suspense writer Eric Ambler, maintained residence in a nearby mews.

Working space was assigned me at Hammer House on Wardour Street. Hammer had slackened feature production on its horror film output and reduced its working staff, appropriately enough, to a skeleton crew. I shared the entire fifth floor with the single occupant of another office, Pamela Anderson. Now Pamela Klacar, resident of Australia and a writer/editor, she still recalls how we nattered about cinema during coffee breaks, very much the way I had with C. L. Moore back at Warner Bros.

The first script I turned out was an adaptation of my own story, *The Indian Spirit Guide*. It met with favor and they asked for another story of mine, subject to approval by Twentieth Century-Fox's resident geniuses back home on Pico Boulevard. Word was not forthcoming; apparently some of the geniuses were doing a long lunch. Since I was on salary, it was suggested I adapt *Girl of My Dreams,* a story by friend Dick Matheson which they already owned.

When not busy at the typewriter I had alternate activities to choose from. The devil finds work for idle hands, but I employed idle feet in exploring London. Longtime fan and friend Alan Dodd conducted me via the Thames as far as Greenwich, where I checked my watch. We also visited Hampton Court, which gave me an opportunity to see how royalty used to live in the days before high taxes. There I actually got lost in its famous maze and couldn't reach the exit. Hours passed, search parties were organized, and finally somebody sent in a Saint Bernard with brandy. I was deeply grateful, even though I am not a Catholic. Eventually the brandy was exhausted and so was I. Three days later I emerged, and swore a mighty oath never to enter a maze again without leaving a trail of bread crumbs. This would make it easier for a Saint Bernard to follow.

The head of Hammer Films, Sir James Carreras, invited me to a party given in his home to celebrate the release of *The Devil Rides Out*. There I met a number of British film personalities along with Dennis Wheatley, author of the novel from which the picture was adapted. Its star was Christopher Lee, and we picked up where we'd left off three years earlier.

Later I visited with Christopher and Gitte, had dinner at John Brunner's home and spent a memorable afternoon in the mews residence with Eric Ambler, discussing the structure of the suspense novel.

Some of my evenings were spent at the National Film Theatre, but I also scouted the legitimate playhouses to select suitable entertainment for Elly, who joined me by prearrangement during the last three weeks of my stay.

The first thing she did was win over, then take over, the entire dining-facilities staff of the Dorchester, which resulted in my receiving superlative service and Elly walking off with the chef's secret recipe for spaghetti sauce. After that she was free to go shopping with Gitte Lee again. Christopher took us to a restaurant run by a Chinese hippie where Guinness Stout was served in individual half-gallon bottles.

Now that there was nothing more for me to do except make minor revisions on the second teleplay, Elly and I were able to supplement regular sightseeing with almost nightly theater attendance. In addition we went to Covent Garden for ballet and Albert Hall for concerts, but avoided opera.*

Shortly before we left for home, the Karloffs invited Elly and me to spend the day with them at their summer cottage near Liphook. They picked us up at the station and conducted a guided tour of the quaint little English village, with Boris pointing out "ye olde" this and "ye olde" that. "And look," he exclaimed. "There's ye olde Woolworth's!"

The remark was typical, as was his warmth and lack of pretension, but for some odd reason Elly was only able to address him as "Mr. Karloff." Perhaps it was a carryover from childhood trauma after seeing the monster on screen. "Call me Boris!" he insisted, but fond of him as she was, to her they remained "Mr. Karloff and Evie."

While Mr. Karloff and I were occupied downstairs, Evie took Elly upstairs for a thorough examination of the premises. Arthritic problems and a touch of acrophobia kept Boris grounded. Following luncheon he and I repaired to the garden, which was bordered by a recently constructed wall. Boris had watched the work in progress and admired the handicraft of the artisan. "Now that's a real contribution," he said. "Long after you and I are dead and forgotten, that wall will still be there."

Later, en route back to the station, the subject of mortality was touched upon again. Driving into town Boris drew our attention to a house as we passed by. "Something rather odd happened there," he told us.

"Odd?" I said.

Boris shrugged. "Let's see what you make of it."

According to his story the Karloffs were acquainted with friends who knew the woman occupying the house in question. One afternoon they came to call on her and were met at the door

---

*I like opera, but not the parts with the singing in them.

by a maid, who invited them into the parlor until the lady of the house came downstairs.

The maid left and the couple sat waiting. Perhaps five minutes passed before their hostess descended the hall staircase and entered the room. Halting there, she stared at them, surprised. "How did you get in here?" she asked.

"The maid let us in."

"But I don't have a maid."

"Then who was that young lady?"

"What young lady? I'm living here alone."

At least that's what she thought at the time. But her visitors had seen, heard, and been admitted to the house by someone else whose appearance both agreed upon.

Only later did they and their hostess discover that a girl answering to her description had met death in this dwelling.

"A ghost?" I said.

Boris smiled. "All I can tell you is that since then others have encountered the young lady, sometimes at night and sometimes in broad daylight."

"You've never seen her?"

His smile broadened. "I'm not anxious to do so."*

We left Liphook, then London, then flew home to climb a mountain of mail.

Only a few months later we were to see the Karloffs again, this time for dinner at our home. The other guests were the Ackermans, the Peepleses and—by last-minute invitation—Fritz

---

*As for me, I have never seen a ghost, though years ago author Charles Higham entertained Elly and me in a home once belonging to playwright Vicki Baum. Her apparition was apparently still in residence, and we definitely felt an inexplicable chill which emanated from upper rooms which should have been sweltering in summer heat, though we heard none of the noises which plagued Charles frequently. He soon sought quieter quarters.

Lang and Lily. Much to our surprise, Fritz and Boris had never met and were eager to do so.

Confronting one another for the first time in our living room, Boris beamed and Fritz thrust out his hand. "We are the last of the dinosaurs!" he proclaimed.

During the course of the evening the two remaining reptiles recapitulated cinematic history from the Late Triassic to the end of the Cretaceous Period, with frequent digressions into the Jurassic and the idiosyncrasies of Darryl F. Zanuck.

Aside from a brief detour into politics, where Fritz and Sam collided left and right, the evening sped by all too swiftly. Boris and Evie were soon to depart for Mexico, where, despite his now-severe infirmities, he was under contract for four films. "And I'm going to make them," he told us. "When it comes to work, I have no shame."

Boris kept his word, did his work, and went home to England where he died at the beginning of the second month of the new year. As best I know, his ghost has never returned, nor would it need to. A part of Karloff still remains very much alive today, more than twenty years after his passing, and continues to exist on screen. Those who have seen him there will not forget the monster. Those who were privileged to know him will not forget the man.

FORTY

Within months we had another visitor, this time a house guest in the six-foot-four form of Christopher Lee.

Christopher, who actively disliked flying following his wartime service as an officer in the RAF, has been traveling by air all over the world ever since. He came to us by way of Hong Kong, after doing a film role there, and spent the next ten days or so here. Aside from the obligatory studio rounds he was free to socialize or indulge in his favorite pursuit, *i.e.*, chasing after golf balls. During the course of his career he'd exercised his expertise on famous courses throughout the world, and now had an opportunity to test the local links.

This was actually Christopher's second trip to Los Angeles, but the first visit had brought him no nearer to a golf course than the back lot of Universal Studios. There, in 1963, the "Alfred Hitchcock Hour" starred him in "The Sign of Satan," adapted from "Return from the Sabbath," a short story by somebody named Robert Bloch.

We didn't know one another then; as a matter of fact I was working elsewhere and hadn't even been informed of his casting.

When not before the camera Christopher spent a miserable stay across the street in a motel infested by termites and supporting actors.

This time around we were able to introduce him to people. Cecil Howard dined us at the Bel Air Country Club overlooking their greens and secured an opportunity for Christopher to golf, which suited him to a tee. Others, like Dan Duryea, extended similar invitations and helped make his stay pleasant.

He proved to be an interesting guest, full of amusing anecdotes about British film people and surprisingly well informed about us colonials. His favorite American performer was W. C. Fields, whom he imitated better than Bradbury did, and he was well versed in the artistry of Laurel and Hardy. He'd worked twice with Boris and shared our personal regard for him; he also shared both regard and his birthday with Vincent Price. A multilinguist with a fine singing voice, Christopher could have enjoyed a career in music as well as films; every morning he sang Wagner in the shower.

As a versatile professional, Christopher chafed at the bit identifying him as a star of horror films. Despite his success in the Dracula role and his portrayal of other illegal aliens in pictures pounded out by Hammer, he rightly considered himself capable of "straight" performances. It was his hope that he'd find wider opportunity to demonstrate this in American films, and declared his intention to return.

Speaking of returns, I was beginning to consider filling out income tax forms. Having squandered most of my ill-gotten gains on such luxuries as food and clothing, there was a problem concerning upcoming payments to the Feds. At the moment Gordon Molson informed me that present demands for my services were nugatory.

Promptly on cue my New York literary agent, Harry Altshuler, called with an offer to novelize a screenplay. Having done that once before, with *The Couch*, I had no particular desire to repeat the experience, but Harry assured me the circumstances were different. What I was to adapt was more a lengthy, in-depth story treatment by mainstream novelists Joan Didion and John Gregory Dunne. Husband and wife, they were collaborating on a film to be produced by Collier Young. It was he who had approached publishers offering to supply them with a novel version for paperback release.

Didion and Dunne had already begun to gain recognition. Their proposed film dealt with the then relatively new and definitely daring procedure of heart transplants. In addition, it was to be edited by Larry Shaw, a science fiction fan who had gone straight, and a friend as well as a colleague. These considerations helped make the project more interesting to me. The flat fee offered for writing the book was less attractive, but with so many of the elements already detailed and in place, I could undoubtedly move ahead without confronting major problems. The parsimonious payment was for paperback publication only; Altshuler had already been promised there would be no hardcover edition. The bottom line was that I needed the money, immediately if not sooner.

To that end I repaired one morning to the Polo Lounge of the Beverly Hills Hotel and seated myself at a table overlooking the cleavage. Joining me were a publisher's representative and Collier Young. "Collie," as he was so aptly nicknamed, wore a tattersall vest and a cordial smile, both of which pleasantly impressed me during our breakfast. By the time I cut into my eggs Benedict we'd already cut a deal.

Had I known what I was letting myself in for I would have ordered eggs Benedict Arnold.

Writing the novel was no problem, once I learned the publishers wanted no major changes or additions to the very serviceable story line and characterization provided to me. Although Collier Young had spoken about arranging a meeting with Ms. Didion and Mr. Dunne, it never occurred, nor did I convene again with the producer. Sirens shrieking, the publishers cornered my manuscript in hot pursuit. What they collared was titled *The Todd Dossier* and adapted "by Robert Bloch from the story by Joan Didion and John Gregory Dunne." Such credit to the original source is usually subordinated in most screenplay novelizations, but in this instance I felt theirs to be a major contribution which deserved notice. There the matter, and I, rested.

The Hollywood Reporter had duly noted my deal to write the novel and I awaited news of its speedy release in paperback. Instead I got a speedy phone call from none other than Collier Young. With deep embarrassment and abject apology he informed me that the publishers had insisted on crediting authorship of the book to him. He had protested their decision, but to no avail, and just wanted to let me know how sorry he was. Before I could recover from my initial shock and formulate a few questions, he hurried on. His closing line, prior to hastily terminating the conversation, was something I'd heard and read about before, but only as a gag. "We've got to get together for lunch sometime."

I couldn't believe my ears, but while they still echoed I hastened to consult a copy of the brief book contract. Sure enough, nowhere in the not-so-fine print was it written in stone that my name must be used as author of *The Todd Dossier*. I'd just automatically assumed that if I wrote the book I'd be identified as the writer.

Harry Altshuler had been a literary agent for twenty-five years and never run into anything like this before. When I called to tell him, he was stunned, but he gave as good as he got. Altshuler had just learned that the paperback outfit's publishing subsidiary was bringing out the book in a hardcover edition. This too was a move not expressly forbidden by the contract; it seemed an unnecessary precaution at the time because the publisher's representative had given his word that the novel would only appear in paperback.

My agent and I weren't the only ones reacting to these

developments. Larry Shaw, who had striven for years to gain an editorial post with a major publishing firm, was so disgusted that he promptly left the job. And after vainly trying to reach those responsible, Harry Altshuler himself closed up his agency. "When they start lying while looking you straight in the eye, it's a sure sign the business has changed, and I want no part of it anymore," he told me.

I was beginning to get the message, but leaving my profession seemed impractical. The only other job I could get at my age was as a school-crossing guard. And even for that I'd probably have had trouble with the civil service application form.

Thus did Collier Young become the author of what *Publishers Weekly* called a "gripping" first novel. "Griping" would probably be a better description of its effect on me, particularly when I later learned it had been published in a British hardcover edition and a German translation as well.

Harry Altshuler was right; the business had changed. But sooner or later, everything changes. Can you see George Washington ordering a Big Mac? Would Abraham Lincoln eat a pizza?

I got new representation with the Scott Meredith Literary Agency, but made no immediate move to supply them with anything to agent. I needed a while to regain enthusiasm for another venture into semi-literature. My feelings of depression continued to deepen for a time. Friends and associates alike were beginning to depart in ever-increasing numbers. Tony Boucher, Charles Beaumont, Karloff and Ferde Grofe were already gone. Soon Doc Smith, August Derleth, John Campbell and Joan Crawford would follow.

I was, of course, not the only one to experience a sense of loss. All of these people had a devoted following in their own field, and their passings were commemorated in a variety of ways.

Tony Boucher, who had made a reputation as an editor and writer of fantasy and science fiction, was equally well known for similar outstanding activities in the mystery field. It was his friends, fans and colleagues in this genre who joined forces to create a mystery aficionados' convention bearing his name. Affectionately termed the "Bouchercons," these annual affairs have endured and flourished.

As guest of honor at the very first Bouchercon I had the opportunity to voice my appreciation for Tony, and this, in some small measure, assuaged my personal sense of loss, something I'd not been able to do when Stanley Weinbaum, H. P. Lovecraft, Henry Kuttner and others left gaps in our ranks.

Another slight elevation in spirits accompanied a 2,400-foot elevation in body as Forrest J Ackerman and I climbed the interminable stone steps to the Monument of Christ the Redeemer overlooking the city of Rio De Janeiro. Atop Corcovado Mountain the ninety-nine-foot-high statue on its thirty-foot base towered above us as we surveyed the city, standing in the shadow of one fifteen-foot hand.

The trip to Rio was part of an expensive circus sponsored by the Brazilian government; a ten-day film festival was the main attraction, the big show under the big top. A gathering of twenty-odd science fiction writers had been added as a sort of sideshow. My fellow freaks (some accompanied by their spouses) included Robert A. Heinlein, Frederick Pohl, Philip José Farmer, Harlan Ellison, Alfred Bester, Robert Silverberg, Arthur C. Clarke, and others of that ilk. Lurking in the shadows were directors noted for their fantasy or science fiction efforts: Fritz Lang, George Pal, Roger Corman, Roman Polanski and Alberto Cavalcanti.

Josef von Sternberg consorted only with the star performers, as befitted a director of his standing. But the only time I encountered him, he was sitting down.

Fritz Lang and I were chauffeured to the newly built modern-art museum where a gala reception was hosted under the auspices of the American Embassy. The decor of the multilevel structure was spectacular, but lacking one element of furnishing—there were no chairs. Hundreds of guests milled around, ice in glasses tinkling over a continuous babble of conversation. I'd had a long day of sightseeing and my feet hurt.

Fritz surveyed the scene, a monocle firmly affixed to one bad eye. How he did it I still don't know, but as he scanned the crowd in that huge hall he found a solitary figure sitting at the far end in a single straight-back chair. "Come," he said.

We made our way through the mob scene and approached the seated figure. It was Josef von Sternberg, who on this particular occasion was sporting a white goatee.

Fritz nodded to him. "Hello, Santa Claus," he said. "My friend here is tired. Get up and give him your seat."

Von Sternberg obeyed without a murmur, I sat down and eased my arches, and Fritz rewarded himself with a martini from the tray of a passing waitress. Even now I find myself wondering at the vagaries of Fritz's vision. He had carefully memorized the route from his hotel to the restaurant chosen for nightly dining, and led me along the crowded Copacabana, dodging the VWs parked at random in the middle of the walk and the VWs which lunged at random through the cross streets. The traffic in Rio was democratic, dealing death to drivers, passengers and pedestrians alike as horns screeched, brakes squealed and mellow voices blended in a chorus of Portuguese obscenities.

But the trip was worth the risk. On the second floor of the continental restaurant we took our meal at a table loaded with *haute cuisine* and flanked by Lotte Eisner, Henri Langlois and a changing cross section of performers and film functionaries from all over the world. The conversation was multilingual, predominantly in German, French and English with occasional interjections in Italian. This was indeed a cosmopolitan crowd; after the meal they belched in four languages.

But my fellow diners had one thing in common—their love

of films. Fritz had made them. Henri Langlois collected them.*
Lotte Eisner chronicled their history. Among the three, they represented an entire era of cinema, augmented by the presence of
actors and actresses who had aided in its creation.

I enjoyed such sessions but much of the stay was spent in the
company of my fellow writers, as passengers in those lunging VWs.
Days were divided between talks, lectures and seminars which I
attended both as a member of the audience and, at times, a
participant. Nights were given over to cocktail parties, dinners and
receptions at various national embassies.

Brazil seemed to have its share of every political and ethnic
category on the face of the earth. But mostly Rio itself had people.
Wall-to-wall people, mountain-to-Sugar-Loaf people, thronging
the walks, jamming the traffic, regally housed in *fazendas* or miser-
ably massed in *fazelas* overlooking the city, crowding the
Copacabana beach.

It was in an effort to avoid such crowding that Arthur Clarke
and I rose early one Sunday morning to enjoy a solitary stroll along
the sands across from our hotel. He snapped a photo of me with
his new camera and sent it to Elly as evidence of the monsters he
had discovered on Brazilian shores.

I discovered a monster of my own. Returning from some late
Saturday-night soirée† with the Pohls, I emerged from the cab
before the entrance to our hotel. At that moment, bathed in
tropical moonlight, a gigantic brown rat scurried across the
Copacabana walk from the beach behind us and disappeared amidst
the shadows of the doorway ahead. Somehow this creature in this
setting seemed to symbolize the contrasts and incongruities which
Rio afforded.

---

*The moving spirit of the Cinémathèque Française, he rescued countless films
from oblivion, was recognized worldwide for his efforts to preserve them, and was
known to regularly store the overflow in his bathtub.
†I don't know the Portuguese word for this, so am using its Polish equivalent.

Incidentally, upon entering the hotel I took an elevator directly to the ninth floor. But the rat had already beaten me to my room.

After this and other exotic experiences it was something of a let-down to return to more mundane matters at home.

Amicus Films, encouraged by the comparative success of *Torture Garden,* sent along another wraparound premise for an anthology offering, and I incorporated four of my stories into *The House That Dripped Blood.* Needless to say, again it was producer Max Rosenberg who gave the title a transfusion. When it came to actual on-screen blood, the film was positively anemic. But due credit must be given to the director for deftly turning the final segment into a send-up of my vampire story, "The Cloak," and thereby improving it a hundred percent.

For reasons unclear, I had been selected to serve as president of the Mystery Writers of America. My tenure of office bridged 1970 and 1971, and one of my duties was to appear at the annual Edgar Awards banquet. Here, in '71 as in previous years, the prestigious Edgar Allan Poe busts were bestowed for the year's best efforts in the field of who-did-its.*

What I won personally was the opportunity to meet with friends old and new, at the banquet and during my stay. Here were such notables as Fred Dannay, who was half of the famed but pseudonymous writing team of Ellery Queen. Here too was James M. Cain, whose *The Postman Always Rings Twice* and other works had so definitely influenced the style of my own first novel. Here was the prolific Michael Avallone, already well on his way to racking up over two hundred novels of his own. It was the last time I saw my former editor Clayton Rawson and his successor, Barbara Norville; the first time I encountered such colleagues as Lucy Freeman,

---

*A little grammar never hurt nobody.

354 / Robert Bloch

Robert L. Fish, Edward D. Hock, Hillary Waugh, and the two Lawrences, Treat and Block.

Awaiting me at home was an offer from William Castle. Bill had come up in the world as producer of the highly successful *Rosemary's Baby,* and was now about to launch a television anthology series called "Ghost Stories." He asked me to become its story editor, an invitation I promptly declined. The position traditionally involved eighteen-hour days, lost weekends and an endless chain of last-minute rewrites.

"Don't hurt Bill's feelings," Gordon Molson said. "Let's bow out of this graciously. I'll just ask him to double his salary offer."

It was a fine idea but it didn't work. Bill met the offer, which would make me one of the best-paid story editors in the business at that time. He also volunteered to throw in a guarantee of employment for the run of the show and six story-and-teleplay assignments per season in addition.

In the end I still had to decline his generous proposal, but he did extract a promise that I would at least do a couple of scripts for him upon completing work on a new novel.

The book, which I called *Nightworld,* appeared the following year. By that time I had already delivered Bill a teleplay, which he rechristened "House of Evil." He had also made several other changes.

The story I concocted was, in a sense, a modernized version of the Hansel and Gretel fairy tale. Its witch was a kindly grandmother whose cookies, properly prepared, took on the powers of voodoo dolls; harming them brought harm to the humans they were molded to resemble.

My dual-natured wicked witch and lovable old lady was written with someone like Bette Davis in mind, this being before she portrayed a harridan for Disney. But Bill Castle made a slight witch-switch. Employing some magic of his own, he transformed my grandmother into a grandfather and gave the role to Melvyn Douglas. There went my main character.

Another wave of the cigar Bill used as a magic wand, and my cookie-dolls no longer represented specific individuals. There went the supernatural logic of my story.

And after the show was aired, there went I, trying to distance myself as much as possible from the necessity of doing any further scripting. I didn't have to go too far, because the series itself soon gave up the ghost.

FORTY-ONE

Undaunted by my failure to get the proper poppets for the teleplay witch, I had my sculptor-scientist mold and animate miniature clay model figures for the next Amicus anthology film, *Asylum*. Needless to say, the clay models became small windup toys, but in many other respects *Asylum* stayed closer to my script as written.

I was onstage for its premiere in 1972, in the company of such then-notables as Wolfman Jack. Offstage I was able to help Elly maintain domesticity and hospitality with the frequent aid of Micaela Novarro.

We still managed to keep up our social schedule. At the monthly Pinkard salons I was more apt to make a solo appearance at local science fiction events along with Craig Miller, Bill Warren, Milt Stevens, Marty Cantor, Bruce Pelz and the secret master of all fandom, Bongo Wolf.*

Shortly after its publication, *Nightworld* was bought by

---

*No matter how many events and names I omit, this book grows exponentially. Problem is, I probably lived too long. The poet Thomas Chatterton died at seventeen. He could have written his autobiography in a pocket notebook.

MGM and I was called upon to write the screenplay. At my brief meeting with producer Saul David I asked for input and suggestions. He merely tapped the novel's dust jacket and said, "Just write it like the book."

David was obviously a man of few words, but these were ones I welcomed, words seldom heard in Hollywood. Overjoyed, I hastened home and went to work. The script posed few problems and I turned it over to Molson for submission without delay.

The delay came from the other end. Neither Molson nor I heard a word from MGM, and several months had passed before I asked my agent to politely inquire just what the hell was going on down there. After getting Saul David on the phone he asked why we hadn't received any response regarding the script. The producer replied to the effect that he'd been reluctant to voice his great disappointment. Molson reread my script and saw that it indeed followed the book as requested. Aside from that one short initial meeting I never saw Saul David again; he didn't ask me to make changes, work on a second draft or do a complete rewrite. But the project was not abandoned, because in the months ahead Molson learned indirectly of two further attempts by two different writers to "fix" the screenplay. Maybe it couldn't be fixed because it wasn't busted. Not too long thereafter MGM changed ownership, dozens of plans for pictures were abandoned, and Saul David retired.

The film was never made, though since then a half-dozen producers here and abroad have inquired regarding availability of motion picture rights. All of them were promptly referred to MGM, and nothing—promptly or otherwise—ever happened as a result. The story behind this entire episode remains shrouded in mystery. Did the producer really want the script to follow the book? Was his decision overruled by other members of the executive echelon? Had the other two writers brought in at separate times both discovered that changing the story resulted in losing its impact? Did they succeed only in coming up with a pale imitation of the real thing, like a small child geeking a canary? Or was the problem maybe just that I had written a nondescript script?

All I know is that a few years later Dwight V. Swain brought out his manual of instruction, *Film Scriptwriting*, and illustrated how to employ dialogue for exposition by using seven pages of my screenplay for *Nightworld*.

While I was busy writing lousy scripts the years had been slipping by. It had now been a quarter of a century since my appearance as guest of honor in Toronto. Time had apparently done its healing work, because now the survivors of the Science Fiction Convention of 1948 wanted to repeat the event. It was very much like San Francisco deciding to have another earthquake. And pushing masochism to its extreme, the Torontoans invited me to return as their guest of honor.

The 1973 World Science Fiction Convention proved somewhat different from its predecessor. This version attracted roughly ten times the number of attendees and I found it advisable to take Elly along for protection. I, in turn, protected her from the lecherous advances of Bob Tucker and Isaac Asimov.

This was her first meeting with a longtime fan named Kirby McCauley and my second meeting with longtime fantasy writer Carl Jacobi. Our friend Judy Lynn Benjamin now coedited and cohabited with her writer-husband Lester del Rey at Ballantine Books. It was Lester who graciously served as toastmaster at the banquet, and this time there was no David H. Keller, MD, to upstage us. Funny thing was, I sort of missed him.

Perhaps what I really missed was the youth, the vitality, the excitement and the sense of wonder which had been part of the luggage I'd carried with me to Toronto in 1948.

But it was still a time for joyful reunions and fond recollection, to say nothing of total exhaustion. In addition, Elly found an added attraction in the presence of several Canadian relatives whom we visited as the convention schedule allowed. The members of her family, who had spread out across Canada very much as the hordes of Genghis Khan swarmed over the Asian steppes, had tended to avoid me until this time. Based on the evidence of what I'd written, they formed a somewhat distorted picture of Elly's married life. Apparently they'd not come to visit because they thought we lived in a two-story house where I was confined to the attic. But after the first contact in Toronto, there was never any dearth of relatives; nieces and nephews appeared regularly to enrich the coffers of Disneyland and Universal Tours.

As the sun sank in the west our plane rose in the south and landed us in Milwaukee for another get-together with old friends; it was to be my last reunion with Herbie Williams, whose death was soon to breach our ranks.

Not too long thereafter Elly and I returned to Milwaukee again for my thirty-ninth high school class reunion. It was in many ways a strange occasion. To begin with, there had never been a reunion of my class in any of the thirty-eight preceding years. And this event wasn't even held at the high school itself, because it no longer existed as an institution of learning. Nearly forty years later our class of '34, cheated of its normal adolescence by the Depression, was still being cheated in late middle age. I gave a little talk in which I took great pains not to refer to a certain book and movie. What I said was deliberately confined to reminiscence and memories of the school days we shared together, with no mention at all of my own life since then.

Voluntarily suppressing one's natural egotism is about as easy as removing one's own appendix, but this time it paid off. When I reseated myself the former classmate at my right leaned over her dinner plate and asked, "What have you been doing since you got out of school?"

I promptly confided that upon graduating from a college of embalming I'd enjoyed a career as a cosmetologist in a mortuary. As a bonus, I offered a few tips about the art of makeup and how those little wire "smilers" placed at each corner of the mouth can enhance the look of enjoyment on the face of the deceased. The face of my former classmate could have used a couple of smilers as she turned away to glance down dubiously at her asparagus. I wonder if she ever found out I was putting her on. For me it was a treasured moment.

After we returned home it was time to go to work. Producer Doug Cramer out at Twentieth wanted to do a movie for television as an homage to the old-time horror films. Along with director Curtis Harrington, he favored an update of the Val Lewton classic *The Cat People*. After discussion we agreed that a totally straight-faced remake was probably a mistake.* Instead I suggested a blending of the elements of several well-remembered films, and came up with a story line which dealt with the Egyptian cat goddess, reincarnation and the first bypass operation ever performed on an artichoke heart. Abandoning this as possibly being offensive to vegetarian viewers, I retained the rest of the story in my teleplay, which was to be modified as a starring vehicle for Diahann Carroll.

By the time the script was completed and approved, Miss Carroll had fulfilled her contractual commitment with the network and I had to rewrite her role. When my revision was completed and approved in turn, Curtis Harrington cast and shot it, taking full advantage of his love affair with old films and friendship with their performers. It was he who suggested transforming an uninspired male villain into an exotic persona along the lines of Gale Sondergaard in *The Letter,* and it was he who got Gale Sondergaard to play the part. Other fine character actors helped to make the curse work in the plot and took the curse off the performance of our leads.

I'd really enjoyed incorporating in-jokes and Curtis had fun noodling out nostalgic touches, but before shooting started the script went through channels and somebody in production came up with a dreadful message.

---

*Years later somebody did such a remake, and it was.

My hour-and-a-half movie for television ran twelve minutes too long.

I couldn't believe it. In terms of dialogue, action and pagination, the script had seemed just about the right length. Of course I'd never taken a course in film production, let alone learned how to estimate on-screen time with scientific accuracy. Director Harrington, I presumed, also relied upon instinct in this matter, together with a competent film editor who helped to assemble the dailies into a rough cut and subsequent versions.

In any case, producer Doug Cramer asked me to pre-edit the film on paper and somehow trim its length by about one-sixth. This was not an easy request to fulfill. With a western, one could merely eliminate a certain amount of fist fights and chase sequences. In a cops-and-robbers epic, one would abridge gun battles and hot pursuits, plus maybe a few car crashes for good measure. It was possible to trim the talk in tragedies, prune the pawing in romances and shear off shtick in comedies. Unfortunately, in the old-fashioned horror film the length problem could not be circumvented by random circumcision.

The secret ingredient of such films, serious or send-ups, is still suspense. In order to achieve it properly a sustained buildup is required; only then do your shock cuts or story twists work as they should. In constructing sequences the pacing is all-important. Put in a seemingly leisurely bit of business here, which will result in an unexpected payoff later on in the scene; add a touch of humor there to throw the audience off guard before you sock it to them. It's also necessary to provide some sort of supernatural or pseudo-scientific inner logic that makes your story momentarily believable, and this too takes time to develop.

The only way I could manage to retain the required buildup for suspense purposes and maintain the equally important interior logic of the story was by delicate surgery. Since the scenes were not repetitious, none could be totally discarded; instead each one had to be gone over very carefully in order to eliminate a word, shorten a line, dispense with a diversion here, a piece of action there. Bit by bit I pared the script down, never subjecting it to a ruthless slicing and dicing but inevitably losing details which would lend a more subtle touch to its humor and its horrific content.

Curtis cooperated in directing the resultant version, which disguised many of my unavoidable alterations. The results exceeded my expectations and at the conclusion of the screening I sat back and heaved a sigh of relief. But before the lights came on in the small theater a querulous voice rose from the darkness behind me. It could only have issued from the mouth of a production staff member; the source was unmistakable. So was the message it conveyed.

"Jesus H. Christ! We're in big trouble—I just timed the show and it runs twelve minutes short!"

I don't know how long it took me to run from the theater to Doug Cramer's office, but then I had no production expert to time me. Upon arrival I found Doug awaiting me, and one look at his face told the story—the too-short story.

"Why didn't you tell me?" I said.

"Better that you see for yourself. At least it'll give you some idea of where additions might be made."

"Does Curtis have outtakes?"

"Maybe a few feet here and there. Nothing we could really use. You'll probably find it easier just to do new scenes from scratch."

"How long am I going to have for scratching?"

"We still have a stage reserved for postproduction during part of next week. Everything's tight, so all they can give us is Tuesday and Wednesday. Curtis thinks he can manage twelve minutes in two days if the setups are simple."

There was a calendar on Doug Cramer's desk, but I didn't need to look at it, nor at my own wristwatch. "It's now five o'clock on Thursday afternoon. You're telling me I have to supply twelve minutes of new material by first thing Tuesday morning—"

"Monday morning." Doug nodded. "Don't forget, we've got to get script approval for the new scenes, negotiate for our cast, do some rehearsing. Which reminds me. They've already torn down most of our interiors. All that's left to use are two sets; one of them's the shop and I'm still trying to find out what the other one is. Casting tells me most of our principals have already gone on to other assignments. I think we can have them put a hold on Miss Sondergaard. Perhaps there's somebody else, but I won't know until they get back to me later. Maybe you and Curtis ought to put your heads together."

It was an unnecessary suggestion. Curtis and I already had our heads together—right there on the chopping block.

I've already hinted that removing twelve minutes of shooting script in bits and pieces wasn't easy. But putting Humpty Dumpty back together again was an impossible task. Much as I would have liked to restore the word I cut out here, the line I eliminated there, the beats and reactions which had once been scattered throughout the script, there was just no way of doing so unless we started all over again, with every set restored and every cast member rehired. Instead, I could count only on two sets and two performers, in totally new scenes. The trick was to make these hitherto unnecessary pages of action and dialogue an intrinsic part of the story, structuring them to add suspense without disturbing the basic plot line and its logical progression.

I finished the new material on Sunday. It was approved on Monday, shot on Tuesday and Wednesday. Thanks to the cooperation of the producer, the creativity of the director and the craft of the two cast members, the show seemed seamless. On the appointed date it went out over the network. Long before then Doug Cramer sent me a case of very good Scotch.

Two years later we teamed up again for another TV movie, this one based on my story "The Dead Don't Die." Maybe they don't, but the show did. Despite Curtis's casting of accomplished character actors, their supporting roles couldn't prop up the lead.

And Ray Milland, who had given such a deftly paced performance in my script for *A Home Away from Home,* merely plodded through his part here like a zombie without a deadline.

While spanning the gap between television movies, I wrote a novel called *American Gothic.* The title came, of course, from Grant Wood's famous painting, and the subject matter was based upon the nefarious career of Herman W. Mudgett, aka H. H. Holmes and a dozen other aliases. The main problem was that in order to make my fictional version convincing I had to omit many of the incredible crimes committed by the story's actual prototype.*

Meanwhile the world whirled on.

Although we still continued to see old movies at the Peepleses', there no longer were any book-hunting expeditions. Gradually the neighborhood secondhand bookshops were closing. Los Angeles had changed as gas stations gave way to minimalls, apartments turned into condominiums and hundreds of high-rises raised their ugly heads. There was so much smog and pollution that apparently nobody noticed what was going on. Attention was divided between drugs and serial killings, the problems of gangs and gridlock. S&Ls sprang up on every street corner, and the whole city became McDonaldized.

Soaring above it for a time was Elly.

Some years before she had received her pilot's license for single-engine aircraft—Spads, Messerschmitts, or whatever they flew back in those days—and now that Erlene Peeples was taking lessons my wife brushed up on her aeronautics and resumed her fly-by-night career in the daytime.

I had every confidence in Elly but none whatsoever in light planes or the air corridors they traversed over southern California.

---

*I made partial amends when, in 1983, my forty-thousand-word factual account, "Dr. Holmes' Murder Castle," was published by Reader's Digest Books in their omnibus, *Tales of the Uncanny.*

She soon grew impatient with radio control towers and, mindful of the ever-increasing flight traffic, she decided to ground herself.

Instead, a few years later, Elly began to develop a new talent. Perhaps it wasn't new, merely latent, but she had never been aware that she possessed it. At no time did Elly ever doodle, make pen or pencil sketches; neither as child or adult had she indulged in crayon drawings or watercolors. Yet here she was, all of a sudden, painting in oils.

Her initial intention was merely to accompany a friend who'd meant to take art lessons. Almost immediately these one-hour sessions resulted in the creation of a portrait. From that point on there was no turning back. Creating proper conditions for working at home was impractical, but the weekly visits to the studio sufficed. Over the years ahead, and under the tutelage of artists Joy Williams and Ruth Masted, Elly turned out a surprisingly steady number of portraits, still-life compositions, landscapes and renderings of flora and fauna.

Eventually she even did a portrait of me. I found it very flattering until I realized that it was just an excuse to have me framed and hung.

FORTY-TWO

Sometimes I think my life is being revised, and not by me. As I go along, bits and pieces are added to smooth the rough edges, hoist up the dangling participles, finish off the unfinished bits of business.

I recall spending one of my dimes at the Jackson Theater in 1933 to see Joan Crawford in *Dancing Lady* and encountering those fugitives from the commedia dell'arte, Ted Healy and His Three Stooges. Wouldn't it be nice, I asked myself, if I could find out where those maniacs came from, how they survive those pokes in the eye and slaps across the chops in triplicate?

Thirty years later, sitting on the studio soundstage during the filming of *Strait-Jacket*, I noted that every morning, promptly at eleven, a tiny elderly man darted in, waited until the red light went off, then ran up to Crawford and whispered something in her ear. She would break up, kiss the little guy on the cheek and watch him scurry away. One morning this occurred while she waited for the shot to be set up, and it was then that she introduced me to the small gentleman.

His name was Moe Howard—the meanest of the Three

Stooges. Thus, a generation later I got an answer to my questions, and in the days that followed had a chance to ask others. The kindly, soft-spoken Mr. Howard was only too happy to talk about his brother Shemp, the early days on the riverboat, and life as one of Healy's *Southern Gentlemen.* I felt somehow as though a part of my life had come full circle.

Again, back in the thirties, I sat in a booth at a record shop, auditioning seventy-eight RPM discs and trying to choose between a Prokofiev piano composition and *The Dagger Dance* from Victor Herbert's opera *Natoma.** The session ended with a final score of Herbert-1, Prokofiev-0, but through the years I regretted there had never been a rematch. Once LP recordings came in, this particular bit of pianistic pyrotechnics was unavailable. Until, one day at a convention, I mentioned it to a fan-friend named Harriet Fellas. She promptly went to the piano and played the whole thing, brilliantly and from memory. Again came the feeling of completion.

Earlier on I recounted my arrival in Hollywood to do what turned out to be six teleplays for a series called "Lock-Up," starring Macdonald Carey. Later he starred in my first "Thriller," and yet for some inexplicable reason the two of us weren't ever in the same place at the same time.

Once more, as in these other instances, a period of thirty years went by. And one day as I sat signing copies of my latest novel in a Westwood bookshop, in walked Macdonald Carey. And presented me with a copy of his third book of poetry! It was a joyful reunion for two people who had never met.

Another serendipitous stitch in time wove its way into the fabric of my life in 1975. It was then that the city of Providence, Rhode Island, played host to the first World Fantasy Convention, chaired by a lifelong fan, Kirby McCauley. Here in the place where

---

*Which, in silent-movie days, was always played as an organ accompaniment at the moment when the Indians came over the hill.

my mentor H. P. Lovecraft was born and lived out his lifetime from cradle to grave, this convocation paid tribute to his memory almost a half century after his passing. Amongst the hundreds of fans and professionals in the rapidly expanding fantasy field were some of the still-surviving members of the Lovecraft Circle: J. Vernon Shea, Frank Belknap Long, Fritz Leiber, H. Warner Munn, Willis Conover. Other genre favorites included Manly Wade Wellman, Karl Edward Wagner, Don Grant, David Hartwell, T.E.D. Klien, Ramsey Campbell, Joseph Payne Brennan, Gahan Wilson and an all-star constellation of luminaries.

As guest of honor I felt painfully inadequate, and was genuinely shocked to receive the convention's very first Life Achievement Award. It came in the form of a bust of HPL, modeled in neo–Easter Island style by Gahan Wilson. I recall admiring these trophies, since christened "Howards" in honor of Howard Phillips Lovecraft, and vowing that some day I'd write something to compete for one of them. It never occurred to me that I had already done so, and the presentation blew my mind. All I could come up with by way of an acceptance was, "I haven't had so much fun since the rats ate my baby sister."

The mayor of Providence came in and presented me with the key to the city, but later on I noticed it still cost me a dime whenever I wanted to get into a pay toilet. Nevertheless it was a memorable occasion in many ways, this meeting and mingling with my peers.

Finally, forty years after Lovecraft had started me on my lifetime career, and almost forty years after his own had ended, I had at last come to the city he called home. Kind hosts conducted Gahan Wilson and me to Lovecraft's final resting place in Swan Point Cemetery and drove us past the church where Lovecraft's character Robert Blake first encountered the horror which would destroy him in *The Haunter of the Dark*.

But it was one evening, at Brown University, that past and present really fused as Fritz Leiber read that story aloud. As his marvelous, theatrically trained voice rose in the darkened auditorium, reciting Lovecraft's description of how I—the "Robert Blake" of the story—met a hideous death only a few blocks away from where this reading was taking place almost four decades later, I felt a mixture of emotions never experienced before or since. Not all that many people have enjoyed the privilege of hearing themselves being killed off that way and lived to tell the tale.

Over the next half-dozen years my convention attendance continued—New York, Atlanta, Washington, Kansas City, Omaha, Louisville, Phoenix, Tucson, St. Louis, Chicago. The latter city hosted a Star Trek affair for sixteen thousand people. The original cast, several moon-landing astronauts, two other writers and I were stashed away on the top floor under round-the-clock security, to be escorted downstairs only for our program appearances or press and TV interviews. It was a sensible precaution, because one afternoon the crowd of Trekkies packed the lobby so tightly that the two-story plate-glass windows were literally pushed out to shatter on Michigan Avenue.

Conventions can be dangerous to your health, and they sure are hard on your feet. Sometimes it can take well over an hour to get from your room to a meeting hall downstairs; there are always people to visit with en route. But that, of course, is what conventions are all about. It's just that sometimes these events have grown to what were once unimaginable and at present have become unmanageable proportions. Such conditions are particularly difficult for the guests of the convention and their spouses, to say nothing of their meaningful relationships (which is sometimes a pretty good idea). Having to stand quietly in the background and listen to a bunch of strangers fulsomely praise your miserable turkey of a husband is insult enough, but listening to *him* sounding off on the platform is added injury. Dressing up, squeezing in and out of elevators, then plowing through crowded corridors to find an uncomfortable seat in an uncomfortable hall—all this can be far from a pleasure to those with no particular interest of their own in fantasy, mystery or science fiction. As the years went by, Elly became less inclined to brave the discomforts of the trip and the fatigue of the festivities, to say nothing of perfecting all of the preliminary arrangements necessitated by our combined absence from home base. Besides, somebody had to stay there to put the bills through the shredder as they came in.

As for me, conventions remained an opportunity for continued contact with readers, colleagues, editors and publishers in the rapidly changing and expanding market for the sort of material I wrote. The changes and expansions were mirrored in the conventions themselves, not only in increased attendance but in the diversity of interests they reflected. No longer were fans united in a common bond of readership. These affairs catered to devotees of film, television, music, comic books, gaming, computers, and to collectors who weren't primarily interested in the content of what they bought, sold, traded, or tried to smuggle out under their jackets.

Several years after the trip to Lovecraft's Providence I found myself in Poe's Baltimore, visiting his home and his churchyard grave. I was surprised to find both residences so small; he'd lived here in what was scarcely more than a doll's house and he rested now within a tiny tract surrounded by the surge of the city. One does not think of Edgar Allan Poe as a little man.

I said that he rested now in his grave, but of course Poe doesn't rest. Like Lovecraft he remains alive within his work, and neither man needs a pyramid to preserve his memory in stone. For better or worse, writers build their own monuments.

Perhaps these somewhat morbid considerations surfaced when I returned from Baltimore and underwent a second cataract surgery. There's something about having a knife stuck in you that evokes intimations of mortality, along with a prayer that they don't screw up your claim forms at Medicare.

There were a number of short-story collections to assemble over the next few years. Many required commentary or introductory material, addressed to readers who might be encountering these efforts for the first time and explaining the circumstances under which they were written. If you've been paying attention to this account, then you already know those circumstances, most of which can be boiled down to a single word: poverty.

Good, bad or indifferent, my work has always had two primary purposes: to entertain others and to sustain my family and myself. Admitting these dual objectives lays me open to the charge of "selling out."

The world out there contains plenty of crooked politicians, corrupt law officers, dishonest bankers, stockbrokers and S&L executives. It offers a broad spectrum of trial attorneys who represent and misrepresent clients they know to be guilty, a judiciary often incompetent or on the take, self-serving ethnic "leaders" or "spokespersons," self-ordained clergymen and televangelists. There's no lack of used-car pitchmen and fake repairmen, high-pressure salesmen of junk merchandise, boiler-room staffs hyping rigged promotions in recordings via telephone or over the airwaves. It abounds in real estate operators, ticket scalpers who gouge customers, unethical lobbyists, computer hackers, parking lot extortionists, exam cheats at West Point, Annapolis and the Air Force Academy. There is a plethora of mail-order fraud peddlers, insurance agents selling worthless policies to the elderly who can't read or interpret the fine print, unqualified "marriage counselors" and "psychological consultants," scientists faking experimental data, economic forecasters, morticians who literally steal the gold from their clients' teeth, unethical operators of rip-off nursing homes, private hospitals and day-care centers. Take heed of disappearing fathers who will never make good on their child-support payments, "professional" people who have no intention of ever repaying their student loans, government contractors who are already faking statements of "cost overruns" before they begin work on their contracts. Note also the steroid-stuffed "amateur" jocks, the labor racketeers, parole violators, the thick-necked goons who have miraculously acquired the capital and licenses to sell liquor to minors and guns to school kids, supermarket owners using crooked scales for meat or produce, physicians who botch plastic-surgery jobs, creative accountants, drug pushers, roofing and siding con men, pharmaceutical manufacturers selling pills at a thousand-percent markup to pharmacists who add another 1,000%. The only thing all these people have in common is their unanimous opinion that anyone who writes a story for a popular magazine, a script for series television or a screenplay for the mass audience is guilty of having "sold out."

The only thing that has saved me from extermination at the hands of these high-principled citizens is the fact that they seldom read books.*

They certainly didn't read *Strange Eons,* the novel I next wrote for a small specialty publisher. Very few people did, and I doubt if any of them would be inclined to accuse me of writing the book just in order to keep up proper maintenance on my second yacht.

Strange Eons was very much a labor of love. Inspired by my Providence visit, I determined to deal with Lovecraftean themes, but unlike his many current imitators, do so in my own style. Neither I nor the book sold out.

The end of the seventies brought changes.

Kirby McCauley took over as my agent.

We lost most of my remaining relatives, including Aunt Lil. A few years earlier, after she suffered a heart attack in Chicago, Elly went there and flew her out to stay with my sister and her family. Now, like Bea and Tess and Aunt Gertrude, she was gone. And missed.

So was Dick Foran, leaving behind a growing son, Tom; wife Suzy took her degree and became a therapist.

---

*Unless the books are extremely dirty. But even then, they don't buy any—just steal them from the public library.

Sometimes it wasn't a matter of mortality. With my daughter and her husband, geography was the factor. She and husband Jim took up residence in the Santa Cruz mountains. From time to time Jim descended into Silicon Valley, returning with contracts as a creative consultant. Sally and local lady friends rode hundreds of miles of interlacing horse trails, starting out from the corral in her own yard. It was in many ways an idyllic existence for them both and would have driven me clinically insane in about 3½ days.

I found life more stimulating as guest of honor at the *Premier Festival du Roman et des Films Policiers* in Reims. Some of the French writers and fans knew English; as a shamefaced monolingist I relied upon my patient and full-time interpreter when talking to others. When I spoke in English to an audience, my remarks were greeted with polite silence. Then the interpreter translated and got all the laughs.

Everything was different in France, including the screening of *Psycho*. Instead of a shower, the French version kills the heroine off on a bidet.

Reims offered other enchantments. There was a tour of the salt mines which have been converted into storage caves for champagne. A group of us were conducted through one such maze, which held no less than twenty-five million bottles. Or did, before we drank most of them up.

Another touch of hospitality I deeply appreciated was a private early-morning tour of the great cathedral. I was escorted by a young man who had been christened there, worshiped at its stations, stood before the altar to repeat his marriage vows. He knew the cathedral's history and made it come alive for me. Several stained-glass windows, demolished during WWII, had been replaced by new creations by Marc Chagall, which didn't detract in the least from the architectural evocation of mystery made manifest. As dawn gave way to sunrise the glass came alive in glory; the smiles of saints took on a radiance and their halos held a golden glow. But beneath them in the sable silence of the cathedral every shadow loomed larger, and when sounds came they took on added meaning. Some miracle of acoustics magnified our heartbeats, added awareness of every breath, and each footstep echoed endlessly into eternity.

Religious feeling? I don't think so. What I felt was the presence of magic.

In Paris I had the pleasure of meeting my French publishers and translators. They and their families offered hospitality which we have since, in some small measure, attempted to reciprocate.

The same holds true for relationships established in Australia. Here, two years later, I was brought over as guest of honor at their first science fiction film festival. It was an Australian fan, Graeme Flanagan, who had compiled my bibliography, and it was Australian fandom that made my stay memorable.

The journey itself was unforgettable, though for other reasons. Taking off for Down Under on a night flight, one arrives to go through customs check in Honolulu at four A.M. Then it's back on the plane for some nonsense with the international date line, which requires either changing your watch or rupturing yourself trying to move your sun dial.

By the time the flight ended in Sydney, I was wiped out. Kind hosts conveyed me to my hotel and I retired immediately. The noonday sky sparkled beyond the window, but it was somewhere around midnight inside my head.

Sleep. Rest. Not since that moment in the Reims cathedral had I known such peace.

The cathedral had no telephone. My Australian hotel room did. Half an hour after retiring I found myself seated beside antipodean science fiction writer Bert Chandler, skimming over Sydney Bay in a hydrofoil. From then on until my departure for Melbourne several days later there was nothing about my stay that resembled a visit to a cathedral.

Escaping alive after speaking at the local university, I flew to Melbourne for the film convention. Again the hospitality overwhelmed me; Mervyn Binns, book dealer and a leading exponent of the occasion, joined with his mates to entertain me. Graeme Flanagan came down from Canberra and we had a lovely tour of the old Melbourne gaol which had once played host to no less a notable than the great Ned Kelly himself. To those of you who think of Australia in terms of Crocodile Dundee let me assure you that it's outlaw and highwayman Kelly who takes pride of place in the annals of Oz. Nowhere is the ambivalent Australian attitude better exemplified than in the gaol, where symbols of law and order are displayed alongside artifacts associated with the lawless and disordered career of its most famous guest. The gaol boasted two other items which remain vivid in my memory. One was small—a pair of tin mittens which could be tightened over the hands of inmates to keep them from masturbating. The other was somewhat larger—a full-sized gallows at the end of a corridor from which prisoners were hung, presumably after being caught masturbating.

Things were much more pleasant at the convention hotel and at the Melbourne university where I spoke and participated in a seminar with Australian filmmakers. The continent was just developing its own cinema, and one could sense an excitement and enthusiasm now sadly lacking in the conglomerate confines of La-La Land.

I'd been doing my best to avoid those confines recently, though not always with complete success. The next novel I turned my hand to had a clumsy title, *But the Serpent Was Cunning,* a genuine Biblical quotation but probably written by King James in one of his less inspired moments. The publishers asked for a substitute and I gave them *There Is a Serpent in Eden.* Later they changed it to *The Cunning* in a subsequent reprint, and I must admit this is better than anything Jimmy and I came up with. But the story, which dealt with the problems of retirees who eventually unite to deal with criminal menace, was too offbeat for the genre readership at which it was arbitrarily aimed. Mindful of my earlier experiences with *The Kidnapper* and *The Star Stalker,* I knew what to expect—or, rather, what not to expect. But as was the case with those two earlier books, this was the novel I wanted to write. I still don't see how anyone can call such an effort a "sellout"; even at its best, the book was really just a "sell-not-very-much."

Being an honored prophet in foreign countries was heady stuff, but I wasn't being honored with many profits in my own. Did this mean I was over the hill? God knows it can happen without your knowing it—and even when you do know, there isn't always very much you can do about it.

A few years earlier a distinguished author inscribed one of his books to me: "For Robert Bloch on his mountain top from Robert Nathan in his valley. And there we sit, looking out at a changing world, and wondering what to do, and how to fit into it—and what's ahead—"

FORTY-THREE

*T*he 1970s wound down and the 1980s wound up, and I was tangled in between. After twenty years in Hollywood it was time to take stock. If I'd had any sense, twenty years ago I would have *bought* stock, but because of my negligence there wasn't a single share in my portfolio.

To be utterly frank, I didn't even have a portfolio. Somehow income had kept abreast of inflation, though not of increasing taxation, and now the IRS had risen from its coffin in search of blood. I got a letter from the local office of the IRS signed, I believe, by a Mr. Lugosi, who wanted to arrange a meeting, preferably after sunset.

Several friends offered suggestions about finding immediate sources of extra cash. Byron Marx, now head of the agency he had built from his father's foundation, was unaware of my predicament, but when he came to dinner he casually volunteered some information. The agency was paying three thousand dollars to writers of one-minute TV commercials; would I like to pick up some spare change?

After thinking it over for a full second, I refused the kind invitation.

Sam Peeples had previously suggested I might follow his example and write scripts for a half-hour animated cartoon series aimed at the Saturday morning kiddie audience. The flat fee was comparable to the one Marx had come up with, and I hesitated for another second before declining.

During one period, Sam spent eighteen months at Universal. Ironically enough, his employer was Frank Price, who had started at the studio as Sam's assistant.

One didn't have to look around for very long without seeing other examples of how the television and film industry had changed. Younger executives now were in the majority, and they wanted to work with writers and directors their own age. With the exception of a few elderly giants, Hollywood was largely in the hands of youthful midgets.

But I still didn't want to write commercials or cartoons. Instead I took a deep breath and sold my collection of Lovecraft letters.

Once the decision was made I acted with the utmost urgency—largely, I suspect, to avoid changing my mind. Between haste and trauma I even neglected the common-sense consideration of having those letters Xeroxed before turning them over to the dealer who purchased them. And I couldn't wait to appease the blood lust of the IRS. Red-fanged and grinning, they slunk away. It was only a temporary respite; I knew that in another year they would rise from the grave again, but by then I hoped to have a stake for them.

Perhaps it was only a rationalization, yet it seemed to me that my literary mentor would have approved what I'd done. The idea of selling his correspondence to save myself from the clutches of the undead could only have amused him. Once more Lovecraft had come to my rescue.

It was during this period that I began working on a project—bankrolled initially, I believe, by Paramount—with director George Pal. "Director" is a misnomer for George, for the term scarcely serves to encompass his abilities. The Hungarian-born Mr. Pal was also an architect, carpenter, cartoonist, animator, creator of a puppet film series and film producer. But above all he was an artist, schooled in the classic European tradition.

Like Fritz Lang, his early training in architecture and fine art caused him to gravitate to the visual medium of film. Inevitably both men were attracted by the spectacular opportunities in science fiction and fantasy.

George and I had met socially on a number of occasions, but this was our first professional relationship. He planned to use a short story by H. G. Wells as the basis for a film to be called *The Day of the Comet*. At this time producer Irwin Allen had made a series of disaster movies, some of which were intentional. George was prepared to jump on the bandwagon or, in this case, the ambulance.

He invited me along for the ride and I came up with a treatment which was approved. We worked singly and together out of one another's homes; thanks to long-suffering wives and George's expert and efficient secretary, Gay, the project proceeded smoothly.

At least it did until word emerged that another studio was already in production on a film with a similar theme and Irwin Allen himself was heaping death and destruction on mankind in a miniseries. So it was back to square one, and there we parted, vowing to meet again.

Meanwhile I pondered further the worsening situation in films and television, particularly as it applied to my particular areas of endeavor. Thanks (if that is the word) to the tremendous commercial success of *The Exorcist*, films of fantasy and the supernatural were becoming increasingly gross, and the level of violence had been depressingly elevated in every category of current cinema. There was even a brief vogue for sleazy cartoons.

In addition, so-called creative control had passed to the hands of the directors, whose names often appeared above the title.

From the very beginning of motion pictures there had been innovative directors, some of whom were responsible for all phases of production, including the script. But until recently they had always been acknowledged as exceptions to the general rule. It was the French who promulgated the *auteur* theory, but vanity is a universal language and now all directors spoke it fluently. Writers didn't get their name above the title and were damned lucky if it appeared somewhere down below unaccompanied by a shared credit with a director, all of whom were *auteurs*.

At times I wondered about this. To me, films and television had a great deal in common. Both were shot on the same kind of soundstage by the same kind of cameras and crews. Both employed similar sets, identical lighting equipment; production differed only slightly, if at all, in any given respect. If you ventured onto a set during a shoot, chances were that you wouldn't know whether they were filming a theatrical feature or a teleplay; you'd see performers who worked in both mediums without any change in their technique. Aside from budget and censorship restrictions, there was no difference between film and television. On that basis I could only ask myself the obvious question: "If all the film directors are *auteurs,* then where in hell are all the *auteur* directors in television?"

I asked myself the question as a last resort; I'd attempted to ask other people but got no answers. Nor did I get any answers as to the possibility of writers regaining any control over their output. The young graduates of cinema courses were all hellbent upon becoming writer-directors and/or writer-producers in order to maintain autonomy, but I lacked both their energy and imperative.

My obvious alternative was the printed word. I consulted my agent, who came up with an obvious suggestion. "Write *Psycho II,*" he said.

He supported the proposal with a variety of reasons. The film industry had already discovered Roman numerals, and book publishers were retaliating with sequels, prequels, and trilogies in ten parts. Hitting closer to home and below the belt, he reminded me that everybody and his illegitimate, half-witted brother was capitalizing on *Psycho* bath towels, *Psycho* shower curtains, *Psycho* room keys, *Psycho* letterheads, *Psycho* cartoons, skits, film rip-offs and title variations. Everybody, that is, except the guy who invented Norman Bates, built him a motel and installed a shower.

I could see the logic of his recommendation, but there was one thing I couldn't visualize, and that was a story to go with the title. Apparently this wasn't bothering the dudes who were doing sequels to successful films; in some cases they brought characters back from the dead, in others they changed events depicted in earlier films, and there were cases when nothing of the original story was used except the title.

Psycho II. I'd have to think about that.

Alexandre Dumas brought D'Artagnan back in *Twenty Years After*. But I wasn't Dumas and Norman Bates would never make it in the Musketeers.

What had old Norman been up to all this time? He'd be getting along in years now. Must be pretty damned dull for him, sitting there in that asylum; even duller if they'd gone ahead and cured him. Or *thought* they'd cured him. But suppose he wasn't cured? And suppose he heard that somebody out in Hollywood intended to make a movie about him? What if he busted out and headed west?

Maybe the answers would add up to a story. And writing such a story would in itself pose and answer other questions. What would Norman Bates think of a world which had become increasingly violent during the long years he'd been shut away from it? Even more intriguing, what would today's world think of him, now that serial murders were commonplace affairs? The bottom line, of course, was whether or not readers would still be interested.

Apparently somebody thought so, because when I reached the bottom line of the novel itself, Warner Books bid for its publication. Agent Kirby McCauley was fully vindicated.

When the news broke, Universal Pictures saw fit to announce that while they owned the movie rights to *Psycho,* they had absolutely no intention of making a sequel. Agent Gordon Molson thought it would be a gesture of courtesy and goodwill if I let Universal see what I was doing with the novel, even though they were free to use my material without payment.

McCauley and I agreed, and Universal got a preview. In short order Molson conducted me to a meeting with a pair of executives connected with film production at the studio. They suggested it would be nice if I rewrote the book to eliminate the Hollywood setting in which much of the story took place. Since the novel had already been enthusiastically accepted by the publishers in its present form I could see no point to this. But clearly they weren't comfortable with my depiction of filmmakers. Confirmation came down from a higher echelon. One of the top executives had also elected to inspect my manuscript. It is usually a matter of common courtesy to return such material with some expression of thanks or even a few words of mild approbation. In this case the gentleman went out of his way to inform my agent that he *hated* the book.

Since I'd never met him, his reaction had to be based on what he'd read, and it was obvious that *Psycho II* was bad news to all those decent God-fearing folks up there in the black tower at Universal. This did not prevent them from announcing that the studio had suddenly decided to produce a sequel to *Psycho* as a movie for television. Apparently one of the resident geniuses had a sudden flash of inspiration.

News about the forthcoming publication of the book was picked up by the foreign press as well as domestic journals. Lo and behold, lightning struck the tower again, and Universal announced the production of a new feature film, *Psycho II,* for worldwide theatrical release. I hope somebody got a raise for coming up with this brilliant idea.

Once a script had been written, the studio sent a copy to me.

This was not intended as mere courtesy; it came with the suggestion that I abandon my book and write a novelization of their screenplay instead.

I met this proposition with a straight face, but upon informing the studio what I'd received as an advance for my own novel there was nothing further except shocked silence on their part.

I didn't have too much time to monitor these developments. The book came out and fared very well. Eventually Universal's film came out and did enough business to result in the production of a *Psycho III*. Believe it or not, they sent me the script of that one too, with the suggestion I write a novelization. Again I declined.

George Pal and I resumed our professional relationship with a property tentatively titled *The Voyage of the Berg*. It dealt with the towing of an Antarctic iceberg to irrigate the barren desert of a kingdom in the Mideast. AIP was set to finance the film and once again George took over production planning while I labored on the script. It was a challenging task but a thankless one. Already the Arab oil countries were falling into general disfavor, and making an Arabian prince the hero seemed ill-advised.

To quiet my concerns, George spoke of a future project he hoped to realize—a film based loosely on the little-known life of the artist who called himself Hieronymus Bosch. Those who persist in thinking of Pal merely as a clever commercial filmmaker with an eye forever cocked towards the juvenile audience may be somewhat surprised to learn of his personal preferences. He had gone so far as to propose publication of a novel about Bosch, to be appropriately illustrated with the artist's work, but proper color reproductions of his paintings made the project too expensive. There was no reason to believe a biographical film would find popular favor, but George knew I shared his enthusiasm for the painter and thought I could inject a screenplay with elements of demonology and witchcraft similar to those found in his canvases.

Contemplating this carrot, I plodded forward with the script of what was now called *Berg*. Dealing with it, I was tempted to call myself *Titanic*. In point of fact it was the relationship between George and me that nearly floundered, sunk by a company employee. This valuable and trusted member of the organization was supposedly monitoring our project, but aside from a single brief luncheon meeting he seemed much too busy to give us an appointment. According to him he spent at least thirty-six hours every day editing AIP's most expensive film for its forthcoming release.

George, although an artist to his fingertips, was still a Hungarian by birth, and as such he found it expedient to maintain contact with a mole in the film company. This particular mole was the accountant, and one day he turned up an item on our errant executive's expense account, charging off a breakfast shared with *me!*

It took George a while to realize that I hadn't entered into a conspiracy to remove him from the project and never met independently with this brilliant young filmmaker. This fact was later confirmed by the accountant, though the filmmaker's brilliance remains open to question. The picture he claimed to have cut and edited went right down the tube, followed shortly thereafter by the company itself. Before George could establish contact with another production outfit he suffered a fatal heart attack. I look back on our association with fond memories, but with deep regret that our names were never fated to be linked together on screen.

Disenchanted with the ways of motion pictures, I accepted a commitment to mount a pilot for a TV series based on Stephen King's *Salem's Lot*. His novel had already duplicated its success in a movie for television. Just how one would go about doing a series was another matter, since recycling a dead town and an undead villain hardly seemed like an original idea.

King and I had first met several years before this. When Steve came west for an initial studio visit he called to invite Elly and me to dinner, asking that I pass a similar invitation along to Ruth and Dick Matheson. We spent a pleasant evening together, during which Dick and I tried to point out some of the perils and pitfalls prevalent in these parts. If he was looking for excitement, we suggested that he go back home to Maine and put in a call to Dial-A-Porn.

Fortunately he didn't take our advice.* On subsequent occasions we got together at conventions and maintained contact. Although King shared my reservations about the *Salem's Lot* caper, he felt somewhat more at ease knowing that I was involved.

As for me, my initial qualms were partially dispelled when I learned that the producer of the opus was Doug Benton, whom I'd worked with back in the days of the "Thriller" shows. I evolved a story line, had it approved, and emerged with a script. But upon learning that thirty-seven copies of that script were to be distributed to network personnel on both the west and east coasts, I realized the project was foredoomed.

Here in Hollywood and back there in Fun City, thirty-seven people were sitting at thirty-seven different desks in thirty-seven different offices, drawing down thirty-seven individual salaries for reading one of the thirty-seven copies of my script. But salaries like theirs weren't being paid merely for a reading without comment. And if the comment consisted merely of approval, those salaries would soon be terminated. In order to hold a job it was best not to hold one's tongue; these people could only prove their worth by offering input, put-downs, criticisms, witticisms, objections and rejections. Certainly no script could ever be run past thirty-seven upwardly mobile executive types without being showered with thirty-seven different complaints and/or suggestions for changes. I took the money and ran, without looking back over my shoulder.

There was no need to. Nothing happened, and I'd already learned what to expect from television in the years ahead.

I faced those years without Gordon Molson at my side; like George Pal, he died of a sudden heart attack and secretary Dorothy

---

*At least I don't think so, although he *did* go home.

Schaff followed within less than a year. Bill Stanton retired and the agency disappeared. I found new representation with the Shapiro-Lichtman Agency but did not encourage them to beat the bushes for new assignments.

A more immediate project was a new novel. *The Night of the Ripper* both summarized and exorcised my professional preoccupation with the prototype of today's mad slashers. In order to underscore the point that throughout history crimes far worse than Jack's had been committed in the name of patriotism, religion, local custom or tradition, I included a number of examples as chapter headings. Researching such material uncovered details which were deleted as unnecessarily gross. Oddly enough, when the novel was published in 1984 most readers seemed to get the point, but some reviewers missed it completely; they thought I'd attempted to add gratuitous gore. I wonder how they would have reacted had they read the unexpurgated accounts in such respectable sources as Will and Ariel Durant's *The Story of Civilization*. One man's sleaze is another man's scholarship.

I was done with the Ripper, but the rippers weren't finished with me. After the lens implant in my left eye came loose and injured the cornea I was strapped to an operating table, given half a children's-strength aspirin as an anesthetic, and subjected to corneal transplant surgery. I can assure you that the entire procedure was no worse than a high colonic with a Roto-Rooter.

FORTY-FOUR

Survival, like every other phenomenon, is selective. Since our marriage Elly and I waited hand and foot on three different dogs in turn. Miniature pinschers almost identical in appearance, all were named Zander. By the time we lost the third her grief prompted me to advise against a fourth facsimile. It seemed that a less demanding, more distant and aloof sort of pet would be preferable as a replacement. I suggested acquiring an innocuous house cat, perhaps a Burmese Blue, a short-haired species not given to displays of temperament or shedding.

No sooner said than done. Elly set out on her quest and promptly purchased a long-haired Himalayan with more temperament than Madonna. The tiny kitten, immediately named Zan, seemed harmless enough, until its mouth opened to display the fangs of a saber-toothed tiger.

Gradually our new pet grew into a four-legged furball, vain, moody and aloof. It was then that my wife decided Zan might be in need of a feline companion. Once again she set out on a hunting expedition. This time she returned from her safari with a Singapura.

Christened Beau, he soon became Bobo, and was Zan's opposite in appearance, personality and behavior.*

Owning two cats instead of one involves five times as much work. Elly designed a condo for their use—a wire-enclosed solarium and runway with three levels of basking shelves. This structure was affixed to a bedroom door leading out onto a patio and equipped with sailcloth drapes which could be raised or lowered to meet exigencies of weather. The whole contraption was constructed for less than it cost Shah Jahan to build the Taj Mahal.

In order to pay for the job and put something away in case Elly decided the cats might need a Great Pyramid, I accepted an offer to novelize the script of *Twilight Zone: The Movie*. The four parts of the screenplay were not shown in the same sequence when the film was released, and only two of these segments were screened for me. Nobody bothered to mention there was also a wraparound for the anthology format, any more than they revealed the fact that one of the leading characters in the film was the black performer Scatman Crothers. They merely stipulated that I take the four unrelated episodes, originally dramatized from individual short stories possibly totaling twenty-thousand words in length, and expand them into a sixty-thousand-word novel without adding any new characters or plot developments. Needless to say, it would be wise if the result in no way resembled any of the original sources, but I could work out this and other problems as I went along. After all, they didn't need the finished novel for six weeks.

To complicate matters further there was a tragic accident during the filming of the first episode, when a helicopter crash killed actor Vic Morrow and two children. As a result the final portion of that story was cut entirely, and I had to rewrite the section with even less material to work from.

---

*There is no real reason for going into all this business about the cats, but I promised them they'd be in the book.

There was only one way for me to adhere to the constraints imposed upon my novelization, and that was to wade into various characters' streams of consciousness. Somehow I managed to get my feet wet, but wasn't particularly ecstatic over the results. I can only hope the cats appreciated these efforts.

Shortly afterwards I was a guest, along with A. E. van Vogt and wife Lydia, at a science fiction film festival in Metz. Once again there was an opportunity to enjoy French hospitality, limited by Lydia's promise to Elly that she would monitor my activities. Later, in Paris I again visited with my editors and translators, then did some sightseeing. The serendipitous discovery at Napoleon's tomb was the War Museum, inconspicuously tucked away behind it. But the main attraction this time around was the Louvre.

Visiting it was the culmination of an ambition held since my earliest excursions to the Art Institute in Chicago. Ever since first hearing of its wonders I had yearned for an opportunity to smile at the Mona Lisa and shake hands with the Venus de Milo. Viewing the treasures of the Louvre was like reviewing my childhood through adult eyes.

Such a childhood was undoubtedly more pleasant than the one experienced by the gypsy urchins who descended out of nowhere one morning on the rue de Rivoli, expertly enveloping me in cacophonous confusion as they ripped off my wallet. These youngsters, smuggled into France from Eastern Europe, roamed the streets and Metro stations of Paris. Trained by Yugoslavian counterparts of the fictional Fagin, a score of such bands preyed continuously upon unsuspecting tourists like me. Robbery at the grimy hands of juvenile delinquents so outraged me that upon returning home I immediately sat down and recouped my losses by writing a story called "The Yugoslaves."*

---

*One pleasant note: my wallet, with credit cards, was found in a trash bin by a student, and she kindly brought it to the American Embassy for return to me.

390 / Robert Bloch

It was one of the few times when personal experience prompted me to convert fact into fiction, but the actual event served to springboard me into the fantasy which followed.

Another actual event took a fantastic turn which I still find inexplicable. Towards the end of my Paris sojourn I was wined and dined by a gentleman named Pierre Grimblat, head of Hamster Productions. He and his associate were producing series for French and Belgian television, and showed me some impressive examples of current efforts. They had in mind a series based on my own published stories and had already selected the first half-dozen vehicles. Upon returning home I was to choose the remainder; meantime they would contact my agent with an offer. The financial arrangement quoted me seemed attractive, and true to their word, it was immediately dispatched to the agency. A follow-up cable stated that their British representative would be arriving in Hollywood after the July fourth holiday, prepared to consummate the deal.

Whether or not he did fly in I'll never know. Nor do I know what happened to the whole proposal. There was nothing more heard from Hamster Productions, despite our inquiries, and the entire event remains an unsolved mystery.

What sales I subsequently made to television consisted of stories presented on "Tales from the Dark Side" and its successor, "Monsters." After several years I finally agreed to adapt one of the stories myself, just to see if I still possessed the knack. I didn't see "Beetles," but since it was aired I presume the script passed muster.

Meanwhile my appearances, conventional and otherwise, culminated in a stint at the Los Angeles Worldcon. Amongst the eleven thousand-odd attendees were longtime writer friends Poul Anderson and Gordon Dickson, whose past collaborations included a series of stories about Hokas. These lovable little aliens, roughly equivalent to intelligent teddy bears, had a penchant for role-playing derived from earthly fiction; thus their planet was populated with everything from cowboys to Sherlock Holmeses, and the adventures of such characters were imitated and emulated in appropriate settings.

The Walker brothers, Jeff and Michael, had acquired story rights, made a film deal, and commissioned me to fashion a screenplay from components of all this material. It was a demanding and difficult task; the siblings and various novae at the production company had conflicting views as to which elements and characters should be incorporated. Even with compromise and combination the script sprawled to an inordinate length. Since every change had to meet with multiple approvals, I was tempted to title the screenplay *Revise and Consent.*

The Walkers were considerate, enthusiastic and supportive, but the time arrived when they also became apprehensive. Our project had been turned over to a lady executive who, they believed, might not be captivated with the venture. When the lady issued an invitation to a Saturday luncheon at her home their forebodings mounted. The best they could do was to present an excuse for one brother's absence and suggest I make a guest appearance in his place. Or, more precisely, in *her* place, where we duly arrived on Saturday, noonish.

The boss lady opened the door of a quietly elegant home at a trendy address. She was young, attractive and quite charming. The luncheon she served was fabulous, accompanied by just the right wine; we were in the presence of the perfect hostess. And there was no need to presume upon her hospitality with a sales pitch about the film project. If anything, she was intent on stressing her own commitment to the venture. Her comments were intelligent and pertinent; this was not just another pretty face but a competent and knowledgeable executive. When we left our Saturday meeting we were greatly relieved.

On Monday morning the boss lady was relieved—of her job. Apparently control of the production company had passed into new hands, and last week's executive was this week's applicant for unemployment benefits. Nobody bothered to fill in the details, but the picture was clear. Our project was obviously about to be put into turnaround. It would have plenty of company; nine out of every ten film scripts commissioned for production never reach the screen.

All this was scant consolation to my friends who had created the Hokas, or to the Walker brothers who invested their hopes and efforts in the enterprise. For me the outcome of the venture was particularly disappointing, because it had represented a long-awaited opportunity to get out of the shower stall.

I could only feel fortunate that I hadn't been consigned to limbo along with the unproduced film. There were matters requiring attention, including the assembly of several new short-story collections, plus the introduction to *Unholy Trinity,* this last being an omnibus volume reprinting three earlier novels. In addition friend John Stanley wanted to publish my *Lefty Feep* series in book form. Personally I tended to believe these yarns were not meant to be unraveled again, but he overrode my objections and insisted I write a new story for the first* volume. There was also the matter of supplying information—and misinformation, it turned out—for a bibliography. Randall Larson spent several years in compilation, at the same time assembling a second offering consisting solely of previously published interviews. People were surprised at the amount of material I had written, but nobody who knew me was surprised at the number of times I had opened my mouth.

My old friend Frank M. Robinson sent a couple of newspaper clippings about a pregnant woman's unusual medical problem. He felt there might be a springboard for a novel here, and suggested I let my imagination jump off it. I developed the story line, while turning out introductions or forewords to a variety of anthologies.

---

*And, as if in proof of my dire predictions, probably the last.

Rest and recreation came in convention attendance. At least I thought so, until two Florida functions in a row brought me into contact with my colleague Andre Norton and her business associate, Ingrid Zierhut. Andre, famed for her *Witch World* series, was editing an anthology of original stories by other fantasy writers based on the characters and settings she had created. Following our first meeting both Andre and Ingrid invited me to do a *Witch World* story. That was decided upon in Tampa; by the time we met later in Fort Lauderdale the story had been written. Here it was proposed that Andre and I collaborate on a novel together. The sheer audacity of such a notion was irresistible; combining that lady's delicate fantasy with my own raunchy approach would not only constitute a mutual challenge but evoke curiosity on the part of our readers.

Writing the short story for Andre's anthology had been a relatively simple matter entailing only the assumption of her narrative style and the retelling of her own tale from the viewpoint of another character. Obviously the same method wasn't practical in a collaborative novel. I couldn't maintain her style, nor could she utilize mine; would there be any point in either of us imitating the other? Bearing this in mind, we decided to meet on common ground. I had researched Victorian London for *The Night of the Ripper*. Andre not only had a great affinity for that place and period, but also a remarkable array of reference material. In addition she was particularly adept in developing female characters while I preferred dealing with the males. What we needed was a plot, and it was already obvious we weren't about to do a rewrite of *Alice in Wonderland*. Instead I proposed a sequel to *The Strange Case of Dr. Jekyll and Mr. Hyde,* and with Andre's assent did an outline on which the publisher offered a contract.

Our plans involved writing alternate chapters in sequence, but before starting we had other commitments to complete. Complicating matters a bit more, both Ingrid Zierhut and Kirby McCauley had casually suggested to me that I do a third book to round out the *Psycho* saga, and in short order that was contracted for.

Just to keep me from drowsing off, the convention committee in Boston intimated that they would like their guest of honor to prepare a special book; it was customary to issue such volumes in limited editions. Not having the spare time to write another novel on that particular afternoon, I instead assembled a sequel to my earlier collection of pieces from fan magazines. *Out of My Head* did well in Boston and so did I.

The next convention was in Minneapolis. It was Elly's first outing to such an affair since our junket to Tucson several years earlier. I had a long phone conversation with the ailing Donald Wandrei and a final meeting with Clifford Simak, whom I'd first visited more than forty years before. We returned home by way of Milwaukee and another reunion with friends, plus meeting expatriate members of Elly's family from there and Chicago.

Another commitment took me to Huntsville, Alabama, and a convention held on the grounds of the Space Center there. Andre and I put the finishing touches on our plans for collaboration. Then, for a time, it looked as though something might put the finishing touch on me.

Thanks to various eye problems I'd become increasingly aware of venerable vulnerability. Now they targeted me for herniorrhaphy, which is almost as hard to spell as it is to endure, but not quite. The prospect did not afford any particular pleasure.

There is no dignity in the impairment of physical functions or mental faculties. There are few of my contemporaries who would hesitate to strike Faust's bargain. I was beginning to wonder whether the time had come for me to say good-bye while I was still able to wave. As a child I always hated vegetables, and now I had no desire to be one.

Nevertheless, the surgery seemed necessary and perhaps it might serve as a holding operation. Elly took me to the hospital as an outpatient and before you could say rigor mortis I found myself rolling down the hall strapped to a gurney. I don't find this particularly comfortable, and the same goes for the flimsy "hospital gown," which is really just a cross between a child's shroud and a body bag.

Wheeled along by the overworked and underpaid, one stares at the ceiling and contemplates how quickly it is possible to be robbed of the illusion of security, stripped of everything including one's very identity. The people who tie you down and prepare you to go under the knife don't even know your name; to them you're merely a number. You enter the operating room as a vital statistic, and whether you'll still be vital when you come out is not their problem. But suddenly it sure as hell has become yours. And you face that problem utterly alone. There is no scapegoat to suffer pain in your stead, no surrogate to fill your grave.

Local anesthesia helps minimize such morbidity, but after abandoning the gurney for the luxurious comfort of the operating table there is usually plenty of time for reflection as they get cutting. In this particular instance I found myself thinking about a game plan for the future, if any.

Recent experience indicated it was time for me to eliminate film and television assignments from the agenda. Far too many efforts had been shelved, and I couldn't expect to escape that fate myself. There were quite a few people in Hollywood who made a living—sometimes a rather handsome one—by writing scripts that never reached the screen. Some of them had similarly survived in television for many years, and the valet service at the pricey restaurants had never refused to park their Mercedes because of this.

But I couldn't feel comfortable writing material which would never find an audience. There was something vaguely unsatisfactory about it—like making an obscene phone call to an answering machine.

All of which didn't mean that I'd quit working. Obviously I write because I cannot accept my own mortality. Putting stories on paper is one way of temporarily extending my existence. It was comforting to realize that once I was sewn up and thrown out there were three books in the future.

In retrospect it sounds silly to be stewing about such inconsequentialities while somebody was busily carving into my guts like a Roman priest inspecting entrails for omens. On the other hand it averted the usual reflections associated with this sort of grand opening—admission of past mistakes and pious resolutions for the future.

There was plenty of time for such considerations after I returned home. Somewhat to my surprise recuperation was a slow process. This bothered me because I was mindful of the fact that time was running short. Maybe there was no way to avoid dropping dead, but I didn't like the idea of doing it on page 145. As if to emphasize the situation Judy Lynn del Rey died of a sudden coronary, and Jack Denton passed away, followed by my brother-in-law, Frank Marcus. Alice Gauer was soon to go; so were Elly's last two sisters.

For a while I took notes on the book project but couldn't summon the strength to actually begin working on it. And I certainly didn't have the strength, let alone the spare time, to consider a sudden and unexpected offer from Australia. A producer wanted me to work on a suspense film which would utilize Sydney Harbor as a background—specifically Sydney Harbor on New Year's Eve, at which time $500,000 worth of fireworks would be launched there to celebrate the bicentenary. Despite my reservations regarding screenplays I probably would have emulated a kangaroo and jumped at the chance had time and health permitted. As it was, I can only assume some fortunate fellow writer scrawled the script 'midst the rockets' red glare, bombs bursting in air, and regular beer runs to Hell's Half-Mile.

FORTY-FIVE

Our own New Year came in with so little fireworks as to barely get by on a pyrotechnicality. I celebrated it by returning a hefty advance payment to my publishers.

Another project first fomented in Florida had been the editing of an anthology of original short stories dealing with mental disturbance. The notion brought me a contract and promises of contributions by an imposing number of authors. But once again I was forced into an attitude of Buddhist resignation as I sat there contemplating my novel.

So the money went back, but I didn't go forward. Instead I assembled more collections of short stories. During recovery from various eye surgeries I'd eschewed novels in favor of turning out more fragmentary fiction. Now it was time to combine some of this recent output with older items which had escaped prior reprint. *Midnight Pleasures* went to one firm, *Fear and Trembling* to another. My first publisher, Arkham House, ended a decade of indecision with an offer to bring out a 250,000-word collection, containing forty or more stories. This merited serious consideration, but Underwood-Miller topped it with a proposal for a

500,000-word venture in three volumes. That could include around a hundred efforts. Together with the two collections already published by Arkham House and the two collections just assembled, the aggregate would encompass just about every short story I felt might bear republication.

After I signed the contract, my recuperation continued while I read stories instead of writing them. This proved to be a more demanding task than I'd expected. Titles like "Yours Truly, Jack the Ripper," "The Cloak," "Enoch" and "That Hellbound Train" were in the earlier collections, which meant they weren't included; nor were any of the stories destined for the forthcoming new collections. Still, the three-volume set was representative enough to serve its purpose. Putting it together reminded me of my preference for the short-story form, and of how infrequently it could be indulged because of economic considerations.

At the time I started typing for a living there were literally thousands of writers whose chief or sole source of income lay in selling short stories. Now I doubted that forty full-time writers in the country supported themselves by such work. And yet, oddly enough, the market had not disappeared. Genre fiction in particular was represented by the publication of anthologies like the one I'd just decided not to edit; these offered outlets for many new tales in addition to evergreen reprints. For some reason collections by individual authors generally did less well, but I'd been lucky both in my own compendiums and the editorial choices made by others.

In spite of limitations it seemed that popular short stories enjoyed a longer life span than popular novels. Items written by me and others thirty, forty or even fifty years ago still popped into print, which was more than could be said for such best-sellers as *The Hucksters, Forever Amber* or *Anthony Adverse.**

---

*Many people do their reading in the bathroom: Writers should do everything to encourage constipation.

Anyway, to make a short story long, once I completed my selections there was no excuse for stalling the three novels. I embarked on the venture initiated by Frank Robinson and did my best to come up with ninety thousand words. As usual the book had been broken down into chapter outlines which would guide me in the actual writing. And so they did—until around the end of Chapter Four.

It was at that point in the narrative that the phone rang, surprising both the heroine and me.

My heroine, Lori, hadn't been expecting the call and I certainly didn't, but there you are; these things happen just the way they do in real life. And when they happen, in fact or fiction, chances are you'll pick up the receiver and answer the phone.

That's what my girl Lori did, and then the trouble started. Out of left field (or was it the left lobe of my brain?) came this total stranger with a flaky idea which had no place in the outline of my story. Only it wasn't my story anymore, nor Lori's, because this intruder took over. If I'd had any sense I would have saved all this trouble by giving my girl an answering machine; she could've had the best model on the market without it costing me a dime. But now it was too late; she'd taken the call and the consequences. In a few short chapters this new character jerked both Lori and the story around to such a point that I was forced to kill the interloper off about thirty-five pages later. I am not normally inclined towards violent measures, but in this instance there was no other choice. Even so, the damage had been done and I had to continue the book in another direction as best I could.

Then, gradually, I couldn't.

Writing continued, but at a much slower pace. It reached a point where the novel would have been completed more quickly if it had been typed by a snail. Much to the frustration of would-be punsters I was not suffering from a writer's block. My problem was eye strain and fatigue, and what I needed was a secretary to take dictation.

To make a long story shorthand, it took close to nine months to find one and rescue Lori from her plight. But my own plight had worsened; I'd fallen still further behind on my commitments to subsequent novels.

Andre Norton had already commenced working on the collaboration and established the pattern we were to follow throughout. She wrote a chapter, and sent it to me for editing and edification. I then wrote the next chapter and consigned it to her tender mercies. We continued this process of alternation, at times writing two chapters instead of one when a situation required lengthier narration. Somewhere along the line I suggested a working title—*The Jekyll Legacy*—to which Andre agreed.

Also, somewhere along the line, I was writing another novel. After I sent my chapter of the collaboration to Andre in Florida there would frequently be an interval of anywhere from ten days to three weeks until her follow-up chapter arrived and I could continue our story. These interim periods gave me an opportunity to forsake the blinding fog of Victorian London for the sunlit streets of Fairvale, where there's always good visibility for making a body count.

The bodies I counted were installed in what I called *Psycho House.* Having severed ties with Jack the Ripper in my previous novel, it was now advisable to cut loose from Norman Bates. It was difficult to let this generous gentleman go—after all, the man had showered me with many blessings over the years—but the time had come. Meanwhile, thanks to Andre, I was also slicing a longtime connection with Messrs. Jekyll and Hyde which dated back to the introduction of my very first book. Perhaps by amputating these various unsavory aspects of my personality I could start a new career as ghostwriter for a televangelist.

Getting various criminal characters off my case was a secondary consideration, but catching up on my writing schedule remained the primary objective. To achieve it I cut out starch, cholesterol and conventions. All holidays were ignored except Bastille Day.

Such complete concentration on work presented new problems; making the crossover from one story to the other occasionally brought about some curious results. Sometimes, much to my surprise, I might find Henry Jekyll, MD, signing in at the Bates Motel while old Norman was creeping up on Queen Victoria in her bathtub.

Andre too was moonlighting with other books when not working on our novel. Mutual salvation lay in the fact that we were both following Stevenson's style as well as incorporating his characters and settings with our own. The task grew easier for me once the collaboration neared its midpoint, for it was then that I finished *Psycho House.*

But saying good-bye to the leading celebrator of Mother's Day left me with those continuing empty stretches until Andre's chapters arrived. Since the meter was still ticking away on the secretary I decided to fill the time gaps by starting an autobiography. It seemed to me the easiest choice of subject matter.

I was wrong.

As a matter of fact, all these months and all these pages later, it's quite possible that the entire content of my autobiography could be summarized in just those three short words: I was wrong. That's one of the things I've concluded from reviewing not just my life but the lives of others that have intertwined with it over long years. Many of them, as was very much the case with me, had warped self-images, misdirected goals, and consciously or unconsciously kept revising their life histories as they went along. Most of us are so fond of believing we're the arbiters of our destinies that we refuse to concede how much of our lives seems governed by happenstance.

Mine certainly was. And I think that I had at least a subliminal awareness of chance as a determining factor in existence, because this has always been the premise of my work. Everything I've ever written has depended on answering a basic question: *What if?*

Applying that query to this account, I came up with some revelations. For example, the factors governing my choice of a career are a series of what ifs.

When my Aunt Lil offered to buy me a magazine from the depot newsstand, what if I had been attracted to any one of several hundred others instead of *Weird Tales*? Quite possibly I might never have known it existed. What if I'd never written to H. P. Lovecraft? But as chance had it, I did.

Up until the time I began this book, I have always believed that he could be held responsible for my becoming a writer. And that Aunt Lil, indirectly and inadvertently, shared that responsibility. Unfortunately these were mistaken notions on my part. I still believe chance was largely responsible for shaping my life, but it goes far deeper than just selecting a magazine and corresponding with one of the contributors.

It seems to me that my writing career began at a baseball game.

Dad took me to the ballpark one summer afternoon for a special father's-and-son's-day exhibition game between the Milwaukee Brewers and I-don't-remember-who. I only remember it was hot, we sat in the bleachers, and Cokes were going for the outrageous price of a dime apiece. I also remember I had recently acquired my first pair of glasses, and my newfound acuity of vision was focussed on that cynosure of all eyes, big-league ballplayer and guest-star, Hack Wilson.

During the seventh inning stretch he came over to face the bleachers and toss an autographed baseball into the mob of eager and adoring youngsters. The ball came directly to me—and I dropped it.

Watching it plummet down into the depths beneath the open bleacher seats, my father said nothing, nor did he ever reproach me by so much as a look. If he felt disappointment it was well and permanently concealed. But that, I now realized, was the turning-point—the moment when I must have made an unconscious decision to abandon further interest in sports and take the introverted course which set the pattern for much of my life yet to come.

What if that ball hadn't slipped through my fingers? If I'd caught it would I have also caught the self-confidence necessary to pursue athletics instead of retreating further into reading? Might I have—God forbid—ended up leading a "normal" existence?

In retrospect what happened seems largely a matter of luck. But what is luck, really? Chances are we'll never know.

All I know is that while H. P. Lovecraft became my literary mentor, it was a baseball player named Hack Wilson who really helped me to become a writer.

FORTY-SIX

1989 sneaked past me when I wasn't looking.

My attention had been diverted by the publication of *Lori* in midyear, followed by *Screams,* an omnibus of three novels in reprint which arrived in early autumn.

Psycho House was published in 1990 and *The Jekyll Legacy* appeared in '91. So did *Psycho-Paths,* the first of the two anthologies of stories by other writers. Meanwhile I was editing the second volume, *Monsters in Our Midst.* My choices were passed on to Martin H. Greenberg, who was in charge of payments, notifications and other messy details. During my spare time I wrote a few new short stories and a variety of introductory essays for other anthologies, and prepared to work on a new novel in 1992.*

Along the way I accepted a few convention invitations in Tulsa, Denver, Long Island and other exotic places. There was a New York symposium for a *Harper's Magazine* article. But before

---

*I'll try to avoid this "and then I wrote" sort of thing from now on. And I promise you there won't be any more footnotes, either.

I could retire to become a school crossing guard, the problem of completing this bit of autobiograffiti remained.

One of the things I lacked was a grand finale. My fiction often offered unexpected twists and surprise endings, but dealing with the facts of life I came up empty-handed. Some of the most treasured moments are too private to be shared.

The fantasies I created in short stories or novels never won me a mass-market audience; now I was finding that my realities lacked the necessary appeal—the skeletons in my closet didn't rattle loudly enough to attract general attention.

Between '89 and '92 I picked up a Life Achievement Award from the Horror Writers of America in Providence, and the Grand Master Award from the first World Horror Convention in Nashville, but that didn't assure me fame and fortune as a pop-culture celebrity. The same can be said of a ten-day trip to Viareggio as a guest of Italy's *Festival In Noir*, which was a delight, but all such journeys are admittedly ego trips. I'm still taking them in '92 and '93.

One of the anticipated joys of autobiography—in addition to patting oneself on the back—is the opportunity to set the record straight. Like most of us, I've sometimes suffered at the hands of others and yearned for a chance to strike back.

I've been plagiarized, deprived of credit and payment for work performed in good faith, ripped off by debtors, conned for a sucker. Some of these episodes provide a tempting opportunity to present myself as an innocent victim of various sons or daughters of bitches whom I can now expose to public scorn.

But running through my injustice collection, I note that time takes its toll, and I find it difficult to summon the necessary malice towards elderly ladies and white-haired old men. Some of them can no longer harm me, because they are dead. Ghost-fighting is a thankless task.*

---

*This is not a footnote.

Autobiographies can also serve the purposes of parlor psychoanalysts. In their eyes my writing can be dismissed as a simple striving for attention, a substitute for the performing career I was unable to follow. It can also serve as an outlet to ventilate fear and release suppressed hostility in seriocomic fashion. While I do not claim to be a candidate for canonization, this account of my personal activities can be seen as a more direct effort to secure approval according to the old-fashioned standards laid down by parents and elders: *Don't spit on the sidewalk, pay your bills, keep your bowels open and your pants shut.*

This is what an analyst might make of my life, but I hope I made more of it than that. Whatever my motivations, I tried to break down the barriers between myself and others, tried to communicate, to entertain. And whatever I did or failed to do, somewhere along the way I found love, and friends, and satisfaction in work. I managed to enter the magic realms which had enchanted me from the start, even to meet some of the magicians I admired. And lived to tell the tale.

That in itself is a pleasant realization. In an era where every star of rock, every jock, every politician or other major criminal becomes an instant autobiographer with a little help from a collaborator whose name appears in smaller type or not at all, I can still honestly say that my life was my own.

They tell me it's not over until the fat lady sings. Well, she's not singing yet, but there are times when I think I can hear her clearing her throat.

So now's the time to stop, I guess. But that reminds me.

Before I go, there's something I forgot to tell you—

INDEX